COST ACCOUNTING

HARCOURT BRACE JOVANOVICH COLLEGE OUTLINE SERIES

COST ACCOUNTING

Mark L. Frigo, Ph.D., CPA, CMA

School of Accountancy
De Paul University

Harcourt College Publishers

Fort Worth   Philadelphia   San Diego   New York   Orlando   Austin   San Antonio
Toronto   Montreal   London   Sydney   Tokyo

ISBN 0-15-601566-8

0 1 2 3 4 5 6 7 8 9   145   20 19 18 17 16 15 14 13 12

PREFACE

The purpose of this book is to help you learn, in the most efficient manner, the basic cost accounting and managerial accounting concepts and techniques. To make this book easier to use, it is written in the clear, concise format of an outline. The topics outlined have been carefully selected to provide coverage of the most important concepts included in the leading cost accounting and managerial accounting textbooks. The hundreds of solved problems and examples that further explain and clarify these topics are representative of the material found in college examinations, textbooks, and professional accounting examinations.

This outline will be useful to students taking a course in cost accounting or managerial accounting at a college or university. Also, this outline provides an excellent review of cost accounting for the Uniform CPA or CMA Examinations. Finally, this outline will be invaluable to those professionals and students who have an interest in increasing their knowledge of cost accounting and managerial accounting through independent study.

A special feature of this outline is a sample **Midterm Examination** and sample **Final Examination**, with solutions. These sample examinations are designed to cover the major topics in a cost accounting or managerial accounting course and to give you the opportunity to develop your abilities to apply your knowledge to various types of questions that you are likely to encounter in a typical college examination. The sample examinations are based on actual examinations that have been developed by the author and used at a major university.

Other features of this outline are the useful study aids that appear at the end of each chapter:

RAISE YOUR GRADES   This feature consists of a checkmarked list of open-ended, thought-provoking questions. This feature will allow you to compare concepts, assimilate concepts and techniques, and prepare for class discussions, quizzes, and examinations.

SUMMARY   This feature provides a brief restatement of the main ideas in the chapter, including definitions of key terms. It is presented in the efficient form of a numbered list so that you can use it to refresh your memory quickly before a quiz or an examination.

RAPID REVIEW   This feature is designed to provide you with a quick review of the concepts and techniques presented in each chapter. The rapid review consists of multiple-choice and true-false questions (with answers at the end of the section) and allows you to test your memory and reinforce your learning of the concepts and techniques presented in the chapter. Each question is cross-referenced to the relevant section in the chapter so that you can locate and review the text material related to that question.

SOLVED PROBLEMS   Each chapter of this outline includes a series of solved problems that require you to apply the concepts and techniques presented in the chapter. The solved problems are similar to problems you may encounter in homework assignments, quizzes, college examinations, and professional examinations such as the CPA and CMA Examinations. Complete solutions with explanations are included for all problems. In addition, each problem is cross-referenced to the section in the chapter that covers the topic of the problem. The solved problems provide you with the opportunity to improve your ability to solve cost accounting and managerial accounting problems.

This outline provides a clear guide to important concepts and techniques and a convenient structure to organize your knowledge in cost accounting and managerial accounting. The format and the many useful features of this outline, including the glossary located at the end of the outline and the numerous examples and solved problems in each chapter, combine to make this college outline a valuable supplement to your college course work and textbook.

DE PAUL UNIVERSITY   MARK L. FRIGO

CONTENTS

Transfer Price.

1 INTRODUCTION TO COST AND MANAGEMENT ACCOUNTING

THIS CHAPTER IS ABOUT

- ☑ **The Purpose of Accounting**
- ☑ **Cost Accounting for Planning and Control**
- ☑ **Organizational Aspects of Accounting**
- ☑ **Economic Aspects of Cost Accounting**
- ☑ **Cost Accounting in Professional Examinations**

1-1. The Purpose of Accounting

The purpose of accounting is to provide information for decision making. Financial accounting is concerned with providing information to external decision makers, such as stockholders, creditors, and governmental agencies. In contrast, cost accounting and management accounting are primarily concerned with providing information to internal decision makers—that is, to management. However, cost accounting information is also used in the preparation of financial accounting reports.

A. Financial accounting

The information that financial accounting provides is usually presented to external decision makers in the form of financial statements. Financial accounting information must conform with *generally accepted accounting principles* (*GAAP*), which are established by the accounting profession. Generally accepted accounting principles encompass the conventions, rules, and procedures that define accepted accounting practice at a particular time. Currently, the Financial Accounting Standards Board (FASB) is responsible for establishing standards for financial accounting.

B. Cost accounting and management accounting

The primary purpose of cost accounting and management (managerial) accounting is to provide information to management for planning and control. The National Association of Accountants (NAA) defines management accounting, in part, as follows:

> Management accounting is the process of identification, measurement, accumulation, analysis, preparation, interpretation, and communication of financial information used by management to plan, evaluate, and control within an organization and to assure appropriate use of and accountability for its resources.

Cost accounting is primarily concerned with the recording and reporting of the cost of manufacturing goods and performing services. It includes methods for recognizing, classifying, allocating, and reporting such costs and comparing them with standard costs.

Although there are differences between cost accounting and management accounting, the two terms are often used interchangeably by accounting practitioners and academicians.

1-2. Cost Accounting for Planning and Control

Cost accounting plays an important role in the interrelated processes of planning and control. *Planning* involves the identification of goals for an organization and the development of plans for achieving those goals. An important part of the planning process is the development of budgets (or plans) for the operations of an organization. Cost accounting provides much of the information needed to develop budgets, as when standard costs (see Chapters 6 and 7) are used to determine budgeted production costs.

Control involves the comparison of actual results with planned results (plans) and the reporting of performance measurements. More specifically, it involves the comparison of actual costs with standard costs and the computation of variances. Cost accounting provides the information needed to accomplish these tasks.

In some cost accounting textbooks, planning and control are divided into three components: strategic planning, management control, and operational (or task) control. *Strategic planning* is the process of identifying organizational goals and the strategies for achieving those goals. *Management control* is the process of assuring that resources are used effectively and efficiently to implement organizational strategies and to attain organizational goals. *Operational control* is the process of assuring that specific operations, or tasks, are completed effectively and efficiently.

1-3. Organizational Aspects of Accounting

In order to understand the role of the accountant in an organization, two different types of authority must be defined. *Line authority* is management authority over subordinates. Line managers have direct decision-making authority for the principal operations of an organization. *Staff authority* is the authority to advise management and to provide information; it generally does not involve direct decision-making authority. Accounting positions within an organization usually have staff authority, since the accountant's primary role is to advise management and to provide information.

An *organization chart* describes the lines of authority and the positions within an organization. An example of a partial organization chart for a corporation is presented in Exhibit 1-1. The marketing vice-president and manufacturing vice-president are line management positions, since they have direct decision-making authority for principal operations (i.e.,

EXHIBIT 1-1

Organization Chart of a Corporation

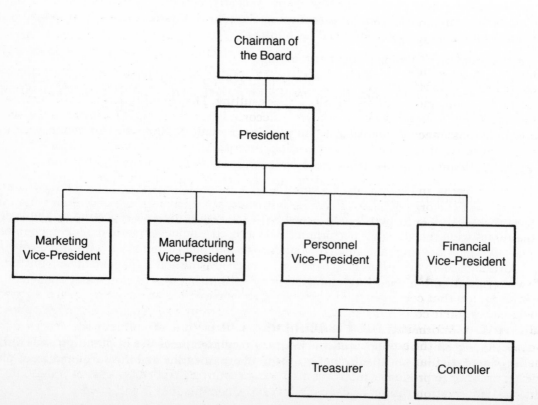

sales and manufacturing) of the firm. In contrast, the financial vice-president and personnel vice-president are staff positions. Two major accounting positions are often discussed in cost accounting textbooks: (1) the controller, and (2) the treasurer.

A. Controller

The controller is usually the chief accountant within an organization. The organization chart of a typical controller's department is presented in Exhibit 1-2.

EXHIBIT 1-2

Organization Chart of a Controller's Department

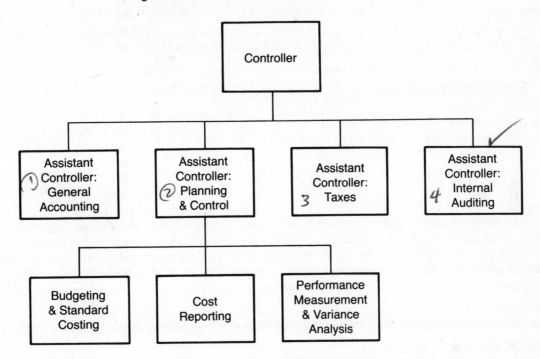

The controller holds a staff position, and serves as an advisor to management and does not have direct management decision-making authority. However, the controller is very influential in management decision making, since the primary source of the information needed for decision making is the controller's department. The principal functions of a controller's department are generally planning and control, general accounting, tax administration, and internal auditing and consulting. The planning and control function of the controller's department is primarily accomplished through accounting analysis. In addition, cost accounting can be useful in the other functions of the controller's department.

B. Treasurer

The treasurer is an accounting position that carries with it responsibility for the financial activities of the organization. These activities usually include short-term financing, long-term financing, banking and investor relations, cash management and investments, and insurance.

1-4. Economic Aspects of Cost Accounting

The information that cost accounting provides can be viewed as an economic commodity with associated economic costs and benefits. The cost of a particular set of information is the cost of producing that information. The benefits of a particular set of information represent the economic impact of the better decisions resulting from the use of the information. Ideally, the benefits of a particular set of information should be greater than its cost. For example, when deciding whether to produce a more detailed cost-accounting report, the cost of producing the additional information should be compared with the benefits that it will yield.

1-5. Cost Accounting in Professional Examinations

Cost accounting represents a significant part of professional accounting examinations. The two major professional accounting examinations that include topics on cost accounting are the Uniform CPA (Certified Public Accountant) Examination and the Certificate in Management Accounting (CMA) Examination. This outline is useful in preparing for both the CPA and CMA examinations.

A. Uniform CPA Examination

The CPA Examination consists of four parts: accounting practice; auditing; business law; and accounting theory. Cost accounting topics represent approximately 10% of accounting practice and 10% of accounting theory, based on the content specification outlines developed by the AICPA (American Institute of Certified Public Accountants) Board of Examiners.

B. Certificate in Management Accounting (CMA) Examination

In 1972, the National Association of Accountants (NAA) established the Institute of Management Accounting (IMA) to administer the Certificate in Management Accounting (CMA) program. The CMA program has the following objectives:

1. To establish management accounting as a recognized profession by identifying the role of the management accountant and the underlying body of knowledge, and by outlining a course of study by which such knowledge can be acquired.
2. To foster higher educational standards in the field of management accounting.
3. To establish an objective measure of an individual's knowledge and competence in the field of management accounting.

The CMA Examination consists of five parts: economics and business finance; organization and behavior, including ethical considerations; public reporting standards, auditing, and taxes; internal reporting and analysis; and decision analysis, including modeling and information systems. Cost accounting (including quantitative methods) represents approximately 40% of the examination content.

RAISE YOUR GRADES

Can you explain...?

☑ the purpose of financial accounting
☑ the purpose of cost and management accounting
☑ how cost accounting and management accounting are defined
☑ the role of cost accounting in the planning and control processes
☑ what strategic planning, management control, and operational control are
☑ the difference between staff authority and line authority
☑ what an organization chart describes
☑ the controller's position within an organization
☑ the treasurer's position within an organization
☑ the role of the controller and the treasurer
☑ why the costs and benefits of cost accounting information are important
☑ the content of the Uniform CPA Examination
☑ the content of the Certificate in Management Accounting Examination
☑ the objectives of the CMA program

SUMMARY

1. The purpose of accounting is to provide information for decision making.
2. The purpose of financial accounting is to provide information to external decision makers, such as stockholders, creditors, and governmental agencies.

3. Generally accepted accounting principles (GAAP) have been established for financial accounting information.
4. The primary purpose of cost and management accounting is to provide information to internal decision makers (management).
5. Cost accounting and management accounting play an important role in the planning and control processes.
6. The terms *cost accounting* and *management accounting* are often used interchangeably.
7. The planning process involves the identification of goals and the development of plans for achieving those goals.
8. The control process involves the comparison of actual results with planned results and the reporting of performance measurements.
9. Planning and control can be divided into three components: strategic planning, management control, and operational control.
10. Line authority is management authority over subordinates; it involves direct decision-making authority for the principal operations of an organization.
11. Staff authority is the authority to advise management and to provide information; it does not involve direct decision-making authority.
12. Accounting positions generally have staff authority within an organization.
13. An organization chart describes the lines of authority and the positions within an organization.
14. The controller is generally the chief accountant of an organization.
15. The controller is an advisor to management and provides information needed for decision making.
16. The controller's department usually includes the following functions: planning and control, general accounting, tax administration, and internal auditing and consulting.
17. The treasurer is primarily responsible for the financial activities of the organization.
18. The primary economic consideration in providing cost accounting information is that the benefits of the information outweigh the costs of producing it.
19. The Uniform CPA Examination and the Certificate in Management Accounting Examination have significant coverage of cost and management accounting.

RAPID REVIEW

1. The primary purpose of cost and management accounting is to provide information to (**a**) stockholders, (**b**) creditors, (**c**) management, (**d**) none of the above. [See Section 1-1.]
2. The primary purpose of financial accounting is to provide information to (**a**) stockholders, (**b**) creditors, (**c**) governmental agencies, (**d**) all of the above, (**e**) none of the above. [See Section 1-1.]
3. Cost accounting plays an important role in planning and control: (**a**) true, (**b**) false. [See Section 1-2.]
4. Using cost accounting information to compare standard costs with actual costs and to compute cost variances is an example of (**a**) the planning process, (**b**) the control process, (**c**) neither of these. [See Section 1-2.]
5. The identification of organizational goals and the strategies for achieving those goals is the process of (**a**) strategic planning, (**b**) management control, (**c**) operational control. [See Section 1-2.]
6. Assuring that resources are used effectively and efficiently to implement organizational strategies and to achieve organizational goals is the process of (**a**) strategic planning, (**b**) management control, (**c**) operational control. [See Section 1-2.]
7. The authority to advise and to provide information is (**a**) line authority, (**b**) staff authority. [See Section 1-3.]
8. Most accounting positions within an organization have primarily (**a**) line authority, (**b**) staff authority. [See Section 1-3.]
9. The accounting position responsible for planning and control, general accounting, tax administration, and internal auditing and consulting is the (**a**) treasurer, (**b**) controller. [See Section 1-3.]

10. The cost of producing a particular set of information should be compared with the benefits of the information: **(a)** true, **(b)** false. [See Section 1-4.]

11. Cost accounting represents the following percentage of the accounting practice and the accounting theory parts of the Uniform CPA Examination: **(a)** 25%, **(b)** 10%, **(c)** 40%. [See Section 1-5.]

12. Cost accounting represents the following percentage of the CMA Examination: **(a)** 25%, **(b)** 15%, **(c)** 40%. [See Section 1-5.]

Answers:

1. **(c)**   2. **(d)**   3. **(a)**   4. **(b)**   5. **(a)**   6. **(b)**   7. **(b)**   8. **(b)**   9. **(b)**   10. **(a)**
11. **(b)**   12. **(c)**

SOLVED PROBLEMS

PROBLEM 1-1: What is the purpose of (*1*) cost and management accounting and (*2*) financial accounting?

Solution: The primary purpose of cost and management accounting is to provide information to internal decision makers (management). In contrast, the purpose of financial accounting is to provide information to external decision makers, such as stockholders, creditors, and governmental agencies. Therefore, these two classes of accounting are concerned with two different groups of decision makers. [See Section 1-1.]

PROBLEM 1-2: Describe the planning and control processes. Give examples of how cost accounting provides information for planning and control.

Solution: The planning process involves the identification of goals and the development of plans for achieving those goals. The control process involves the comparison of actual results with planned results and the reporting of performance measurements.

Cost accounting information is used in the planning process when standard costs are used to develop budgets and to determine budgeted production costs. In the control process, cost accounting provides information needed to compare actual costs with standard costs and to compute cost variances. [See Section 1-2.]

PROBLEM 1-3: Define each of the following components of the planning and control processes: strategic planning, management control, and operational control.

Solution: Strategic planning is the process of identifying organizational goals and the strategies for achieving those goals. Management control is the process of assuring that resources are used effectively and efficiently to implement organizational strategies and to attain organizational goals. Operational control is the process of assuring that specific operations, or tasks, are completed effectively and efficiently. [See Section 1-2.]

PROBLEM 1-4: Describe the position of controller within an organization. Identify the primary functions of the controller's department.

Solution: The controller is usually the chief accountant of an organization. The controller holds a staff position, serving as an advisor to management and having no direct management decision-making authority. The controller is very influential in management decision making, since the primary source of the information needed for decision making is the controller's department.

The principal functions of a controller's department are generally planning and control, general accounting, tax administration, and internal auditing and consulting. [See Section 1-3.]

PROBLEM 1-5: Describe the primary functions of the treasurer.

Solution: The treasurer is primarily responsible for the financial activities of the organization. These activities usually include short-term financing, long-term financing, banking and investor relations, cash management and investments, and insurance. [See Section 1-3.]

PROBLEM 1-6: Describe the content of the Uniform CPA Examination and the Certificate in Management Accounting (CMA) Examination. What percentage of the content of each examination represents cost and management accounting topics?

Solution: The CPA Examination consists of four parts: accounting practice; auditing; business law; and accounting theory. Cost and management accounting topics represent approximately 10% of accounting practice and 10% of accounting theory. The CMA Examination consists of five parts: economics and business finance; organization and behavior, including ethical considerations; public reporting standards, auditing, and taxes; internal reporting and analysis; and decision analysis, including modeling and information systems. Cost and management accounting represent approximately 40% of the examination content. [See Section 1-5.]

2 COST ACCOUNTING CONCEPTS AND TERMINOLOGY

THIS CHAPTER IS ABOUT

- ☑ **Cost Terminology**
- ☑ **Variable Costs and Fixed Costs**
- ☑ **Average Costs**
- ☑ **Product Costs and Period Costs**
- ☑ **Accounting for Product Costs**

2-1. Cost Terminology

In general, accountants define *costs* as resources foregone to acquire goods or services.

A. Costs expressed in monetary units

In accounting, costs (foregone resources) must be expressed in terms of monetary units (such as dollars). For example, suppose that it takes 100 pounds of material (a foregone resource) at \$5.00 per pound to manufacture a certain product. An accountant must express that foregone resource in terms of monetary units so that, say, material costs = 100 lb × \$5.00/lb = \$500.

B. Cost accumulation

Cost accumulation is the collection of cost data within the accounting system. The specific cost data that will be collected depends on a company's cost objectives.

C. Cost objectives

A *cost objective* is any activity for which a separate measurement of costs is desired. The determination of cost objectives assists the decision-making process. For example, a common cost objective is *product costing* for inventory valuation and gross income determination. In product costing, costs incurred in the manufacture of a product are accumulated and applied to the units of production.

Another example of a cost objective is *production department cost control*, in which production costs are accumulated for each production department in order to evaluate production department efficiency.

2-2. Variable Costs and Fixed Costs

In cost accounting, it is important to distinguish between variable costs and fixed costs. You can do this by observing how a cost changes in response to changes in the level of production activity (i.e., production output), within the relevant range of activity.

A. Relevant range

The *relevant range* refers to the levels of production activity within which a firm expects to operate. For example, a company may expect to operate within the range of an annual production activity of 100,000 to 120,000 units. On the basis of the relevant range, a company's costs can be classified as either variable or fixed. This classification into variable cost and fixed cost components is valid only within the relevant range.

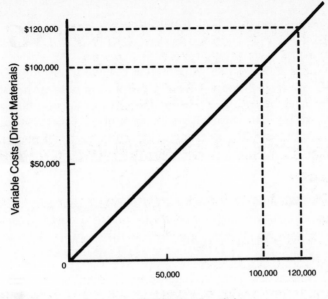

Figure 2-1
Variable Cost Behavior

B. Variable costs

Variable costs are costs that, *in total*, change in direct proportion to changes in production activity, within the relevant range. An example of a variable cost is a material cost of $100,000 at a production level of 100,000 units and $120,000 at a production level of 120,000 units. The graphical representation of this cost behavior is presented in Figure 2-1. In general, accountants assume a *linear* (as opposed to curvilinear) variable cost behavior, as Figure 2-1 shows.

C. Fixed costs

Fixed costs are costs that, *in total*, remain unchanged when significant changes in production activity occur, within the relevant range. For example, if property taxes for a factory remain constant regardless of its production activity, the taxes are a fixed cost. Figure 2-2 illustrates fixed cost behavior. Notice that the fixed cost behavior is linear.

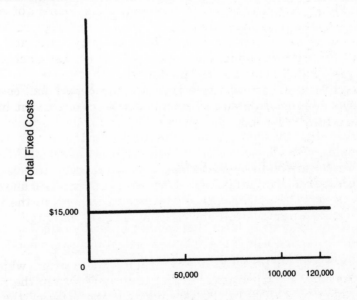

Figure 2-2
Fixed Cost Behavior

2-3. Average Costs

In cost accounting, several types of cost averages are useful.

A. Average cost

You generally compute *average cost* (also called *unit cost*) by dividing total costs by a measure of output. Examples of measures of output include units of production (for a manufacturing company), hours of service completed (for a service company), and academic credit hours generated (for a university). So, for example, if total costs are $10,000 and there are 5,000 units of production, the average cost would be $2.00 per unit ($10,000 ÷ 5,000 units).

B. Average variable cost

You compute *average variable cost* (also called *variable cost per unit*) by dividing total variable costs by the units of output. Average variable costs are constant within the relevant range, since total variable costs change in direct proportion to changes in output. Thus, in Figure 2-1 the average variable cost is $1.00 per unit at all levels of output.

C. Average fixed cost

You compute *average fixed cost* (also called *fixed cost per unit*) by dividing total fixed costs by the units of output. Since total fixed costs are constant within the relevant range, the average fixed cost will decrease as output increases. For example, in Figure 2-2 the average fixed cost at an output level of 10,000 units is $1.50 per unit ($15,000 ÷ 10,000 units). At an output level of 15,000 units, the average fixed cost is $1.00 per unit ($15,000 ÷ 15,000 units).

2-4. Product Costs and Period Costs

It is important to distinguish between product costs and period costs.

A. Product costs

Product costs are all the costs incurred in producing a product that are recorded in *inventory accounts*, or *asset accounts* (Direct Materials, Work-in-Process, Finished Goods) until the output is sold. Then the product costs are transferred from the inventory accounts to an *expense account* (Cost of Goods Sold).

There are three categories of product costs: (1) direct materials costs, (2) direct labor costs, and (3) indirect manufacturing costs. Different combinations of these categories are called prime costs and conversion costs.

1. DIRECT MATERIALS COSTS

Direct (or *raw*) *materials costs* are the costs of materials that can be physically traced to the finished output. Examples of direct materials are sheet steel for an automobile manufacturer or crude oil for an oil refinery. Direct materials cost is a variable cost.

Generally, direct materials must be traceable to the finished product in an economical manner. This means that the small amount of lubricant used to manufacture an automobile, for example, would *not* be a direct material, but an indirect material. All materials that are not direct materials are indirect materials, and their costs are classified as indirect manufacturing costs.

2. DIRECT LABOR COSTS

Direct labor costs are the costs of labor that can be physically traced to the finished output. An example of direct labor is a production line assembler in an automobile production plant. Direct labor cost is a variable cost.

All labor that *cannot* be physically traced to the finished output in an economically efficient manner is indirect labor, and its cost is classified as an indirect manufacturing cost. An example of indirect labor is the factory floor sweeper in a lumber mill. Although the floor sweeper did not contribute directly to the production of the product, the floor sweeper did contribute indirectly to production.

3. INDIRECT MANUFACTURING (FACTORY OVERHEAD) COSTS

Indirect manufacturing costs are all product costs that are not classified as direct materials or direct labor costs. Indirect manufacturing costs are also called *factory overhead, factory burden,* or *manufacturing overhead* costs. For the purposes of this outline, the term *factory overhead costs* will be used.

There are two categories of factory overhead costs:

1. *Variable factory overhead* is an indirect product cost that changes in direct proportion to the activity level. Examples are the costs of electric power, supplies (indirect materials), and indirect labor.
2. *Fixed factory overhead* is an indirect product cost that does not change with changes in the activity level. Examples are factory rent, insurance costs, and straight-line depreciation.

4. PRIME COSTS AND CONVERSION COSTS

In cost accounting, the three product cost categories can be combined as follows:

- *Prime costs* consist of direct materials costs plus direct labor costs.
- *Conversion costs* consist of direct labor costs plus factory overhead costs.

B. Period costs

Generally, *period costs* are nonproduction costs, such as selling and administrative expenses. Therefore, period costs are *not* recorded in inventory accounts but are immediately expensed in the period in which the costs are incurred

Examples of period costs are sales commissions, corporate administrative expenses, marketing and advertising expenses, and accounting department salaries.

2-5. Accounting for Product Costs

Product costs are recorded initially in inventory accounts (asset accounts) and later in the Cost of Goods Sold account (an expense account). Therefore, product costs affect both the balance sheet (asset accounts) and the income statement (expense account).

A. Product costs in inventory accounts

Product costs are recorded in three inventory accounts: (1) Direct Materials Inventory, (2) Work-in-Process Inventory, and (3) Finished Goods Inventory. Direct materials costs are first recorded in the Direct Materials Inventory account and later, when the direct materials are being used in production, are transferred to Work-in-Process Inventory. Direct labor costs and factory overhead costs are recorded in the Work-in-Process Inventory account during the production process. When production is complete, product costs are transferred from the Work-in-Process Inventory account to the Finished Goods Inventory account.

Exhibit 2-1 summarizes the use of inventory accounts in accounting for product costs. The three inventory accounts are generally presented in the balance sheet (statement of financial position).

B. Product costs as a cost-of-goods-sold expense

Generally, you will use three steps to compute the cost of goods sold for a manufacturing company. In *Step 1,* you would compute the cost of the direct materials used in the production process (the direct materials cost that is transferred to Work-in-Process Inventory). In *Step 2,* you would compute the cost of goods manufactured (the cost that is transferred to the Finished Goods Inventory account). Finally, in *Step 3* you would compute the cost of goods sold.

Exhibit 2-2 presents the specific computations involved in each of these steps. Study these steps carefully, as they form the basis for much of the material that follows in this outline.

EXHIBIT 2-1

Accounting for Product Costs

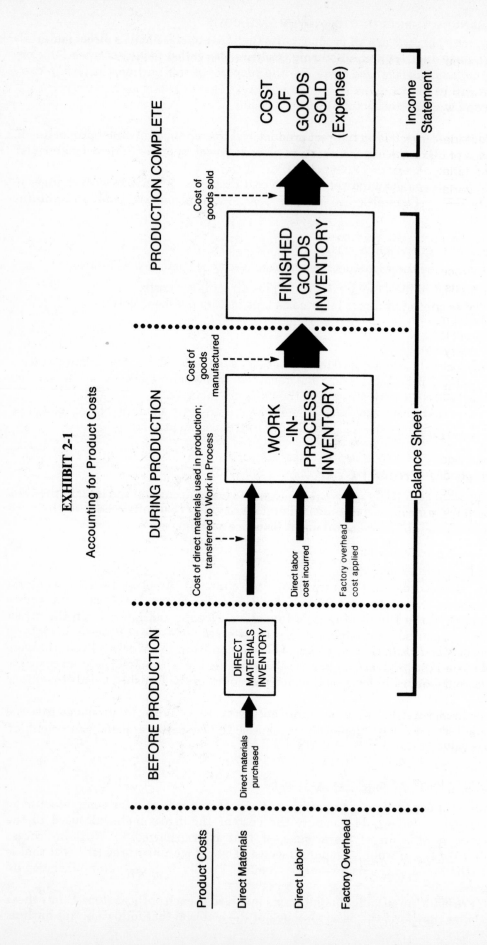

EXHIBIT 2-2

Computing Cost of Goods Sold for a Manufacturing Company

STEP 1: COMPUTE COST OF DIRECT MATERIALS USED IN PRODUCTION (DIRECT MATERIALS COST TRANSFERRED TO WORK-IN-PROCESS INVENTORY).

    Direct Materials Inventory, beginning balance
+ Purchases of direct materials
− Direct Materials Inventory, ending balance
= Direct materials used in production

STEP 2: COMPUTE COST OF GOODS MANUFACTURED.

    Work-in-Process Inventory, beginning balance
+ Product costs transferred to Work-in-Process
    Inventory
    (1) Direct materials
    (2) Direct labor
    (3) Factory overhead
− Work-in-Process Inventory, ending balance
= Cost of goods manufactured

STEP 3: COMPUTE COST OF GOODS SOLD.

    Finished Goods Inventory, beginning balance
+ Cost of goods manufactured
− Finished Goods Inventory, ending balance
= Cost of goods sold

EXAMPLE 2-1: The Boston Company had the following costs and inventories for 19X3:

	January 1, 19X3 balance	December 31, 19X3 balance
Direct Materials Inventory	$12,000	$10,000
Work-in-Process Inventory	80,000	70,000
Finished Goods Inventory	60,000	50,000

Direct labor costs transferred to Work-in-Process Inventory were $30,000, and factory overhead transferred to Work-in-Process Inventory was $20,000. Direct materials purchases were $38,000. What was the cost of goods sold for the Boston Company in 19X3?

STEP 1: COMPUTE COST OF DIRECT MATERIALS USED IN PRODUCTION.

Direct Materials Inventory, January 1	$12,000
+ Purchases of direct materials	+ 38,000
− Direct Materials Inventory, December 31	− 10,000
= Direct materials used in production	$40,000

STEP 2:   COMPUTE COST OF GOODS MANUFACTURED.

Work-in-Process Inventory, January 1	$ 80,000
+ Product costs transferred to Work-in-Process Inventory:	
(1) Direct materials	+ 40,000
(2) Direct labor	+ 30,000
(3) Factory overhead	+ 20,000
− Work-in-Process Inventory, December 31	− 70,000
= Cost of goods manufactured	$100,000

STEP 3:   COMPUTE COST OF GOODS SOLD.

Finished Goods Inventory, January 1	$ 60,000
+ Cost of goods manufactured	+ 100,000
− Finished Goods Inventory, December 31	− 50,000
= Cost of goods sold	$110,000

C. Statement of cost of goods manufactured

This statement of cost of goods manufactured includes the computation of the cost of direct materials used in production (Step 1 in Exhibit 2-2) and the cost of goods manufactured (Step 2). The purpose of this statement is to summarize the accounting for product costs. In particular, this statement summarizes the three components of product costs: (1) direct materials, (2) direct labor, and (3) factory overhead.

Exhibit 2-3 presents the statement of cost of goods manufactured for the Boston Company, using the data from Example 2-1. The factory overhead costs of $20,000 are broken down as follows: indirect labor, $10,000; supplies, $2,000; utilities, $2,000; depreciation, $3,000; miscellaneous, $3,000.

EXHIBIT 2-3

Boston Company
Statement of Cost of Goods Manufactured
For the Year Ended December 31, 19X3

Direct materials:		
Inventory, January 1	$12,000	
Purchases of direct materials	38,000	
Cost of direct materials available for use	$50,000	
Less: Inventory, December 31	10,000	
Direct materials used		$ 40,000
Direct labor		30,000
Factory overhead:		
Indirect labor	$10,000	
Supplies	2,000	
Utilities	2,000	
Depreciation	3,000	
Miscellaneous	3,000	20,000
Manufacturing costs incurred during 19X3		$ 90,000
Add: Work-in-Process Inventory, January 1		80,000
Manufacturing costs accounted for		$170,000
Less: Work-in-Process Inventory, December 31		70,000
Cost of goods manufactured		$100,000

RAISE YOUR GRADES

Can you explain...?

☑ what *costs* are
☑ the purpose of cost objectives
☑ the concept of relevant range
☑ the difference between variable and fixed costs
☑ how to compute average variable and fixed costs
☑ the difference between product costs and period costs
☑ the three categories of product costs
☑ how the three inventory accounts are used to account for product costs
☑ how to compute the cost of direct materials used
☑ how to compute the cost of goods manufactured
☑ how to compute the cost of goods sold
☑ how to prepare a statement of cost of goods manufactured

SUMMARY

1. Costs are generally defined as resources foregone to acquire goods or services and are expressed in terms of monetary units.
2. Cost accumulation involves the collection of cost data in the accounting system.
3. A cost objective is any activity for which a separate measurement of costs is desired.
4. An example of a cost objective is product costing.
5. Variable costs are costs that, in total, change in direct proportion to changes in production activity (output).
6. Fixed costs are costs that, in total, do not change during significant changes in production activity.
7. The relevant range is the range of production activity within which variable cost and fixed cost classifications are valid.
8. Average variable costs are computed by dividing total variable costs by units of output.
9. Average variable costs are constant within the relevant range.
10. Average fixed costs are computed by dividing total fixed costs by units of output.
11. Average fixed costs decrease with increases in production activity.
12. Product costs are production costs that are inventoried until the products are sold.
13. Product costs consist of the costs of direct materials, direct labor, and factory overhead.
14. Prime costs equal direct materials plus direct labor costs.
15. Conversion costs equal direct labor plus factory overhead costs.
16. The Work-in-Process Inventory account records product costs for units of production that have been started but are not complete.
17. The Finished Goods Inventory account records product costs for completed units of production.
18. The cost of goods manufactured equals beginning Work-in-Process Inventory, plus product costs transferred to Work-in-Process Inventory, minus ending Work-in-Process Inventory.
19. The cost of goods sold equals beginning Finished Goods Inventory, plus cost of goods manufactured, minus ending Finished Goods Inventory.

RAPID REVIEW

1. Costs are generally defined as resources foregone to acquire goods or services: **(a)** true, **(b)** false. [See Section 2-1.]
2. Any activity for which a separate measurement of cost is desired represents **(a)** a cost, **(b)** a cost objective, **(c)** cost accumulation, **(d)** the relevant range. [See Section 2-1.]

3. Costs that, in total, do not change during significant changes in production activity, within the relevant range are (a) variable costs, (b) fixed costs, (c) all production costs. [See Section 2-2.]

4. Costs that, in total, change in direct proportion to changes in production activity are (a) variable costs, (b) fixed costs, (c) all production costs. [See Section 2-2.]

5. In general, accountants assume that variable costs and fixed costs are (a) linear, (b) curvilinear, (c) both of the above. [See Section 2-2.]

6. Average costs are computed by dividing total costs by units of output: (a) true, (b) false. [See Section 2-3.]

7. Average costs that are constant during changes in production activity are (a) average variable costs, (b) average fixed costs, (c) all average production costs. [See Section 2-3.]

8. Average costs that decrease with increases in production activity are (a) average variable costs, (b) average fixed costs, (c) all average production costs. [See Section 2-3.]

9. Which of the following is a product cost? (a) direct materials, (b) direct labor, (c) factory overhead, (d) all of the above. [See Section 2-4.]

10. Both direct materials and direct labor are variable costs: (a) true, (b) false. [See Section 2-4.]

11. Prime costs consist of the following costs: (a) direct materials + direct labor, (b) direct materials + factory overhead, (c) direct labor + factory overhead. [See Section 2-4.]

12. Conversion costs consist of the following costs: (a) direct materials + direct labor, (b) direct materials + factory overhead, (c) direct labor + factory overhead. [See Section 2-4.]

13. Factory overhead costs are (a) direct product costs, (b) indirect product costs, (c) period costs. [See Section 2-4.]

14. Cost of goods sold is (a) an expense, (b) an asset, (c) a period cost. [See Section 2-5.]

15. Cost of goods sold equals beginning Finished Goods Inventory + cost of goods manufactured − ending Finished Goods Inventory. (a) true, (b) false. [See Section 2-5.]

Answers:

1. (a)   2. (b)   3. (b)   4. (a)   5. (a)   6. (a)   7. (a)   8. (b)   9. (d)   10. (a)
11. (a)   12. (c)   13. (b)   14. (a)   15. (a)

SOLVED PROBLEMS

PROBLEM 2-1: Classify the following costs as variable costs (V) or fixed costs (F).

1. Salary of factory safety manager _____
2. Sheet steel used in manufacturing automobiles _____
3. Factory rent _____
4. Wages of assembly-line workers _____
5. Insurance expense on factory equipment _____
6. Straight-line depreciation expense on factory equipment _____
7. Wages of factory storeroom personnel _____
8. Wages of factory janitors _____
9. Salaries for factory industrial engineering department _____
10. Paper used in the production of textbooks _____

Solution: In order to determine whether a cost item is a variable cost or a fixed cost, you must ask how the cost would change in response to a change in production activity. If the cost would change in direct proportion, then it is a variable cost. If the cost would *not* change with changes in production activity, then it is a fixed cost.

1. F—Salaries are generally fixed costs.
2. V—This is a direct materials cost.
3. F—Factory rent is generally a fixed cost.
4. V—This is a direct labor cost.
5. F—Insurance expense is generally a fixed cost.
6. F—Straight-line depreciation is a fixed cost.
7. V—This is a variable overhead cost, if more personnel are needed to handle greater factory output.
8. V—This is a variable overhead cost, if more janitors are needed when more factory capacity is used.
9. F—Salaries are generally fixed cost.
10. V—This is a direct materials cost.

[See Section 2-2.]

PROBLEM 2-2: Classify the following costs as direct costs (D) or indirect costs (I).

1. Salary of factory safety manager   _____
2. Sheet steel used in manufacturing automobiles   _____
3. Factory rent   _____
4. Wages of assembly-line workers   _____
5. Insurance expense on factory equipment   _____
6. Straight-line depreciation expense on factory equipment   _____
7. Wages of factory storeroom clerks   _____
8. Wages of factory janitors   _____
9. Salaries for factory industrial engineering department   _____
10. Paper used in the production of textbooks   _____

Solution: In order to answer this question, you must distinguish between direct costs—costs for materials or labor that are directly traceable to the finished output—and indirect costs—factory overhead costs, whether variable or fixed.

1. I—fixed factory overhead
2. D—direct materials
3. I—fixed factory overhead
4. D—direct labor
5. I—fixed factory overhead
6. I—fixed factory overhead
7. I—variable factory overhead
8. I—variable factory overhead
9. I—fixed factory overhead
10. D—direct materials

[See Section 2-4.]

Problems 2-3 and 2-4 are based on the following data.

Producto Company recorded the following inventories for 19X5.

	Inventory Balance	
	January 1, 19X5	December 31, 19X5
Direct Materials Inventory	$50,000	$52,000
Work-in-Process Inventory	74,000	70,000
Finished Goods Inventory	67,000	54,000

During 19X5, the company incurred the following costs:

Direct material purchases	$300,000
Direct labor costs	120,000
Indirect factory labor costs	60,000
Other indirect factory costs	50,000

PROBLEM 2-3: Compute the cost of goods manufactured for Producto Company.

Solution: In order to solve this problem, you would first compute the amount of direct materials used in the production process.

Direct Materials Inventory, beginning balance	$ 50,000
+ Purchases of direct materials	+ 300,000
− Direct Materials Inventory, ending balance	− 52,000
= Direct materials used in production	$298,000

Now you can compute the cost of goods manufactured.

Work-in-Process Inventory, beginning balance	$ 74,000
+ Direct materials used in production	298,000
+ Direct labor costs incurred	120,000
+ Indirect labor costs	60,000
+ Other indirect factory overhead	50,000
− Work-in-Process Inventory, ending balance	− 70,000
= Cost of goods manufactured	$532,000

[See Section 2-5.]

PROBLEM 2-4: Compute the cost of goods sold for Producto Company.

Solution: Compute the cost of goods sold following Step 3 in Exhibit 2-2. Use the cost of goods manufactured found in Problem 2-3.

Finished Goods Inventory, beginning balance	$ 67,000
+ Cost of goods manufactured	+ 532,000
− Finished Goods Inventory, ending balance	− 54,000
= Cost of goods sold	$545,000

[See Section 2-5.]

PROBLEM 2-5: The following information applies to MLF Company for 19X7:

Work-in-Process Inventory:	
January 1, 19X7	$ 50,000
December 31, 19X7	60,000
Direct materials used	170,000
Direct labor costs incurred	190,000
Cost of goods manufactured	450,000

What was the amount of factory overhead costs incurred by MLF Company in 19X7?

Solution: You would solve this problem by using Step 2 of Exhibit 2-2.

Work-in-Process Inventory, January 1, 19X7	$ 50,000
+ Production costs transferred to Work-in-Process:	
Direct materials used	+ 170,000
Direct labor costs incurred	+ 190,000
Factory overhead costs incurred	+ X
− Work-in-Process Inventory, December 31, 19X7	− 60,000
= Cost of goods manufactured	$450,000

You can solve for X to find the amount of factory overhead costs incurred:

$$\$450,000 = \$50,000 + \$170,000 + \$190,000 + X - \$60,000$$
$$X = \$100,000$$

[See Section 2-5.]

PROBLEM 2-6: Alpha Beta Fraternity is planning a party at which a band will perform. The cost of hiring the band for the party is $2,000. Based on previous parties, it has been determined that the cost of refreshments consumed by each person attending will be $8.00. What will be the average cost per person if (1) 500 people attend; (2) 1,000 people attend?

Solution: This problem involves computing the average (unit) cost for the party. There are two cost components in the problem: (a) fixed cost of $2,000 for the band and (b) variable cost of $8.00 per person for refreshments.

You would find the total costs for the party as follows:

	500 people	1,000 people
Variable cost (refreshments)*	$4,000	$ 8,000
Fixed cost (band)	2,000	2,000
Total cost	$6,000	$10,000

*based on $8.00 per person

Thus, you would compute the average (unit) cost for the party for 500 people as follows:

$$\text{Average cost} = \frac{\text{Total cost}}{\text{Number of people}}$$
$$= \frac{\$6,000}{500}$$
$$= \$12.00 \text{ per person}$$

Similarly, the average cost per person for 1,000 people attending would be:

$$\text{Average cost} = \frac{\$10,000}{1,000}$$
$$= \$10.00 \text{ per person}$$

Note that the average total cost per person decreases as the number of people increases. Also, note that the average variable cost is the same ($8.00) for 500 people or 1,000 people, but that the average fixed cost is $4.00 per person for 500 people ($2,000/500) and is $2.00 per person for 1,000 people ($2,000/1,000). [See Section 2-3.]

PROBLEM 2-7: ABC Company manufactures a product that requires the raw material X-101. The accounting system of ABC Company has a specific inventory account, Direct Materials, for this raw material. Based on an analysis of the accounting records of ABC Company, the following information for 19X2 was obtained.

Direct Material—X-101 Inventory, beginning balance	$ 354,000
Direct Material—X-101 Inventory, ending balance	321,000
X-101 transferred to Work-in-Process	961,000
Work-in-Process Inventory, beginning balance	1,751,000
Work-in-Process Inventory, ending balance	1,552,000

Based on this information, what was the amount of raw materials X-101 purchased in 19X2?

Solution: In order to solve this problem, you must remember that you compute the amount of direct materials used in production as follows:

Direct Materials Inventory, beginning balance
+ Purchases of direct materials
− Direct Materials Inventory, ending balance
= Direct materials used in production

We can rearrange this equation to compute the purchases of direct materials.

Direct Materials Inventory, ending balance	$321,000
+ Direct materials used in production	+ 961,000
− Direct Materials Inventory, beginning balance	− 354,000
= Purchases of direct materials	$928,000

[See Section 2-5.]

PROBLEM 2-8: The following information is available for direct materials costs for 19X1 operations of XYZ Corporation:

Direct Materials Inventory, January 1, 19X1	$125,000
Direct Materials Inventory, December 31, 19X1	103,000
Direct materials used in production	410,000

What amount of direct materials did XYZ Corporation purchase in 19X1?

Solution: Begin by using Step 1 from Exhibit 2-2:

Direct Materials Inventory, beginning balance	$125,000
+ Purchases of direct materials	+ X
− Direct Materials Inventory, ending balance	− 103,000
= Direct materials used in production	$410,000

Now you can solve for direct materials purchased:

$$\$410,000 = \$125,000 + X - \$103,000$$
$$X = \$388,000$$

[See Section 2-5.]

PROBLEM 2-9: The following production cost information is available for the 19X8 operations of XYZ Company:

Work-in-Process Inventory, January 1, 19X8	$350,000
Work-in-Process Inventory, December 31, 19X8	370,000
Cost of goods manufactured	610,000
Direct materials used in production	388,000
Factory overhead costs	200,000

Based on this information, what was the amount of direct labor costs incurred?

Solution: Use Step 2 from Exhibit 2-2 to solve this problem.

Work-in-Process Inventory, January 1, 19X8	$350,000
+ Product costs transferred to Work-in-Process:	
Direct materials used in production	+ 388,000
Direct labor costs incurred	+ X
Factory overhead costs	+ 200,000
− Work-in-Process Inventory, December 31, 19X8	− 370,000
= Cost of goods manufactured	$610,000

Now you can solve for direct labor costs incurred:

$$\$610{,}000 = \$350{,}000 + \$388{,}000 + X + \$200{,}000 - \$370{,}000$$
$$X = \$42{,}000$$

[See Section 2-5.]

PROBLEM 2-10: The following product cost information is available for ABC Company.

Direct materials used in production	$167,000
Direct labor costs incurred	200,000
Factory overhead costs	193,000
Total production costs	$560,000

What were the amounts of prime costs and conversion costs for ABC Company?

Solution: To answer this question, use the definitions of prime costs and conversion costs.

Prime costs = Direct materials costs + Direct labor costs
= $167,000 + $200,000
= $367,000

Conversion costs = Direct labor costs + Factory overhead costs
= $200,000 + $193,000
= $393,000

[See Section 2-4.]

Problems 2-11 to 2-14 are based on the following data.

The following information is available for Hi-Tech Company for 19X5.

Direct Materials Inventory:	
January 1, 19X5	$11,000
December 31, 19X5	8,000
Direct materials purchased	73,000
Work-in-Process Inventory:	
January 1, 19X5	6,000
December 31, 19X5	7,000
Direct labor costs	18,000
Factory Overhead Costs:	
Indirect labor	4,000
Supplies	1,000
Utilities	2,000
Depreciation	4,000
Finished Goods Inventory:	
January 1, 19X5	18,000
December 31, 19X5	22,000

PROBLEM 2-11: What was the amount of direct materials used in production by Hi-Tech Company?

Solution: Use Step 1 of Exhibit 2-2 to find the amount of direct materials used in production.

Direct Materials Inventory, January 1, 19X5	$11,000
+ Direct materials purchased	+ 73,000
− Direct Materials Inventory, December 31, 19X5	− 8,000
= Direct materials used in production	$76,000

[See Section 2-5.]

PROBLEM 2-12: What was the cost of goods manufactured for Hi-Tech Company?

Solution: Use Step 2 of Exhibit 2-2 to find the cost of goods manufactured.

	Work-in-Process Inventory,	
	January 1, 19X5	$ 6,000
+	Production costs transferred to	
	Work-in-Process:	
	Direct materials used	+ 76,000
	Direct labor costs incurred	+ 18,000
	Factory overhead costs incurred	+ 11,000
−	Work-in-Process Inventory,	
	December 31, 19X5	− 7,000
=	Cost of goods manufactured	$104,000

Note that the amount of $76,000 for the direct materials used was obtained from the solution to Problem 2-11. [See Section 2-5.]

PROBLEM 2-13: What is the amount of cost of goods sold for Hi-Tech Company?

Solution: Use Step 3 of Exhibit 2-2 to find the cost of goods sold.

	Finished Goods Inventory,	
	January, 1, 19X5	$ 18,000
+	Cost of goods manufactured	+ 104,000
−	Finished Goods Inventory,	
	December 31, 19X5	− 22,000
=	Cost of goods sold	$100,000

Note that the amount of $104,000 for the cost of goods manufactured was obtained from the solution to Problem 2-12. [See Section 2-5.]

PROBLEM 2-14: Prepare a Statement of Cost of Goods Manufactured for Hi-Tech Company for 19X5.

Solution:

Hi-Tech Company
Statement of Cost of Goods Manufactured
For Year Ended December 31, 19X5

Direct materials:		
Inventory, January 1	$11,000	
Purchases of direct materials	73,000	
Cost of direct materials available for use	$84,000	
Less: Inventory, December 31	8,000	
Direct materials used		$ 76,000
Direct labor costs		18,000
Factory overhead:		
Indirect labor	$ 4,000	
Supplies	1,000	
Utilities	2,000	
Depreciation	4,000	11,000
Manufacturing costs incurred during 19X5		$105,000
Add: Work-in-Process Inventory, January 1		6,000
Manufacturing costs accounted for		$111,000
Less: Work-in-Process Inventory, December 31		7,000
Cost of goods manufactured		$104,000

[See Section 2-5.]

3 *JOB-ORDER COSTING*

THIS CHAPTER IS ABOUT

☑ **Production Costing**
☑ **Source Documents for Job-Order Costing**
☑ **Journal Entries for Job-Order Costing**
☑ **Ledger Accounts for Job-Order Costing**
☑ **Underapplied and Overapplied Factory Overhead**
☑ **Cost of Goods Manufactured Statement and Income Statement**

3-1. Production Costing

Production costs are generally accumulated for two purposes: (1) product costing and (2) planning and control. Cost accumulation for product costing involves applying production costs to units of production. Cost accumulation for planning and control involves accumulating costs by various responsibility centers (e.g., production departments) within the organization for planning and control uses.

There are two primary systems of production costing: (1) job-order costing and (2) process costing. This chapter will describe the job-order costing system; process costing will be discussed in detail in Chapter 4.

A. Job-order costing systems

Job-order costing is used by organizations whose production and services can be identified by individual jobs (batches) or units. Each job generally receives varying amounts of direct materials, direct labor, and factory overhead. An organization using a job-order costing system would accumulate production costs for each job produced. Since units in different jobs generally receive different amounts of direct materials, direct labor, and factory overhead, the cost per unit for different jobs will differ. Industries that usually use job-order costing include printing, construction, and custom machinery production.

B. Process costing systems

Process costing is used by organizations whose products or services are mass-produced through a continuous series of production steps (i.e., processes). In general, process costing is used where the units of production contain approximately the same amount of direct materials, direct labor, and factory overhead. In this system, production costs are accumulated for all units produced in a period, and the cost per unit is generally the same for all units. Process costing is commonly used in industries such as oil refining, chemical processing, and steel manufacturing.

3-2. Source Documents for Job-Order Costing

A job-order costing system uses source documents to accumulate product costs for individual jobs. There are three primary source documents in job-order costing: (1) the job cost sheet, (2) the materials requisition form, and (3) the labor cost sheet. These documents are used in manual systems; similar source documents can be used in a computerized system.

A. Job cost sheet

The job cost sheet is used to accumulate and summarize product costs (direct materials, direct labor, and factory overhead) for each job. The job cost sheet usually contains the following information:

1. Job identification number
2. Customer name
3. Date/time started
4. Date/time completed
5. Direct materials costs
6. Direct labor costs
7. Factory overhead costs

The job cost sheet is used to accumulate all production costs for a specific job. The producing company usually must quote a price for the job to the buying company before all production costs for that job are incurred. The summary of the job cost sheet can be used to determine the profit or loss on a specific job.

B. Materials requisition form

The materials requisition form is used to accumulate the amount and cost of materials used in a particular job. The materials requisition form usually includes the following information:

1. Job identification number
2. Dates of materials issuance
3. Authorization for materials issuance
4. Physical quantity of materials used
5. Unit and total cost of materials used

C. Labor cost sheet

The labor cost sheet (work ticket) is used to accumulate the amount and cost of direct labor for a particular job. The labor cost sheet usually contains the following information:

1. Job identification number
2. Employee identification number
3. Date and times of work performed
4. Number of hours worked
5. Hourly rate and total labor costs

3-3. Journal Entries for Job-Order Costing

There are eight basic journal entries to record the production process in a job-order costing system. These entries are:

(A) PURCHASE OF MATERIALS

(B) ISSUANCE OF DIRECT AND INDIRECT MATERIALS TO PRODUCTION

(C) ACCRUAL OF DIRECT AND INDIRECT FACTORY LABOR PAYROLL COSTS

(D) PAYMENT OF ACCRUED FACTORY LABOR PAYROLL COSTS

(E) INCURRENCE OF FACTORY OVERHEAD COSTS OTHER THAN INDIRECT MATERIALS AND INDIRECT LABOR

(F) APPLICATION OF FACTORY OVERHEAD COSTS, USING A PREDETERMINED RATE

(G) COMPLETION OF JOB AND TRANSFER TO FINISHED GOODS INVENTORY

(H) COST OF GOODS SOLD

EXAMPLE 3-1: The following information is available for Seaside Company for the year 19X4:

Budgeted factory overhead costs	$135,000
Budgeted direct labor hours	50,000
Budgeted direct labor costs	150,000

Direct materials purchased	$260,000
Indirect materials purchased	$ 40,000
Direct materials issued to production	$240,000
Indirect materials issued to production	$ 20,000
Direct labor costs accrued	$196,000
Indirect labor costs accrued	$ 25,000
Accumulated depreciation incurred for factory building	$ 40,000
Accumulated depreciation incurred for factory equipment	$ 30,000
Prepaid insurance expired on factory building	$ 3,000
Prepaid insurance expired on factory equipment	$ 2,000
Utilities payable	$ 7,000
Miscellaneous factory expenses payable	$ 3,000
Selling and administrative expenses	$ 56,730
Job #101 was sold in 19X4	$680,760
Direct labor hours used in production	49,000

Assume that job #101 was the only job produced in 19X4.

Using this information you would prepare the following journal entries under a job-order costing system. (The T-accounts for these entries are shown in Exhibit 3-1.)

(A) PURCHASE OF MATERIALS

The Materials Control account is the inventory account for materials. The word *control* indicates that this general ledger controlling account is supported by subsidiary ledger accounts. The Materials Control account represents the total dollar amount of all materials in inventory. The subsidiary ledger accounts *Direct Materials Inventory* and *Indirect Materials Inventory* represent the specific dollar amounts of the specific types of materials in inventory. The following journal entry records the purchase of materials.

Materials Control (Direct Material)	$260,000	
Materials Control (Indirect Material)	40,000	
Accounts Payable		$300,000
To record purchase of materials.		

(B) ISSUANCE OF DIRECT AND INDIRECT MATERIALS TO PRODUCTION

Direct Materials issued to production are recorded in the Work-in-Process (WIP) Control account, which is an inventory account. Indirect materials issued to production are recorded in the Factory Overhead Control account because all production costs except direct materials and direct labor are accumulated in the Factory Overhead Control account.

WIP Control (Direct Material)	$240,000	
Factory Overhead Control (Indirect Material)	20,000	
Materials Control (Direct Material)		$240,000
Materials Control (Indirect Material)		20,000
To record issuance of materials to production.		

(C) ACCRUAL OF DIRECT AND INDIRECT FACTORY LABOR PAYROLL COSTS

Labor costs earned are accrued for factory production at the end of a period. Direct labor costs accrued are debited to Work-in-Process Control. Indirect labor costs accrued are debited to Factory Overhead. Accrued Payroll is a liability account that reflects the total (direct and indirect) labor costs accrued.

WIP Control (Direct Labor)	$196,000	
Factory Overhead Control (Indirect Labor)	25,000	
Accrued Payroll		$221,000
To record factory payroll earned.		

(D) PAYMENT OF ACCRUED FACTORY LABOR PAYROLL COSTS

This entry simply reflects the payment of the accrued payroll.

Accrued Payroll	$221,000	
Cash		$221,000
To record factory payroll earned.		

NOTE: For simplification, payroll taxes are not shown in these journal entries.

(E) INCURRENCE OF FACTORY OVERHEAD COSTS OTHER THAN INDIRECT MATERIALS AND INDIRECT LABOR

Factory overhead includes all production costs except direct labor and direct materials. Factory overhead may include:

Indirect materials	Payroll taxes on factory worker wages
Indirect labor	Depreciation on factory plant and equipment
Repairs to factory buildings and equipment	
Insurance on factory plant and equipment	Utilities

Factory overhead does not include selling and administrative expenses.

The debit to Factory Overhead Control represents the total of other factory overhead costs incurred. The credit to Prepaid Insurance reflects the amount of prepaid insurance that has expired during the accounting period. The credit to Accumulated Depreciation represents the amount of depreciation expense for the accounting period.

Factory Overhead Control	$85,000	
Prepaid Insurance–Factory Building		$ 3,000
Prepaid Insurance–Factory Equipment		2,000
Accumulated Depreciation–Building		40,000
Accumulated Depreciation–Equipment		30,000
Utilities payable		7,000
Miscellaneous factory expenses payable		3,000
To record factory overhead.		

(F) APPLICATION OF FACTORY OVERHEAD COSTS, USING A PREDETERMINED RATE

As you can see from the journal entry in (E), the overhead costs incurred are for the benefit of all jobs produced during the period and cannot be related to any particular job. Also, some overhead costs such as utilities and other factory overhead costs will not be known until the end of the period. Rather than hold a finished job in inventory until all costs can be attributed to it, it is necessary to develop a method of allocating oberhead costs to jobs on a predetermined basis.

The predetermined overhead application rate is determined as follows:

1. Estimate budgeted factory overhead.
2. Choose a base–such as direct labor hours, direct labor dollars, or machine hours.
3. Estimate budgeted direct labor hours (or direct labor dollars or machine hours).
4. Use one of the following equations to determine the predetermined overhead rate:

$$\text{Predetermined overhead rate} = \frac{\text{Budgeted factory overhead}}{\text{Budgeted direct labor hours}} \tag{3.1}$$

$$\text{Predetermined overhead rate} = \frac{\text{Budgeted factory overhead}}{\text{Budgeted direct labor costs}} \tag{3.2}$$

$$\text{Predetermined overhead rate} = \frac{\text{Budgeted factory overhead}}{\text{Budgeted machine hours}} \tag{3.3}$$

Seaside Company's budgeted factory overhead costs are $135,000. Budgeted direct labor hours are 50,000, and budgeted direct labor costs are $150,000. Compute the predetermined overhead rate using budgeted direct labor hours and budgeted direct labor costs. The predetermined overhead rate based on direct labor hours is:

$$\text{Predetermined overhead rate} = \frac{\text{Budgeted factory overhead}}{\text{Budgeted direct labor hours}}$$

$$= \frac{\$135,000}{50,000}$$

$$= \$2.70 \text{ per direct labor hour}$$

The predetermined overhead rate based on direct labor costs is:

$$\text{Predetermined overhead rate} = \frac{\text{Budgeted factory overhead}}{\text{Budgeted direct labor costs}}$$

$$= \frac{\$135,000}{\$150,000}$$

$$= 90\% \text{ of direct labor costs}$$

You now know that for Seaside Company, the predetermined overhead rate is $2.70 per direct labor hour used in production. The direct labor hours used in production were 49,000. Therefore, the journal entry to record Factory Overhead Applied would be:

WIP Control (Factory Overhead Applied)	$132,300	
Factory Overhead Applied ($2.70 × 49,000)		$132,300
To record applied factory overhead.		

(G) COMPLETION OF JOB AND TRANSFER TO FINISHED GOODS INVENTORY

When job #101 has been completed, the costs associated with this job are transferred from the WIP Control account to the Finished Goods Control inventory account.

Finished Goods Control	$568,300	
WIP Control (Direct Material)		$240,000
WIP Control (Direct Labor)		196,000
WIP Control (Factory Overhead Applied)		132,300
To record transfer of completed goods.		

(H) COST OF GOODS SOLD

When job #101 has been sold, the costs of that job are transferred from the Finished Goods Control account—an inventory account—to the Cost of Goods Sold account—an expense account.

Cost of Goods Sold	$568,300	
Finished Goods Control		$568,300
To record cost of sale.		

To record the sale of job #101, make the following journal entry:

Cash	$680,760	
Sales		$680,760
To record sale of goods.		

To record the payment of selling and administrative expenses, make the following journal entry:

Selling and Administrative Expenses	$56,730	
Cash		$56,730
To record payment of selling and administrative expenses.		

3-4. Ledger Accounts for Job-Order Costing

Exhibit 3-1 illustrates the general ledger accounts used to make the journal entries in Example 3-1. The letters are references to the journal entries in Example 3-1. Remember the following points when tracing these journal entries.

1. Materials Control, Work-in-Process Control, and Finished Goods Control are inventory accounts.
2. Cost of Goods Sold is an expense account, which will be found on the income statement.
3. Factory Overhead Applied is found by using a predetermined overhead rate multiplied by an appropriate base such as direct labor hours. This amount is credited to the Factory Overhead Applied account and debited to the Work-in-Process Control account.
4. Factory Overhead Applied represents an estimate of costs. Factory Overhead Control represents actual costs incurred. The amounts in these accounts will rarely be equal. Section 3-5 will explain the concept of overapplied factory overhead and underapplied factory overhead.

EXHIBIT 3-1

General Ledger Accounts for Job-Order Costing

Material Control

(A)	260,000	240,000	(B)
(A)	40,000	20,000	(B)

Work-in-Process Control

(B)	240,000	240,000	(G)
(C)	196,000	196,000	(G)
(F)	132,300	132,300	(G)

Finished Goods Control

(G)	568,300	568,300	(H)

Cost of Goods Sold

(H)	568,300	

Factory Overhead Applied

	132,300	(F)

Factory Overhead Control

(B)	20,000	
(C)	25,000	
(E)	85,000	

Accounts Payable

	300,000	(A)

Accrued Payroll

(D)	221,000	221,000	(C)

Cash

(H)	680,760	221,000	(D)
		56,730	(H)

Prepaid Insurance–Factory

	3,000	(E)
	2,000	(E)

Accumulated Depr.–Factory

	40,000	(E)
	30,000	(E)

Misc. Factory Exp. Payable

	3,000	(E)

Utilities Payable

	7,000	(E)

Selling & Admin. Expenses

(H)	56,730	

Sales

	680,760	(H)

3-5. Underapplied and Overapplied Factory Overhead

The factory overhead costs that are applied to the jobs produced during the year using a predetermined overhead rate are recorded in the Factory Overhead Applied account. Actual factory overhead costs incurred are recorded in the Factory Overhead Control account. Generally, the amount recorded in Factory Overhead Applied during the year will differ from the amount recorded in Factory Overhead Control. This condition means that factory overhead will be either underapplied or overapplied.

A. Underapplied overhead

If the ending balance in the Factory Overhead Control account exceeds the ending balance in Factory Overhead Applied, overhead is *underapplied*. In other words, the amount of factory overhead cost *applied* to production is *less* than the actual factory overhead costs *incurred*.

At the end of the period, the amount of underapplied overhead is either:

1. closed to Cost of Goods Sold or
2. allocated proportionately to Work-in-Process Control, Finished Goods Control, and Cost of Goods Sold.

The most accurate treatment is to prorate the underapplied overhead amount. This approach is used if the underapplied overhead is material in amount. However, a widely practiced course of action is to close the underapplied overhead to Cost of Goods Sold.

EXAMPLE 3-2: Bassel Company has the following year-end balances:

Factory Overhead Applied

$324,000	

Factory Overhead Control

$326,000	

Work-in-Process Control

$30,000	

Finished Goods Control

$70,000	

Cost of Goods Sold

$900,000	

Factory overhead has been underapplied, since the balance in Factory Overhead Control is greater than the balance in Factory Overhead Applied. You compute the amount of underapplied overhead as follows:

$$\text{Underapplied overhead} = \text{Factory Overhead Control} - \text{Factory Overhead Applied} \quad \text{(3.4)}$$
$$= \$326,000 - \$324,000$$
$$= \$2,000 \text{ underapplied factory overhead}$$

1. CLOSE UNDERAPPLIED OVERHEAD TO COST OF GOODS SOLD

Debit the $2,000 of underapplied factory overhead to Cost of Goods Sold. Debit Factory Overhead Applied to close that account, and credit Factory Overhead Control to close that account.

Factory Overhead Applied	$324,000	
Cost of Goods Sold	2,000	
Factory Overhead Control		$326,000
To close factory overhead accounts.		

This journal entry accomplishes two things: (1) It adjusts Cost of Goods Sold for the difference between actual and applied factory overhead, and (2) it closes the Factory Overhead Applied and Factory Overhead Control accounts.

2. ALLOCATE UNDERAPPLIED OVERHEAD PROPORTIONATELY TO WORK-IN-PROCESS CONTROL, FINISHED GOODS CONTROL, AND COST OF GOODS SOLD ACCOUNTS.

Theoretically, this is the preferred method; however, it is generally not used when the amount of underapplied (or overapplied) overhead is immaterial, or when the process of proration is too complicated.

Prorate the underapplied overhead in proportion to the amount of factory overhead costs in each of these three accounts. The amounts of factory overhead costs in the year-end account balances for the Bassel Company are:

Account	Factory overhead costs	Percentage
Cost of Goods Sold	$275,400	85%
Finished Goods Control	32,400	10
Work-in-Process Control	16,200	5
Total factory overhead applied	$324,000	100%

Using the percentages of factory overhead cost in each account, you would prorate the underapplied overhead as follows:

Cost of Goods Sold	$2,000 × 85% = $1,700
Finished Goods Control	$2,000 × 10% = 200
Work-in-Process Control	$2,000 × 5% = 100
Total	$2,000

Your would record the proration of the underapplied overhead to the three accounts with the following journal entry:

Cost of Goods Sold	$ 1,700	
Finished Goods Control	200	
Work-in-Process Control	100	
Factory Overhead Applied	324,000	
Factory Overhead Control		$326,000
To close factory overhead accounts.		

B. Overapplied overhead.

If the ending balance in Factory Overhead Applied is greater than the ending balance in Factory Overhead Control, overhead has been *overapplied*. In other words, the factory overhead cost *applied* is *greater* than actual factory overhead cost incurred. The accounting treatment for overapplied overhead is the same as for underapplied overhead, except that the adjustments to the Work-in-Process Control, Finished Goods Control, and Cost of Goods Sold accounts would be credits instead of debits.

EXAMPLE 3-3: Lausanne Company had the following year-end balances:

Factory Overhead Applied	Factory Overhead Control	Finished Goods Control
91,280	90,720	19,600

Work-in-Process Control	Cost of Goods Sold
8,400	252,000

Overapplied overhead = Factory Overhead Control − Factory Overhead Applied

= $90,720 − $91,280

= $560 overapplied factory overhead

1. CLOSE OVERAPPLIED OVERHEAD TO COST OF GOODS SOLD.

Factory Overhead Applied	$91,280	
Factory Overhead Control		$90,720
Cost of Goods Sold		560
To close factory overhead accounts.		

2. ALLOCATE OVERAPPLIED OVERHEAD PROPORTIONATELY TO WORK-IN-PROCESS CONTROL, FINISHED GOODS CONTROL, AND COST OF GOODS SOLD.

The amounts of factory overhead costs in the year-end account balances for the Lausanne Company are:

	Factory overhead costs	Percentage
Cost of Goods Sold	$73,024	80%
Finished Goods Control	13,692	15
Work-in-Process Control	4,564	5
Total factory overhead applied	$91,280	100%

Using the percentages of factory overhead cost in each account, you would prorate the overapplied overhead as follows:

Cost of Goods Sold	$560 × 80% = $448
Finished Goods Control	$560 × 15% = $ 84
Work-in-Process Control	$560 × 5% = $ 28
Total	$560

You would then record the proration of the overapplied overhead to the three accounts with the following journal entry:

Factory Overhead Applied	$91,280	
Cost of Goods Sold		$ 448
Finished Goods Control		84
Work-in-Process Control		28
Factory Overhead Control		90,720
To close factory overhead accounts.		

3-6. Cost of Goods Manufactured Statement and Income Statement

A. Cost of goods manufactured statement

The purpose of a cost of goods manufactured statement is to summarize all production costs for a period. The production costs consist of direct material, direct labor, and factory overhead. Following is a model Cost of Goods Manufactured statement.

Company Name
Cost of Goods Manufactured
For the Period Ended, Date

Direct Materials Control, Beginning Inventory	$XXX	
Add: Purchases	+ XXX	
Direct Materials Available for Use	$XXX	
Less: Direct Materials Control, Ending Inventory	− XXX	
Direct Materials Used		$XXX
Direct Labor		+ XXX
Factory Overhead Costs:		
Indirect Materials Used	$XXX	
Indirect Labor	+ XXX	
Depreciation	+ XXX	
Insurance	+ XXX	
Miscellaneous	+ XXX	
Total Overhead Costs		+ XXX
Total Manufacturing Costs		$XXX
Add: Work-in-Process Control, Beginning Inventory		+ XXX
Total costs to account for		$XXX
Less: Work-in-Process Control, Ending Inventory		− XXX
Cost of Goods Manufactured		$XXX

B. Income statement

A company's income statement shows whether the business earned net income or incurred a net loss for the period covered. For a manufacturing company, the cost of goods manufactured is included in the income statement under the cost of goods sold section. Following is a model income statement.

Company Name
Income Statement
For the Period Ended, Date

Sales		$XX,XXX
Less: Cost of Goods Sold:		
Finished Goods Control, Beginning Inventory	$XX,XXX	
Add: Cost of Goods Manufactured	+ XXX	
Cost of Goods Available for Sale	$XX,XXX	
Less: Finished Goods Control, Ending Inventory	− XX,XXX	
Cost of Goods Sold		− XX,XXX
Gross Margin		$XX,XXX
Administrative and Selling Expenses:		
Less: Administrative Expenses	$ X,XXX	
Less: Selling Expenses	XXX	− X,XXX
Income before Taxes		$XX,XXX
Income Taxes		− X,XXX
Net Income		$XX,XXX

EXAMPLE 3-4: Cubbie Company is in the business of manufacturing baseball pennants. The following information is available for the year ended December 31, 19X4:

	Account Balances	
	January 1	December 31
Direct Materials Control	$2,000	$10,000
Work-in-Process Control	3,500	2,000
Finished Goods Control	1,500	30,000

The following information is also available:

Direct labor costs	$ 30,000
Direct materials purchased	$100,000

Other actual factory overhead costs include:

Indirect materials used	$ 900
Indirect labor	20,000
Insurance	5,000
Depreciation	1,000
Miscellaneous	500

The year 19X4 proved to be very disappointing for Cubbie Company. They had budgeted sales of $1,000,000, but actual sales were only $50,000. Administrative expenses and selling expenses were $25,000 and $20,000, respectively. Cubbie Company's tax rate is 15%.

Based on this information and using the model statements, we can prepare a Cost of Goods Manufactured statement and an Income Statement for Cubbie Company for 19X4.

Cubbie Company
Cost of Goods Manufactured Statement
For the Year Ended, December 31, 19X4

Direct Materials Control, Jan. 1	$ 2,000	
Add: Purchases	100,000	
Direct Materials Available for Use	$102,000	
Less: Direct Materials Control, Dec. 31	10,000	
Direct Materials Used		$ 92,000
Direct Labor		30,000
Factory Overhead Costs:		
Indirect Materials Used	$ 900	
Indirect Labor	20,000	
Insurance	5,000	
Depreciation	1,000	
Miscellaneous	500	
Total Overhead Costs		27,400
Total Manufacturing Costs		$149,400
Add: Work-in-Process, Jan. 1		3,500
Total costs to account for		$152,900
Less: Work-in-Process, Dec. 31		2,000
Cost of Goods Manufactured		$150,900

Cubbie Company
Income Statement
For the Year Ended, December 31, 19X4

Sales		$ 50,000
Less: Cost of Goods Sold:		
Finished Goods Control, Jan. 1	$ 1,500	
Add: Cost of Goods Manufactured	150,900	
Cost of Goods Available for Sale	$152,400	
Less: Finished Goods Control, Dec. 31	30,000	
Cost of Goods Sold		122,400
Gross Margin		$ (72,400)
Administrative and Selling Expenses:		
Less: Administrative Expenses	$ 25,000	
Less: Selling Expenses	20,000	
Income before Taxes		45,000
		$(117,400)
Income Taxes (15%)		–0–
Net Loss		$(117,400)

RAISE YOUR GRADES

Can you explain...?

☑ the two purposes of cost accumulation
☑ the differences between job-order costing and process costing
☑ the source documents that are used in a job-order costing system
☑ how to prepare journal entries to record the purchase and issuance of materials costs in a job-order costing system
☑ how to prepare journal entries to record factory labor costs in a job-order costing system
☑ how to prepare journal entries to record factory overhead costs in a job-order costing system
☑ how to prepare journal entries to record the completion and sale of jobs in a job-order costing system
☑ how to compute a predetermined overhead rate
☑ how to determine whether factory overhead is underapplied or overapplied
☑ what journal entries are acceptable to account for underapplied or overapplied overhead
☑ how to prepare a cost of goods manufactured statement
☑ how to prepare an income statement

SUMMARY

1. Production costs are accumulated for product pricing purposes and for planning and control purposes.
2. The two primary systems of production costing are job-order costing and process costing.
3. Job-order costing is used by organizations whose products can be identified by individual jobs (or batches).
4. Process costing is used by organizations whose products are mass-produced through a continuous series of production steps.
5. The job cost sheet, the materials requisition form, and the labor cost sheet are source documents for job-order costing and are used to accumulate production costs for individual jobs.
6. There are eight basic journal entries used to record the production process for job-order costing.

    (a) Purchase of materials
    (b) Issuance of direct and indirect materials to production
    (c) Accrual of direct and indirect factory labor payroll costs
    (d) Payment of accrued factory labor payroll costs
    (e) Incurrence of factory overhead costs other than indirect materials and indirect labor
    (f) Application of factory overhead costs, using a predetermined rate
    (g) Completion of job and transfer to finished goods inventory
    (h) Cost of goods sold

7. The term *control* in ledger account titles means that subsidiary ledger accounts provide detailed records that support the control account.
8. Direct materials costs used in production are recorded in the Work-in-Process Control account.
9. Direct labor costs incurred in production are recorded in the Work-in-Process Control account.
10. All production costs *except* direct materials and direct labor are accumulated in the Factory Overhead Control account.

11. Use one of the following equations to determine the predetermined overhead rate:

$$\text{Predetermined overhead rate} = \frac{\text{Budgeted factory overhead}}{\text{Budgeted direct labor hours}} \qquad \textbf{(3.1)}$$

$$\text{Predetermined overhead rate} = \frac{\text{Budgeted factory overhead}}{\text{Budgeted direct labor costs}} \qquad \textbf{(3.2)}$$

$$\text{Predetermined overhead rate} = \frac{\text{Budgeted factory overhead}}{\text{Budgeted machine hours}} \qquad \textbf{(3.3)}$$

12. Multiply the predetermined overhead rate by the appropriate base (direct labor hours, direct labor costs, or machine hours) to find the amount of Factory Overhead Applied.

13. The amount of Factory Overhead Applied is credited to Factory Overhead Applied and debited to Work-in-Process Control.

14. The difference between the ending balances in the Factory Overhead Applied and the Factory Overhead Control accounts represents underapplied or overapplied factory overhead.

15. Underapplied factory overhead can be allocated in two ways: (1) Debit the amount of underapplied factory overhead to Cost of Goods Sold, or (2) debit the amount proportionately to Cost of Goods Sold, Finished Goods Control, and Work-in-Process Control.

16. Overapplied factory overhead can be allocated in two ways: (1) Credit the amount of underapplied factory overhead to Cost of Goods Sold, or (2) credit the amount proportionately to Cost of Goods Sold, Finished Goods Control, and Work-in-Process Control.

17. The Cost of Goods Manufactured statement summarizes all production costs for a period.

18. The cost of goods manufactured amount is included in the income statement under the cost of goods sold section.

19. The Income Statement shows whether the company earned net income or incurred a net loss.

RAPID REVIEW

1. Production costs are generally accumulated for the purposes of (a) product costing, (b) planning and control, (c) both of the above, (d) none of the above. [See Section 3-1.]

2. Which production costing system would be used by organizations whose products can be identified by individual jobs or batches? (a) process costing, (b) job-order costing, (c) none of the above. [See Section 3-1.]

3. Which production costing system would be used by organizations whose products are mass-produced using a continuous series of production steps? (a) process costing, (b) job-order costing, (c) none of the above. [See Section 3-1.]

4. Which of the following is *not* a source document used in job-order costing? (a) job cost sheet, (b) materials requisition form, (c) labor requisition form, (d) labor cost sheet. [See Section 3-2.]

5. When direct materials are issued to production, the cost of these materials is transferred from Materials Control to (a) Work-in-Process Control, (b) Factory Overhead Control, (c) Factory Overhead Applied, (d) none of the above. [See Section 3-3.]

6. When indirect materials are issued to production, the cost of these materials is transferred from the Materials Control account to (a) Work-in-Process Control, (b) Factory Overhead Control, (c) Factory Overhead Applied, (d) none of the above. [See Secton 3-3.]

7. Actual factory overhead costs incurred are recorded in which of the following general ledger accounts? (a) Factory Overhead Control, (b) Factory Overhead Applied, (c) Work-in-Process Control, (d) none of the above. [See Section 3-3.]

8. If the year-end balance in the Factory Overhead Control account is greater than the balance in the Factory Overhead Applied account, overhead has been (a) overapplied, (b) underapplied, (c) neither overapplied nor underapplied. [See Section 3-5.]

9. The most widely practiced year-end treatment of underapplied factory overhead is to (a) debit Cost of Goods Sold, (b) credit Cost of Goods Sold, (c) prorate the amount between Cost of Goods Sold and Finished Goods Control. [See Section 3-5.]

10. The most accurate year-end treatment of overapplied factory overhead is to (**a**) debit Cost of Goods Sold, (**b**) credit Cost of Goods Sold, Finished Goods Control, and Work-in-Process Control, (**c**) debit Work-in-Process Control. [See Section 3-5.]

11. The predetermined factory overhead rate can be computed by dividing budgeted factory overhead costs by (**a**) budgeted direct labor hours, (**b**) actual direct labor hours, (**c**) actual direct labor costs. [See Section 3-3.]

12. Which of the following is *not* an inventory account within a job-order costing system? (**a**) Work-in-Process Control, (**b**) Finished Goods Control, (**c**) Cost of Goods Sold, (**d**) Materials Control. [See Section 3-4.]

Answers:

1. (**c**)   2. (**b**)   3. (**a**)   4. (**c**)   5. (**a**)   6. (**b**)   7. (**a**)   8. (**b**)   9. (**a**)

10. (**b**)   11. (**a**)   12. (**c**)

SOLVED PROBLEMS

PROBLEM 3-1: Chicago Company uses a job-order costing system. The following transactions occurred during the month of May:

1. Direct materials of $80,000 were issued to production. Indirect materials of $10,000 were issued to production.
2. Direct labor costs of $80,000 were incurred. Indirect labor costs of $15,000 were incurred.
3. Other factory overhead costs incurred during the month were: $25,000 for accumulated depreciation, $10,000 for manufacturing supplies, and $2,000 for miscellaneous.
4. Factory overhead is applied to production at a predetermined overhead rate of $4.00 per direct labor hour. Direct labor hours used in production = 10,000.
5. Jobs with a total cost of $200,000 were completed and transferred during the month.
6. Jobs with a total cost of $180,000 were shipped and invoiced to customers during the month.

On the basis of this information, prepare the journal entries relating to production costs.

Solution: The journal entries for the transactions are as follows:

1.	Work-in-Process Control (Direct Material)	$80,000	
	Factory Overhead Control (Indirect Material)	10,000	
	Material Control (Direct Material)		$80,000
	Material Control (Indirect Material)		10,000
	To record issuance of materials to production.		
2.	Work-in-Process Control (Direct Labor)	$80,000	
	Factory Overhead Control (Indirect Labor)	15,000	
	Accrued Payroll		$95,000
	To record factory payroll earned.		
3.	Factory Overhead Control	$37,000	
	Accumulated Depreciation—Factory		$25,000
	Manufacturing Supplies		10,000
	Miscellaneous Factory Expenses Payable		2,000
	To record factory overhead.		
4.	Work-in-Process Control (Factory Overhead Applied)	$40,000	
	Factory Overhead Applied ($4.00 × 10,000)		$40,000
	To record applied factory overhead.		
5.	Finished Goods Control	$200,000	
	Work-in-Process Control		$200,000
	To record transfer of completed goods.		

6. Cost of Goods Sold $180,000

    Finished Goods Control $180,000

    To record cost of sales.

[See Section 3-3].

PROBLEM 3-2: Following are the year-end balances for the factory overhead accounts of Allanco Company:

Factory Overhead Control $200,000
Factory Overhead Applied $250,000

Assume that Allanco Company adjusts the Cost of Goods Sold account for the total amount of underapplied or overapplied overhead.

Make the journal entry to close the factory overhead accounts.

Solution: The amount of over- or underapplied overhead is found by subtracting the amount of Factory Overhead Applied from the actual amount of Factory Overhead Control. If the amount is positive (actual factory overhead is greater than applied factory overhead), factory overhead has been underapplied. If the amount is negative (actual factory overhead is less than applied factory overhead), factory overhead has been overapplied.

Factory Overhead Control $200,000
− Factory Overhead Applied   250,000

$ (50,000) overapplied factory overhead

The journal entry to adjust Cost of Goods Sold and to close the factory overhead accounts is:

Factory Overhead Applied $250,000

    Factory Overhead Control $200,000

    Cost of Goods Sold 50,000

To close factory overhead accounts.

[See Section 3-5.]

Problems 3-3 and 3-4 are based on the following information.

Northern University Press uses a job-order costing system. The following data pertain to the actual results for 19X8:

Direct materials purchased on account	$ 80,000
Indirect materials purchased on account	6,500
Direct materials issued to production	72,000
Indirect materials issued to production	3,200
Direct labor costs incurred (10,000 hours)	110,000
Indirect labor costs incurred	5,000
Other factory overhead costs incurred	110,000

The budgeted factory overhead costs for 19X8 were $150,000, and budgeted direct labor hours were 15,000. Factory overhead costs are applied to production based on direct labor hours.

PROBLEM 3-3: Prepare the journal entries for the following:

1. Materials purchased
2. Materials issued to production
3. Labor costs incurred
4. Other factory overhead costs incurred
5. Factory overhead costs applied

Solution: The journal entries are as follows:

1. Materials Control (Direct Material) $80,000

    Materials Control (Indirect Material) 6,500

    Accounts Payable $86,500

    To record purchase of materials.

2. | | | |
    |---|---|---|
    | Work-in-Process Control (Direct Material) | $72,000 | |
    | Factory Overhead Control (Indirect Material) | 3,200 | |
    | Materials Control (Direct Material) | | $72,000 |
    | Materials Control (Indirect Material) | | 3,200 |
    | To record issuance of materials to production. | | |

3. | | | |
    |---|---|---|
    | Work-in-Process Control (Direct Labor) | $110,000 | |
    | Factory Overhead Control (Indirect Labor) | 5,000 | |
    | Accrued Payroll | | $115,000 |
    | To record factory payroll earned. | | |

4. | | | |
    |---|---|---|
    | Factory Overhead Control | $110,000 | |
    | Sundry Accounts* | | $110,000 |
    | To record factory overhead. | | |

* Remember that the credit to "Sundry Accounts" represents such accounts as accumulated depreciation, prepaid insurance, and utilities payable—all relating to the factory overhead expenses.

5. Before making this journal entry, you must compute the predetermined factory overhead rate as follows:

$$\frac{\text{Predetermined}}{\text{overhead rate}} = \frac{\text{Budgeted factory overhead}}{\text{Budgeted direct labor hours}}$$

$$= \frac{\$150,000}{15,000}$$

$$= \$10.00 \text{ per direct labor hour.}$$

Next, you compute the amount of factory overhead applied:

$$\frac{\text{Factory}}{\text{overhead applied}} = \frac{\text{Predetermined}}{\text{overhead rate}} \times \frac{\text{Actual direct}}{\text{labor hours}}$$

$$= \$10.00 \times 10,000$$

$$= \$100,000 \text{ factory overhead applied}$$

The journal entry for factory overhead applied is:

Work-in-Process Control (Factory Overhead Applied)	$100,000	
Factory Overhead Applied		$100,000
To record factory overhead applied.		

[See Section 3-3.]

PROBLEM 3-4: Compute the amount of underapplied or overapplied overhead and make the necessary journal entry to allocate that amount to Cost of Goods Sold only.

Solution: To find the amount of over- or underapplied factory overhead, you must first compute the total actual factory overhead costs and then subtract from that amount the factory overhead applied (see journal entry 5 from Problem 3-3).

Actual Factory Overhead Costs:		
Indirect Materials	$ 3,200	
Indirect Labor	5,000	
Sundry Accounts	110,000	$118,200
Factory Overhead Applied		100,000
		$ 18,200 underapplied factory overhead

The journal entry to allocate this amount of underapplied overhead to Cost of Goods Sold is:

Cost of Goods Sold	$ 18,200	
Factory Overhead Applied	100,000	
Factory Overhead Control		$118,200
To close factory overhead accounts.		

[See Section 3-5.]

Problems 3-5, 3-6, and 3-7 are based on the following information.

The DPU Manufacturing Company estimates budgeted direct labor costs of $98,000; budgeted direct labor hours of 24,500; and budgeted factory overhead costs of $147,000.

DPU worked on and completed only one job during the year. The company paid direct labor wages of $5.36 per hour. Actual hours used in production were 25,000. Actual factory overhead costs were $152,000.

PROBLEM 3-5: If DPU applies factory overhead on the basis of direct labor hours,

A. CALCULATE THE PREDETERMINED OVERHEAD RATE.

B. MAKE JOURNAL ENTRIES TO RECORD:

1. actual factory overhead incurred
2. applied factory overhead

C. DETERMINE THE AMOUNT OF OVERAPPLIED OR UNDERAPPLIED FACTORY OVERHEAD AND MAKE THE NECESSARY JOURNAL ENTRY TO ALLOCATE THAT AMOUNT TO COST OF GOODS SOLD ONLY.

Solution:

A. CALCULATE THE PREDETERMINED OVERHEAD RATE.

Calculate the predetermined overhead rate based on direct labor hours using the following equation:

$$\text{Predetermined overhead rate} = \frac{\text{Budgeted factory overhead costs}}{\text{Budgeted direct labor hours}}$$

$$= \frac{\$147,000}{24,500}$$

$$= \$6.00 \text{ per direct labor hour}$$

B. MAKE JOURNAL ENTRIES TO RECORD:

1. actual factory overhead incurred

To record actual factory overhead incurred, make a debit for the entire amount to Factory Overhead Control and a credit to each overhead account involved. (For simplicity, we have made one credit entry to Sundry Accounts.)

Factory Overhead Control	$152,000	
Sundry Accounts		$152,000
To record actual factory overhead.		

2. applied factory overhead

To apply factory overhead using a predetermined overhead rate based on direct labor hours, we must know the predetermined overhead rate ($6.00) and the *actual* number of direct labor hours used in production (25,000).

Compute the amount of applied factory overhead based on direct labor hours using the following equation:

$$\text{Applied Factory Overhead} = \text{Pedetermined overhead rate} \times \text{Actual direct labor hours}$$

$$= \$6.00 \times 25,000$$

$$= \$150,000$$

The journal entry is:

Work in Process (Factory Overhead Applied)	$150,000	
Factory Overhead Applied ($6.00 × 25,000)		$150,000
To record factory overhead applied.		

C. DETERMINE THE AMOUNT OF OVERAPPLIED OR UNDERAPPLIED FACTORY OVERHEAD.

The amount of over- or underapplied overhead is found by subtracting the amount of factory overhead applied from the *actual* amount of Factory Overhead Control. If the amount is *positive* (actual factory overhead is greater than applied factory overhead), factory overhead has been underapplied. If the amount is *negative* (actual factory overhead is less than applied factory overhead), factory overhead has been overapplied.

Actual Factory Overhead	$152,000
— Factory Overhead Applied	150,000
	$ 2,000 underapplied factory overhead

Making the necessary journal entry to allocate the over- and underapplied factory overhead to Cost of Goods Sold only also closes out both the Factory Overhead Control and the Factory Overhead Applied accounts.

The problem in closing the amount of over- or underapplied factory overhead to Cost of Goods Sold arises when deciding whether to debit or credit the account.

REMEMBER: If factory overhead has been underapplied, the Cost of Goods Sold account must be increased. The Cost of Goods Sold account normally has a debit balance, and to increase an account that normally has a debit balance, you must debit that account.

Whenever you make journal entries, always debit and credit the amounts you know for sure. To close the Factory Overhead Control and Factory Overhead Applied accounts, you would make the following journal entry:

Factory Overhead Applied	150,000	
Factory Overhead Control		$152,000

You can see that a debit of $2,000 is needed to balance this journal entry. Because factory overhead was underapplied by $2,000 and the entire amount is closed to Cost of Goods Sold, debit Cost of Goods Sold for the entire amount. The journal entry is:

Cost of Goods Sold	$ 2,000	
Factory Overhead Applied	150,000	
Factory Overhead Control		$152,000
To close factory overhead accounts.		

[See Sections 3-3 and 3-5.]

PROBLEM 3-6: If DPU applies factory overhead on the basis of direct labor costs,

A. CALCULATE THE PREDETERMINED OVERHEAD RATE.

B. MAKE JOURNAL ENTRIES TO RECORD:

1. actual factory overhead incurred
2. applied factory overhead

C. DETERMINE THE AMOUNT OF OVERAPPLIED OR UNDERAPPLIED FACTORY OVERHEAD AND MAKE THE NECESSARY JOURNAL ENTRY TO ALLOCATE THAT AMOUNT TO COST OF GOODS SOLD ONLY.

Solution:

A. CALCULATE THE PREDETERMINED OVERHEAD RATE.

Calculate the predetermined overhead rate based on direct labor costs using the following equation:

$$\text{Predetermined overhead rate} = \frac{\text{Budgeted factory overhead costs}}{\text{Budgeted direct labor costs}}$$

$$= \frac{\$147,000}{\$98,000}$$

$$= 150\% \text{ of direct labor costs}$$

B. MAKE JOURNAL ENTRIES TO RECORD:

1. actual factory overhead incurred

To record actual factory overhead incurred, make a debit for the entire amount to Factory Overhead Control and a credit to each overhead account involved. (For simplicity, we have made one credit entry to Sundry Accounts.)

Factory Overhead Control	$152,000	
Sundry Accounts		$152,000
To record actual factory overhead.		

2. applied factory overhead

To apply factory overhead using a predetermined overhead rate based on direct labor cost, we must first determine actual direct labor costs. To do this we must know the actual direct labor hours used in production (25,000) and the actual direct labor wage rate per hour ($5.36).

Compute actual direct labor costs using the following equation.

$$\frac{\text{Actual direct labor}}{\text{costs used in production}} = \frac{\text{Actual direct labor}}{\text{hours used in production}} \times \frac{\text{Actual direct labor}}{\text{wage rate per hour}}$$

$$= 25,000 \times \$5.36$$
$$= \$134,000$$

The predetermined overhead rate based on direct labor costs is 150%.

Compute the amount of applied factory overhead based on direct labor cost, using the following equation:

$$\frac{\text{Applied Factory}}{\text{Overhead}} = \frac{\text{Predetermined}}{\text{overhead rate}} \times \frac{\text{Actual direct}}{\text{labor costs}}$$

$$= 150\% \times \$134,000$$
$$= \$201,000$$

The journal entry is:

Work in Process (Factory Overhead Applied)	$201,000	
Factory Overhead Applied		$201,000
To record factory overhead applied.		

C. DETERMINE THE AMOUNT OF OVERAPPLIED OR UNDERAPPLIED FACTORY OVERHEAD.

The amount of over- or underapplied overhead is found by subtracting the amount of factory overhead applied from the *actual* amount of Factory Overhead Control. If the amount is *positive* (actual factory overhead is greater than applied factory overhead), factory overhead has been *underapplied*. If the amount is *negative* (actual factory overhead is less than applied factory overhead), factory overhead has been *overapplied*.

Actual Factory Overhead	$152,000
— Factory Overhead Applied	201,000
	$(49,000) overapplied factory overhead

Making the necessary journal entry to allocate the over- and underapplied factory overhead to Cost of Goods Sold only also closes out both the Factory Overhead Control and the Factory Overhead Applied accounts.

The problem in closing the amount of over- or underapplied factory overhead to Cost of Goods Sold arises when deciding whether to debit or credit the account.

REMEMBER: If factory overhead has been overapplied, the Cost of Goods Sold account must be decreased. The cost of Goods Sold account normally has a debit balance, and to decrease an account that normally has a debit balance, you must credit that account.

Whenever you make journal entries, always debit and credit the amounts you know for sure. To close the Factory Overhead Control and Factory Overhead Applied accounts, you would make the following journal entry:

Factory Overhead Applied	$201,000	
Factory Overhead Control		$152,000

You can see that a credit of $49,000 is needed to balance this journal entry. Because factory overhead was overapplied by $49,000, and the entire amount is closed to Cost of Goods Sold, credit Cost of Goods Sold for the entire amount. The journal entry is:

Factory Overhead Applied	$201,000	
Factory Overhead Control		$152,000
Cost of Goods Sold		49,000
To close factory overhead accounts.		

[See Sections 3-3 and 3-5.]

PROBLEM 3-7: Based on your answer to Problem 3-6C, prorate the amount of over- or underapplied factory overhead to the following accounts, based on their respective percentage of factory overhead costs:

	Factory overhead costs
Cost of Goods Sold	$ 60,300
Finished Goods Control	104,520
Work-in-Process Control	36,180
Total factory overhead applied	$201,000

Solution: The amount of overapplied factory overhead in Problem 3-6C was $49,000. To prorate the overapplied factory overhead to Cost of Goods Sold, Finished Goods Control, and Work-in-Process Control, you must find the percentage of factory overhead costs that each of these account balances bears to the total amount of actual factory overhead costs.

This is done using the following equation:

$$\frac{\text{Factory overhead cost in specific account}}{\text{Total amount of factory overhead costs applied}}$$

Cost of Goods Sold

$$\frac{60,300}{201,000} = 30\%$$

Finished Goods Control

$$\frac{104,520}{201,000} = 52\%$$

Work-in-Process Control

$$\frac{36,180}{201,000} = 18\%$$

Multiply each of these percentages separately by the total amount of overapplied factory overhead to find the amount of overapplied factory overhead that should be credited to each account:

Cost of Goods Sold	$49,000 × 30% =	$14,700
Finished Goods Control	$49,000 × 52% =	25,480
Work-in-Process Control	$49,000 × 18% =	8,820
		$49,000

You would record the proration of the overapplied overhead to the three accounts with the following journal entry:

Factory Overhead Applied	$201,000	
Factory Overhead Control		$152,000
Cost of Goods Sold		14,700
Finished Goods Control		25,480
Work-in-Process Control		8,820
To close factory overhead accounts.		

[See Section 3-5.]

PROBLEM 3-8: Husky Printing Company uses a job-order costing system. In 19X2, the company incurred factory overhead costs of $80,000 and applied $100,000 of factory overhead costs to production. Husky Printing Company prorates the underapplied or overapplied factory overhead among the Work-in-Process Control, Finished Goods Control, and Cost of Goods Sold accounts. Analysis of these accounts shows the following percentage of factory overhead costs in each account:

	Factory overhead costs	Percentage
Work-in-Process Control	$ 30,000	30%
Finished Goods Control	20,000	20%
Cost of Goods Sold	50,000	50%
Total factory overhead applied	$100,000	100%

Prepare the journal entry to close the Factory Overhead accounts.

Solution: Find the amount of over- or underapplied overhead. Subtract Factory Overhead Applied from the *actual* amount of Factory Overhead Control.

Actual Factory Overhead	$ 80,000
Factory Overhead Applied	100,000
	$ (20,000) overapplied factory overhead

To prorate the overapplied factory overhead to Cost of Goods Sold, Finished Goods Control, and Work-in-Process Control, you must know the percentage of factory overhead costs that each of these accounts bears to the total amount of actual factory overhead. This was given in the problem. You must then multiply each of these percentages separately by the total amount of overapplied factory overhead to find the amount of overapplied factory overhead that should be credited to each account.

Work-in-Process Control	$20,000 × 30% =	$ 6,000
Finished Goods Control	$20,000 × 20% =	4,000
Cost of Goods Sold	$20,000 × 50% =	10,000
		$20,000

The journal entry to close factory overhead accounts is:

Factory Overhead Applied	$100,000	
Factory Overhead Control		$ 80,000
Work-in-Process Control		6,000
Finished Goods Control		4,000
Cost of Goods Sold		10,000
To close factory overhead accounts.		

[See Section 3-5.]

PROBLEM 3-9: The Corbin Manufacturing Company uses a job-order costing system. Two jobs (job #101 and job #102) were started and completed during May. There was no other production during May. The predetermined overhead rate is $4.00 per direct labor hour. The following information is available:

	Job 101	Job 102
Direct materials	$11,000	$ 8,000
Direct labor costs	$10,000	$ 3,000
Direct labor hours	4,000	1,000
Factory overhead incurred	$13,000	$ 6,000
Total selling price (Revenue)	$40,000	$25,000

Assume that the company follows the practice of closing underapplied or overapplied overhead costs to Cost of Goods Sold. Based on this information, compute the following:

(a) The amount of underapplied or overapplied overhead for each job and the total underapplied or overapplied overhead.

(b) The total gross profit (Sales Revenue minus Cost of Goods Sold) and the gross profit for each job.

Solution: In order to solve this problem, the applied overhead must be computed:

	Job 101	Job 102	Total
4,000 hours × $4.00	$16,000		
1,000 hours × $4.00		$4,000	
5,000 hours × $4.00			$20,000

Next, the underapplied or overapplied overhead would be computed as follows:

	Job 101	Job 102	Total
Actual Factory Overhead	$13,000	$6,000	$19,000
Factory Overhead Applied	16,000	4,000	20,000
(Overapplied) or Underapplied Overhead	($ 3,000)	$2,000	($ 1,000)

The gross profit would be computed as follows:

	Job 101	Job 102	Total
Revenue	$40,000	$25,000	$65,000
Production costs:			
Direct materials	11,000	8,000	19,000
Direct labor	10,000	3,000	13,000
Actual factory overhead	13,000	6,000	19,000
Cost of goods sold	$34,000	$17,000	$51,000
Gross profit	$ 6,000	$ 8,000	$14,000

Gross profit equals sales revenue minus cost of goods sold. Notice that the actual factory overhead incurred was used to compute the gross profit in this problem since the company closes underapplied or overapplied overhead to Cost of Goods Sold. [See Section 3-5.]

Problems 3-10 to 3-12 are based on the following data.

ABC Company uses a predetermined factory overhead rate to apply factory overhead to production on the basis of direct labor costs for Department A and on the basis of direct labor hours for Department B. The following *budgeted* information is provided for 19X0.

	Department A	Department B
Direct labor cost	$12,800	$ 3,500
Factory overhead costs	$16,000	$15,000
Direct labor hours	1,600	500

The job cost sheet for job #118 shows the following amounts:

	Department A	Department B
Direct materials issued	$200	$400
Direct labor costs	$320	$210
Direct labor hours	40	30

PROBLEM 3-10: What are the predetermined overhead rates for Department A and Department B?

Solution: Department A applies factory overhead on the basis of direct labor costs. The predetermined overhead rate for Department A is computed as follows:

$$\text{Department A Predetermined overhead rate} = \frac{\text{Budgeted factory overhead}}{\text{Budgeted direct labor cost}}$$

$$= \frac{\$16,000}{\$12,800}$$

$$= 125\% \text{ of direct labor costs}$$

Department B applies factory overhead on the basis of direct labor hours. The predetermined overhead rate for Department B is computed as follows:

$$\text{Department B Predetermined overhead rate} = \frac{\text{Budgeted factory overhead}}{\text{Budgeted direct labor hours}}$$

$$= \frac{\$15,000}{500}$$

$$= \$30.00 \text{ per direct labor hour}$$

[See Section 3-3.]

PROBLEM 3-11: Compute the total production costs for job #118, and prepare the journal entry to record factory overhead applied to job #118 from Department A.

Solution: Before you can compute total production costs for job #118, you must use the two different predetermined overhead rates found in Problem 3-10 to *apply* factory overhead to job #118.

Department A

To find the amount of factory overhead applied to job #118 from Department A, you use the following equation:

Factory overhead applied = Direct labor costs × Predetermined overhead rate

= $320 × 125%

= $400 factory overhead applied to job #118 from Department A

Department B

To find the amount of factory overhead applied to job #118 from Department B, you use the following equation:

Factory overhead applied = Direct labor hours × Predetermined overhead rate

= 30 × $30

= $900 factory overhead applied to job #118 from Department B

Now you can find the total production costs for job #118.

	Department A	Department B	Total
Direct materials	$200	$ 400	$ 600
Direct labor	320	210	530
Factory overhead applied	400	900	1,300
	$920	$1,510	$2,430

The journal entry to record factory overhead applied to job #118 from Department A is:

Work-in-Process Control (Factory Overhead		
Applied, job #118)	$400	
Factory Overhead Applied (job #118)		$400
To record factory overhead for Department A.		

[See Sections 3-3 and 3-5.]

PROBLEM 3-12: Prepare the journal entry to record factory overhead applied to job #118 from Department B.

Solution: The journal entry to record factory overhead applied to job #118 from Department B is:

Work-in-Process Control (Factory Overhead		
Applied, job #118)	$900	
Factory Overhead Applied (job #118)		$900
To record factory overhead for Department B.		

[See Section 3-3.]

PROBLEM 3-13: The following account balances are available for Urbcon Manufacturing Company, which uses a job-order costing system:

	Account Balances	
	January 1	January 31
Direct Materials Control	$15,000	$30,000
Work-in-Process Control	1,000	2,000
Finished Goods Control	10,000	30,000

The following information is also available:

Indirect materials used	$ 500
Direct labor costs	10,000
Direct materials purchased	35,000
Sales	50,000
Administrative expenses	2,500
Selling expenses	700
Tax rate	18%
Other factory overhead includes:	
Indirect labor	$ 1,500
Depreciation	2,000
Insurance	2,200
Taxes	3,500
Miscellaneous	300

Using the information above, prepare a Cost of Goods Manufactured statement and an Income Statement.

Solution:

Urbcon Manufacturing Company
Cost of Goods Manufactured
For the Month Ended, January 31, 19X7

Direct Materials Control, Jan. 1	$15,000	
Add: Purchases	35,000	
Direct Materials Available for Use	$50,000	
Less: Direct Materials Control, Jan. 31	30,000	
Direct Materials Used		$20,000
Direct Labor		10,000
Factory Overhead Costs:		
Indirect Materials Used	$ 500	
Indirect Labor	1,500	
Depreciation	2,000	
Insurance	2,200	
Taxes	3,500	
Miscellaneous	300	
Total Overhead Costs		10,000
Total Manufacturing Costs		$40,000
Add: Work-in-Process Control, Jan. 1		1,000
Total costs to account for		$41,000
Less: Work-in-Process Control, Jan. 31		2,000
Cost of Goods Manufactured		$39,000

Urbcon Manufacturing Company
Income Statement
For the Month Ended, January 31, 19X7

Sales		$50,000
Less: Cost of Goods Sold:		
Finished Goods Control, Jan. 1	$10,000	
Add: Cost of Goods Manufactured	39,000	
Cost of Goods Available for Sale	$49,000	
Less: Finished Goods Control, Jan. 31	30,000	
Cost of Goods Sold		19,000
Gross Margin		$31,000
Administrative and Selling Expenses:		
Less: Administrative Expenses	$ 2,500	
Less: Selling Expenses	700	3,200
Income before Taxes		$27,800
Income Taxes (18%)		5,004
Net Income		$22,796

[See Section 3-6.]

PROBLEM 3-14: The following information is available for the Blue Demons Company:

	Account Balances	
	January 1	January 31
Direct Materials Control	$10,000	$15,000
Work-in-Process Control	20,000	10,000
Finished Goods Control	9,000	5,000

The costs incurred during the month of January were:

Direct materials purchased	$30,000
Direct labor costs	40,000

Indirect materials used	5,000	
Indirect labor costs	25,000	
Other factory overhead costs:		
Depreciation	10,000	
Miscellaneous overhead costs	5,000	

Based on this information, prepare a Cost of Goods Manufactured statement for the month of January.

Solution: The Statement of Cost of Goods Manufactured for the Blue Demons Company would be:

Blue Demons Company
Statement of Cost of Goods Manufactured
For the Month Ended January 31, 19X1

Direct Materials Control, Jan. 1	$10,000	
Add: Purchases	30,000	
Direct materials Available for Use	$40,000	
Less: Direct Materials Control, Jan. 31	15,000	
Direct Materials Used		$ 25,000
Direct Labor		40,000
Factory Overhead Costs:		
Indirect Materials Used	$ 5,000	
Indirect Labor	25,000	
Depreciation	10,000	
Miscellaneous	5,000	
Total Overhead Costs		45,000
Total Manufacturing Costs		$110,000
Add: Work-in-Process Control, Jan. 1		20,000
Total costs to account for		$130,000
Less: Work-in-Process Control, Jan. 31		10,000
Cost of Goods Manufactured		$120,000

[See Section 3-6.]

Chapter 4 (handwritten)

4 PROCESS COSTING

THIS CHAPTER IS ABOUT

☑ **Process Costing Concepts**
☑ **General Process Costing Procedures**
☑ **Process Costing Using the Weighted-Average and FIFO Methods**
☑ **Transferred-in Costs**
☑ **Process Costing and Standard Costs**
☑ **Spoilage, Waste, and Defective Units**

4-1. Process Costing Concepts

Process costing is a method of product costing. It is used in industries where each unit of production requires approximately the same amounts of direct materials, direct labor, and factory overhead. These industries are characterized by continuous mass production of identical units. You will remember from Chapter 3 that another product costing method, job-order costing, is used in industries where each batch (or unit) requires different amounts of direct materials, direct labor, and factory overhead.

The purpose of any of the product costing methods is to allocate production costs to units of production.

A. Equivalent units of production

Process costing is based on the concept of equivalent units of production. Equivalent units measure the relative amount of production completed. For example, 100 units that are 60% complete represent 60 equivalent units (100 units × 60%) of production.

prime cost = DM + DL (handwritten)

EXAMPLE 4-1: A company has in ending WIP inventory 100 units that are 75% complete. Find equivalent units in ending WIP inventory by multiplying the units in ending WIP inventory by the percentage of completion.

CC = DL + Factory OH (handwritten)

$$\text{Equivalent units in ending WIP inventory} = 100 \text{ units} \times 75\% \text{ completion}$$
$$= 75 \text{ equivalent units}$$

Usually, equivalent units are defined separately for direct materials and conversion costs (conversion costs = direct labor + factory overhead), because direct materials are often applied to production differently than conversion costs. For example, a common assumption is that all (100%) of direct materials are applied to a unit of production when a unit is started, but that conversion costs are applied to a unit uniformly throughout the production process.

Units that are completed are, by definition, 100% complete and are, therefore, already expressed in equivalent units.

EXAMPLE 4-2: EBA completed 5,000 units during the period. In ending WIP inventory, there were 3,000 units that were 100% complete for direct materials and 50% complete for conversion costs. There were no units in beginning WIP inventory. Compute total equivalent units (units completed + ending WIP inventory) separately for direct materials and conversion costs.

48

Direct Materials

Total equivalent units = (5,000 × 100%) + (3,000 × 100%)

= 5,000 + 3,000

= 8,000 total equivalent units for direct materials

Conversion Costs

Total equivalent units = (5,000 × 100%) + (3,000 × 50%)

= 5,000 + 1,500

= 6,500 total equivalent units for conversion costs

B. Average cost per equivalent unit

Process costing uses average cost per unit, which is based on equivalent units of production in a department or process. (Although job-order costing also uses average cost per unit, this average is usually different for each batch and is based on the number of units in a particular batch or job order.) In process costing you would compute the production cost per equivalent unit for a production department or process by dividing production costs by equivalent units of production. You then use this unit (average) cost to allocate costs to ending WIP inventory and units completed.

1. ENDING WIP INVENTORY

Use equation 4.1 to allocate production costs to ending WIP inventory.

$$\frac{\text{Production costs allocated}}{\text{to ending WIP inventory}} = \frac{\text{Equivalent units in}}{\text{ending WIP inventory}} \times \frac{\text{Cost per}}{\text{equivalent unit}} \qquad (4.1)$$

$$\boxed{PC = EWIP \times CPEU}$$

Direct materials costs and conversion costs are allocated separately to ending WIP inventory.

2. UNITS COMPLETED

Use equation 4.2 to allocate production costs to units completed in a production department or process.

$$\frac{\text{Production costs allocated}}{\text{to units completed}} = \text{Units completed} \times \frac{\text{Cost per}}{\text{equivalent unit}} \qquad (4.2)$$

$$\boxed{PC = UC \times CPEU}$$

Direct materials costs and conversion costs are allocated separately to units completed.

EXAMPLE 4-3: The following information is available for a production department:

Ending WIP inventory (100% complete for direct materials; 50% complete for conversion costs)	100 units
Units completed	900 units
Direct materials cost per equivalent unit	$4.00
Conversion cost per equivalent unit	$6.00

Assume that beginning WIP inventory was zero and that direct materials costs of $4,000 and conversion costs of $5,700 were applied to production. The equivalent units in ending WIP inventory are 100 (100 × 100%) for direct materials and 50 (100 × 50%) for conversion costs.

You would compute the production costs allocated to ending WIP inventory by using equation 4.1. Production costs are allocated separately for direct materials and conversion costs. These costs are then added together to find total production costs allocated to ending WIP inventory.

Direct materials		
100 equivalent units × $4.00	$ 400	
Conversion costs		
50 equivalent units × $6.00	300	
Production costs allocated to		
ending WIP inventory		$ 700

Use equation 4.2 to allocate production
costs to units completed.

Direct materials		
900 equivalent units × $4.00	$3,600	
Conversion costs		
900 equivalent units × $6.00	5,400	
Production costs allocated to units completed		9,000
Total production costs allocated		$9,700

You can see that total costs allocated to ending WIP inventory and units completed ($700 + $9,000 = $9,700) equal the total of the direct materials costs and conversion costs applied to production ($4,000 + $5,700 = $9,700).

4-2. General Process Costing Procedures

This section presents four steps for process costing analysis:

1. Summarize physical units
2. Compute equivalent units of production
3. Compute cost per equivalent unit
4. Allocate production costs to ending WIP inventory and units completed

Step 4 is the primary goal of process costing.

A. Step 1: Summarize physical units

Physical units express the physical flow of production. They are a measure of the units of production that have been started and that may or may not be complete. Physical units do not consider the degree of completion of the units. For example, 10 units that are 50% complete represent 10 physical units and 5 (50% × 10) equivalent units.

You would summarize the physical units of production as follows:

	PHYSICAL UNITS
Beginning WIP inventory	XXX
+ Units started	XXX
= Total physical units to account for	XXX
Ending WIP inventory	XXX
+ Units completed	XXX
= Total physical units accounted for	XXX

Total physical units to account for must always equal total physical units accounted for.

EXAMPLE 4-4: The following information is from the production department of Olympic Company for the month ended July 31, 19X4:

Beginning WIP inventory	–0–
Units started in process	10,000
Units completed	8,000
Ending WIP inventory (100% complete for direct materials; 50% complete for conversion costs)	2,000
Direct materials production costs	$24,000
Conversion costs	$28,800

Based on this information, summarize physical units as follows:

	PHYSICAL UNITS
Beginning WIP inventory	–0–
Units started	10,000
Total physical units to account for	10,000
Ending WIP inventory	2,000
Units completed	8,000
Total physical units accounted for	10,000

B. Step 2: Compute equivalent units of production

You would compute equivalent units for each major category of production cost—direct materials and conversion costs—using equation 4.3.

$$\text{Equivalent units} = \text{Physical units} \times \text{Percentage of completion} \qquad \textbf{(4.3)}$$

$$\boxed{EU = PU \times \%C}$$

You compute equivalent units separately for direct materials and conversion costs. The equivalent units of production for direct materials and conversion costs can be summarized as follows:

	EQUIVALENT UNITS	
	direct materials	conversion costs
Beginning WIP inventory	XXX	XXX
+ Current production	XXX	XXX
= Total equivalent units	XXX	XXX
Ending WIP inventory	XXX	XXX
+ Units completed	XXX	XXX
= Total equivalent units	XXX	XXX

The equivalent unit computation for each line is explained below.

1. Equivalent units for beginning WIP inventory and equivalent units for ending WIP inventory would be computed separately using equation 4.3

$$EU = PU \times \%C$$

2. Units completed are 100% complete by definition and are, therefore, already expressed in equivalent units (8,000 physical units × 100% = 8,000 equivalent units).

3. Current production in equivalent units is computed using equation 4.4

$$\frac{\text{Current production}}{\text{equivalent units}} = \frac{\text{Ending WIP inventory}}{\text{equivalent units}} + \frac{\text{Units}}{\text{completed}} - \frac{\text{Beginning WIP inventory}}{\text{equivalent units}} \qquad \textbf{(4.4)}$$

This equation can also be expressed in a table format.

	EQUIVALENT UNITS	
	direct materials	conversion costs
Ending WIP inventory	XXX	XXX
+ Units completed	+ XXX	+ XXX
− Beginning WIP inventory	− XXX	− XXX
= Current production	XXX	XXX

EXAMPLE 4-5: Using the information in Example 4-4, compute equivalent units of production for the Olympic Company as follows:

	EQUIVALENT UNITS direct materials	EQUIVALENT UNITS conversion costs
Beginning WIP inventory	–0–	–0–
Current production	10,000*	9,000*
Total equivalent units	10,000	9,000
Ending WIP inventory		
(2,000 × 100%)	2,000	
(2,000 × 50%)		1,000
Units completed (8,000 × 100%)	8,000	8,000
Total equivalent units	10,000	9,000

* The Current Production amount is computed using equation 4.4. In general, Current Production is not given in problems and must be computed.

	EQUIVALENT UNITS direct materials	EQUIVALENT UNITS conversion costs
Ending WIP inventory	2,000	1,000
+ Units completed	8,000	8,000
– Beginning WIP inventory	–0–	–0–
= Current production	10,000	9,000

C. Step 3: Compute cost per equivalent unit

To compute cost per equivalent unit, you must first summarize production costs.

	direct materials	conversion costs	Total
Beginning WIP inventory	XXX	XXX	XXX
+ Current production costs	XXX	XXX	XXX
= Total production costs	XXX	XXX	XXX

The production costs for beginning WIP inventory were determined at the end of the previous period. The current production costs include production costs that have been applied to production during the current period.

Now you can compute production cost per equivalent unit using equation 4.5

$$\text{Cost per equivalent unit} = \frac{\text{Production costs}}{\text{Equivalent units}}$$

(4.5)

$$CPE = \frac{PC}{EU}$$

You usually compute the cost per equivalent unit separately for direct materials and conversion costs.

	direct materials	conversion costs
Production costs	XXX	XXX
÷ Equivalent units	XXX	XXX
= Cost per equivalent unit	XXX	XXX

EXAMPLE 4-6: Using the information in Example 4-4, compute the cost per equivalent unit. First, total production costs would be summarized.

	PRODUCTION COSTS	
	direct materials	conversion costs
Beginning WIP inventory	–0–	–0–
Current production costs	$24,000	$28,800
Total production costs	$24,000	$28,800

Next, compute the cost per equivalent unit using equation 4.5. Equivalent units were computed in Example 4-5.

	direct materials	conversion costs
Total production costs	$24,000	$28,800
÷ Equivalent units	÷ 10,000	÷ 9,000
= Cost per equivalent unit	$ 2.40	$ 3.20

D. Step 4: Allocate production costs

You would use the cost per equivalent unit to allocate production costs to ending WIP inventory and units completed.

	direct materials	conversion costs	Total
Ending WIP inventory equivalent units	XXX	XXX	
× Cost per equivalent unit	$XXX	$XXX	
= Total production costs allocated to ending WIP inventory	$XXX +	$XXX	= $XXX
Units completed	XXX	XXX	
× Cost per equivalent unit	$XXX	$XXX	
= Total production costs allocated to units completed	$XXX +	$XXX	= XXX
Total production costs allocated			$XXX

EXAMPLE 4-7: Using the information in Example 4-4, allocate production costs to ending WIP inventory and units completed.

	direct materials	conversion costs	Total
Ending WIP inventory equivalent units	2,000	1,000	
Cost per equivalent unit	$ 2.40	$ 3.20	
Total production costs allocated to ending WIP inventory	$ 4,800	$ 3,200	$ 8,000
Units completed	8,000	8,000	
Cost per equivalent unit	$ 2.40	$ 3.20	
Total production costs allocated to units completed	$19,200	$25,600	44,800
Total production costs allocated			$52,800

E. Production cost reports

Production cost reports present a summary of the process costing analysis. In addition, the production cost report can provide the basis for solving process costing problems.

Exhibit 4-1 presents a production cost report of the process costing analysis from Examples 4-4 through 4-7.

EXHIBIT 4-1

Olympic Company
Production Cost Report
For the Month Ended, July 31, 19X4

Summarize physical units and compute equivalent units.

	PHYSICAL UNITS	EQUIVALENT UNITS direct materials	EQUIVALENT UNITS conversion costs
Beginning WIP inventory	–0–	–0–	–0–
Units started	10,000		
Current production		10,000	9,000
Total units to account for	10,000	10,000	9,000
Ending WIP inventory	2,000	2,000	1,000
Units completed	8,000	8,000	8,000
Total units accounted for	10,000	10,000	9,000

Compute cost per equivalent unit.

	direct materials	conversion costs	Total
Beginning WIP inventory	–0–	–0–	–0–
Current production costs	$24,000	$28,800	$52,800
Total production costs	$24,000	$28,800	$52,800
Equivalent units	÷ 10,000	÷ 9,000	
Cost per equivalent unit	$ 2.40	$ 3.20	

Allocate production costs.

	direct materials	conversion costs	Total
Ending WIP inventory equivalent units	2,000	1,000	
Cost per equivalent unit	$ 2.40	$ 3.20	
Total production costs allocated to ending WIP inventory	$ 4,800	$ 3,200	$ 8,000
Units completed	8,000	8,000	
Cost per equivalent unit	$ 2.40	$ 3.20	
Total production costs allocated to units completed	$19,200	$25,600	44,800
Total production costs allocated			$52,800

4-3. Process Costing Using the Weighted-Average and FIFO Methods

In Examples 4-4 through 4-7, it was assumed that beginning WIP inventory was zero. If the beginning WIP inventory balance is not zero, then you will generally use a cost flow assumption such as the weighted-average method or the FIFO (First-In, First-Out) method.

The four steps of the process costing analysis presented in Section 4-2 will be used for the weighted-average method and the FIFO method. For both methods, Step 1, summarizing physical units, and Step 2, computing equivalent units of production, will be the same as presented in Section 4-2. The two methods will differ for Step 3, computing cost per equivalent unit, and Step 4, allocating production costs.

A. Process costing using the weighted-average method

Steps 1 and 2 of the weighted-average method are the same as presented in Section 4-2. Step 3, computing average cost per equivalent unit, is found using equation 4.6.

$$\text{Cost per equivalent unit(Weighted-Average)} = \frac{\text{Total production costs}}{\text{Total equivalent units}} \qquad \textbf{(4.6)}$$

$$\boxed{\text{CPE(WA)} = \frac{\text{TPC}}{\text{TEU}}}$$

Note that the weighted-average method computes cost per equivalent unit based on *total* production costs and *total* equivalent units. This will be contrasted with the FIFO method cost per equivalent unit, which is based on *current* production costs and *current* equivalent units. Cost per equivalent unit is computed separately for direct materials and conversion costs.

EXAMPLE 4-8: The following information is provided for Chicago Manufacturing Company for the month ended June 30, 19X7:

Beginning WIP inventory	10,000
(100% complete for direct materials;	
50% complete for conversion costs)	
Units started in process	30,000
Units completed	35,000
Units in ending WIP inventory	5,000
(100% complete for direct materials;	
40% complete for conversion costs)	
Production costs:	
Direct materials:	
Beginning WIP inventory	$ 36,500
Current production	103,500
Conversion costs:	
Beginning WIP inventory	$ 19,400
Current production	136,000

To allocate production costs, use the 4 steps outlined in Section 4-2.

STEP 1. SUMMARIZE PHYSICAL UNITS.

Physical units are concerned only with whole units. The number of total units to account for and total units accounted for must always be equal.

STEP 2. COMPUTE EQUIVALENT UNITS.

Use equation 4.3 to calculate equivalent units. Remember that equivalent units are calculated separately for direct materials and conversion costs.

$$\text{EU} = \text{PU} \times \%\text{C}$$

REMEMBER: Units completed are 100% complete for both direct materials and conversion costs (35,000 units completed × 100%).

Direct Materials

$$\text{Total equivalent units} = 35,000 + (5,000 \times 100\%)$$
$$= 35,000 + 5,000$$
$$= 40,000 \text{ equivalent units for direct materials}$$

Conversion Costs

$$\text{Total equivalent units} = 35,000 + (5,000 \times 40\%)$$
$$= 35,000 + 2,000$$
$$= 37,000 \text{ equivalent units for conversion costs}$$

Equation 4.4 is used to compute the equivalent units for current production.

| | EQUIVALENT UNITS | |
	direct materials	conversion costs
Ending WIP inventory	5,000	2,000
Units completed	+ 35,000	+ 35,000
Beginning WIP inventory	− 10,000	− 5,000
Current production	30,000	32,000

Steps 1 and 2 are presented below.

| | PHYSICAL UNITS | EQUIVALENT UNITS | |
		direct materials	conversion costs
Beginning WIP inventory	10,000	10,000	5,000
Units started	30,000		
Current production		30,000	32,000
Total units to account for	40,000	40,000	37,000
Ending WIP inventory	5,000	5,000	2,000
Units completed	35,000	35,000	35,000
Total units accounted for	40,000	40,000	37,000

STEP 3. COMPUTE COST PER EQUIVALENT UNIT.

Use equation 4.6 to compute cost per equivalent unit.

$$CPE(WA) = \frac{TPC}{TEU}$$

Cost per equivalent unit is computed separately for direct materials and conversion costs.

	direct materials	conversion costs	Total
Beginning WIP inventory	$ 36,500	$ 19,400	$ 55,900
+ Current production costs	103,500	136,000	239,500
= Total production costs	$140,000	$155,400	$295,400
÷ Total equivalent units	40,000	37,000	
= Cost per equivalent unit	$ 3.50	$ 4.20	

STEP 4. ALLOCATE PRODUCTION COSTS.

You would use the cost per equivalent unit to allocate production costs to ending WIP inventory and units completed.

	direct materials	conversion costs	Total
Ending WIP inventory equivalent units	5,000	2,000	
× Cost per equivalent unit	$ 3.50	$ 4.20	
= Total production costs allocated to ending inventory	$ 17,500	$ 8,400	$ 25,900
Units completed	35,000	35,000	
× Cost per equivalent unit	$ 3.50	$ 4.20	
= Total production costs allocated to units completed	$122,500	$147,000	269,500
Total production costs allocated			$295,400

Exhibit 4-2 presents the production cost report, which summarizes the process costing procedures for the weighted-average method for Chicago Manufacturing Company.

EXHIBIT 4-2

Chicago Manufacturing Company
Production Cost Report (Weighted-Average Method)
For the Month Ended, June 30, 19X7

Summarize physical units and compute equivalent units.

	PHYSICAL UNITS	EQUIVALENT UNITS direct materials	conversion costs
Beginning WIP inventory	10,000	10,000	5,000
Units started	30,000		
Current production		30,000	32,000
Total units to account for	40,000	40,000	37,000
Ending WIP inventory	5,000	5,000	2,000
Units completed	35,000	35,000	35,000
Total units accounted for	40,000	40,000	37,000

Compute cost per equivalent unit.

	direct materials	conversion costs	Total
Beginning WIP inventory	$ 36,500	$ 19,400	$ 55,900
Current production costs	103,500	136,000	239,500
Total production costs	$140,000	$155,400	$295,400
Equivalent units	40,000	37,000	
Cost per equivalent unit	$ 3.50	$ 4.20	

Allocate production costs.

	direct materials	conversion costs	Total
Ending WIP inventory equivalent units	5,000	2,000	
Cost per equivalent unit	$ 3.50	$ 4.20	
Total production costs allocated to ending WIP inventory	$ 17,500	$ 8,400	$ 25,900
Units completed	35,000	35,000	
Cost per equivalent unit	$ 3.50	$ 4.20	
Total production costs allocated to units completed	$122,500	$147,000	269,500
Total production costs allocated			$295,400

Note that the total production costs allocated equal the total production costs summarized in Step 3. The cost per equivalent unit (Step 3) using the weighted-average method is based on *total* production costs divided by *total* equivalent units. The cost per equivalent unit is then used to allocate production costs to ending WIP inventory and units completed (Step 4).

B. Process costing using the FIFO method

Steps 1 and 2 of the FIFO method are the same as presented in Section 4-2. Step 3, computing FIFO cost per equivalent unit, is found using equation 4.7.

$$\text{Cost per equivalent unit(FIFO)} = \frac{\text{Current production costs}}{\text{Current production in equivalent units}} \qquad \textbf{(4.7)}$$

$$\text{CPE(FIFO)} = \frac{\text{CPC}}{\text{CEU}}$$

Note that the FIFO method computes cost per equivalent unit based on *current* production costs and *current* equivalent units. In contrast, the weighted-average method uses *total* production costs and *total* equivalent units to compute the cost per equivalent units. Step 4, allocating production costs, will be illustrated using two different methods.

EXAMPLE 4-9: The information from Example 4-8 will be used to illustrate the FIFO method of processing costing.

Beginning WIP inventory	10,000
(100% complete for direct materials; 50% complete for conversion costs)	
Units started in process	30,000
Units completed and transferred	35,000
Units in ending WIP inventory	5,000
(100% complete for direct materials; 40% complete for conversion costs)	
Production costs:	
Direct materials:	
Beginning WIP inventory	$ 36,500
Current production	103,500
Conversion costs:	
Beginning WIP inventory	$ 19,400
Current production	136,000

To allocate production costs, use the 4 steps outlined in Section 4-2.

STEP 1. SUMMARIZE PHYSICAL UNITS.

Physical units are concerned only with whole units. The number of total units to account for and total units accounted for must always be equal.

STEP 2. COMPUTE EQUIVALENT UNITS.

Use equation 4.3 to calculate total equivalent units. Remember that equivalent units are calculated separately for direct materials and conversion costs.

$$EU = PU \times \%C$$

Direct Materials

Total equivalent units = 35,000 + (5,000 × 100%)

= 35,000 + 5,000

= 40,000 equivalent units for direct materials

Conversion Costs

Total equivalent units = 35,000 + (5,000 × 40%)

= 35,000 + 2,000

= 37,000 equivalent units for conversion costs

Equation 4.4 is used to compute the equivalent units for current production.

	EQUIVALENT UNITS	
	direct materials	conversion costs
Ending WIP inventory	5,000	2,000
Units completed	+ 35,000	+ 35,000
Beginning WIP inventory	− 10,000	− 5,000
Current production	30,000	32,000

Steps 1 and 2 are presented below.

	PHYSICAL UNITS	EQUIVALENT UNITS direct materials	EQUIVALENT UNITS conversion costs
Beginning WIP inventory	10,000	10,000	5,000
Units started	30,000		
Current production		30,000	32,000
Total units to account for	40,000	40,000	37,000
Ending WIP inventory	5,000	5,000	2,000
Units completed	35,000	35,000	35,000
Total units accounted for	40,000	40,000	37,000

STEP 3. COMPUTE COST PER EQUIVALENT UNIT.

Use equation 4.7 to compute FIFO cost per equivalent unit.

$$CPE(FIFO) = \frac{CPC}{CEU}$$

Cost per equivalent unit is computed separately for direct materials and conversion costs.

	direct materials	conversion costs
Current production costs	$103,500	$136,000
÷ Current production equivalent units	30,000	32,000
= FIFO cost per equivalent unit	$ 3.45	$ 4.25

STEP 4. ALLOCATE PRODUCTION COSTS.

Using the FIFO method, the allocation of production costs to ending WIP inventory and to units completed must reflect the First-In, First-Out (FIFO) assumption. The FIFO assumption is that the first units started would be the first units to be completed. The following procedures would be used to allocate production costs using the FIFO method.

1. PRODUCTION COSTS ALLOCATED TO ENDING WIP INVENTORY.

The FIFO cost per equivalent unit would be used to compute the cost allocated to ending WIP inventory as follows:

	direct materials	conversion costs
Ending WIP inventory equivalent units	XXX	XXX
× FIFO cost per equivalent unit	$XXX	$XXX
= Production costs allocated to ending WIP inventory	$XXX	$XXX

2. PRODUCTION COSTS ALLOCATED TO UNITS COMPLETED.

The cost allocated to units completed would be computed as follows:

	direct materials	conversion costs
Total production costs	$XXX	$XXX
− Production costs allocated to ending WIP inventory	XXX	XXX
= Production costs allocated to units completed	$XXX	$XXX

Assume that units in ending WIP inventory were started in the current period.

Using the approach described above, the production costs would be allocated as follows to ending WIP inventory and units completed for the information in Example 4-9.

Allocate production costs—FIFO method.

	direct materials	conversion costs	Total
Ending WIP inventory equivalent units	5,000	2,000	
× FIFO cost per equivalent unit	$ 3.45	$ 4.25	
= Production costs allocated to ending WIP inventory	$ 17,250	$ 8,500	$ 25,750
Total production costs	$140,000	$155,400	
− Production costs allocated to ending WIP inventory	17,250	8,500	
= Production costs allocated to units completed	$122,750	$146,900	$269,650
Total production costs allocated			$295,400

An alternative approach found in some textbooks for allocating production costs to units completed and ending WIP inventory (Step 4) using the FIFO method is summarized below:

	direct materials	conversion costs	Total
1. Beginning WIP inventory costs	XXX	XXX	XXX
+ Current costs added to complete beginning WIP inventory	XXX	XXX	XXX
= Total costs allocated to beginning WIP inventory	XXX	XXX	XXX
2. + Costs allocated to units started and completed in current period	XXX	XXX	XXX
= Total production costs allocated to units completed	XXX	XXX	XXX
3. + Costs allocated to ending WIP inventory	XXX	XXX	XXX
= Total production costs allocated	XXX	XXX	XXX

STEP 1. BEGINNING WIP INVENTORY COSTS

The direct materials cost and conversion costs associated with beginning WIP inventory were given in the example: $36,500 and $19,400, respectively. The current production costs to complete beginning WIP inventory are found using the following equation:

$$\left(\text{Physical units} \times \frac{\text{percentage of completion \textbf{added}}}{} \right) \times \frac{\text{FIFO cost per equivalent unit}}{}$$

Direct Materials

We know that the units in beginning WIP inventory in this example were 100% complete for direct materials. Therefore, those units received no more direct materials in the current period and none of the current production costs are allocated to beginning WIP inventory for direct materials.

Conversion Costs

The 10,000 physical units in beginning WIP inventory were 50% complete for conversion costs. Therefore, the percentage of completion added to those units was 50%. Using the equation in Step 1, you can find the current production costs allocated to finish beginning WIP inventory.

$$\left(\text{Physical units} \times \frac{\text{percentage of completion \textbf{added}}}{} \right) \times \frac{\text{FIFO cost per equivalent unit}}{}$$

Current costs added to
complete beginning WIP inventory
$$= (10,000 \times 50\%) \times \$4.25$$
$$= 5,000 \times \$4.25$$
$$= \$21,250 \text{ current production costs for conversion costs}$$
allocated to beginning WIP inventory

Step 1 is presented below.

	direct material	conversion costs	Total
Beginning WIP inventory costs	$36,500	$19,400	$55,900
Current costs added to complete beginning WIP inventory	–0–	21,250	21,250
Total costs allocated to beginning WIP inventory	$36,500	$40,650	$77,150

STEP 2. UNITS STARTED AND COMPLETED IN THIS PERIOD

To find the number of units started and completed in this period, we must use the physical summary.

Beginning WIP inventory	10,000
Units started	30,000
Total units to account for	40,000
Units completed	35,000
Ending WIP inventory	5,000
Total units accounted for	40,000

We can find the number of units started and completed in the current period by subtracting the beginning WIP inventory from the units completed.

Units completed	35,000
Beginning WIP inventory	− 10,000
Units started and completed	25,000

To find the amount of current production costs for direct materials associated with units started and completed, multiply the units started and completed by the FIFO cost per equivalent unit for direct materials ($3.45).

To find the amount of current production costs for conversion costs associated with units started and completed, multiply the units started and completed by the FIFO cost per equivalent unit for conversion costs ($4.25).

	direct materials	conversion costs
Units started and completed	25,000	25,000
× FIFO cost per equivalent unit	$ 3.45	$ 4.25
= Costs allocated to units started and completed in current period	$86,250	$106,250

Step 2 is shown below.

	direct materials	conversion costs	Total
= Total costs allocated to beginning WIP inventory	$ 36,500	$ 40,650	$ 77,150
+ Costs allocated to units started and completed in current period	86,250	106,250	192,500
= Total production costs allocated to units completed in current period	$122,750	$146,900	$269,650

STEP 3. ENDING WIP INVENTORY

Allocate production costs to ending WIP inventory by multiplying the equivalent units by the FIFO cost per equivalent unit.

	direct materials	conversion costs
Ending WIP inventory equivalent units	5,000	2,000
× FIFO cost per equivalent unit	$ 3.45	$ 4.25
Total production costs allocated to ending WIP inventory	$17,250	$8,500

Using the approach described above, the production costs would be allocated as follows:

	direct materials	conversion costs	Total
Beginning WIP inventory costs	$ 36,500	$ 19,400	$ 55,900
Current costs added to complete beginning WIP inventory	–0–	21,250	21,250
Total costs allocated to beginning WIP inventory	$ 36,500	$ 40,650	$ 77,150
Costs allocated to units started and completed in current period	86,250	106,250	192,500
Total production costs allocated to units completed in current period	$122,750	$146,900	$269,650
Costs allocated to ending WIP inventory	17,250	$8,500	25,750
Total production costs allocated	$140,000	$155,400	$295,400

4-4. Transferred-in Costs

When more than one production department or process exists and units of production are transferred from one department to another for further processing, the costs associated with those units must be accounted for. Transferred-in costs are production costs transferred from one production department to another. For example, if Department 1 transfers 200 units of production with a cost of $1,500 to Department 2, the $1,500 would be considered transferred-in costs for Department 2 and the 200 units would be treated as units started (units transferred-in) in the summary of physical units. When you compute equivalent units, you consider transferred-in costs as a separate production cost category (in addition to direct materials and conversion costs). Transferred-in units are considered to be 100% complete in the equivalent units summary.

A. Transferred-in costs using the weighted-average method

Accounting for transferred-in costs using the weighted-average method uses the same four steps as described in Section 4-3. Transferred-in costs would be added as a separate category for computing the cost per equivalent unit. The following example illustrates the procedures for accounting for transferred-in costs using the weighted-average method.

EXAMPLE 4-10: Assume that the Clemson Company has two production departments, Department A and Department B. Department A completes the first part of the production process and transfers the units to Department B. Department B completes the units. For the month of June, Department A has transferred 30,000 units to Department B with production costs of $60,000. The following information is provided for the month of June for Department B:

Beginning WIP inventory	10,000
(100% complete for direct materials; 50% complete for conversion costs)	
Units started (transferred-in)	30,000
Units completed	35,000
Ending WIP inventory	5,000
(100% complete for direct materials; 40% complete for conversion costs)	

Transferred-in costs:
Beginning WIP inventory	$ 18,000
Current production	$ 60,000

Direct materials costs:
Beginning WIP inventory	$ 36,500
Current production	$103,500

Conversion costs:
Beginning WIP inventory	$ 19,400
Current production	$136,000

Assume that 100% of the direct materials are added to all units when they begin production in Department B. Based on this information, determine the amount of production costs that should be allocated to ending WIP inventory and units completed in Department B.

STEPS 1 AND 2. SUMMARIZE PHYSICAL UNITS AND COMPUTE EQUIVALENT UNITS.

The physical units would be summarized and equivalent units would be computed in the same manner as in Section 4-3. However, "TI costs" (transferred-in costs) is an additional category for computing equivalent units. Notice that production associated with transferred-in costs is 100% complete when transferred to Department B.

	PHYSICAL UNITS	TI costs	direct materials	conversion costs
Beginning WIP inventory	10,000	10,000	10,000	5,000
Units started	30,000			
Current production		30,000	30,000	32,000
Total units to account for	40,000	40,000	40,000	37,000
Ending WIP inventory	5,000	5,000	5,000	2,000
Units completed	35,000	35,000	35,000	35,000
Total units accounted for	40,000	40,000	40,000	37,000

Remember that you would compute the current production in equivalent units using equation 4.4 as follows:

$$\text{Current production} = \text{Ending WIP inventory equivalent units} + \text{Units completed} - \text{Beginning WIP inventory equivalent units}$$

This equation can be used to compute current production for each of the production cost categories (TI costs, direct materials, and conversion costs) as follows:

	TI costs	direct materials	conversion costs
Ending WIP inventory	5,000	5,000	2,000
+ Units completed	35,000	35,000	35,000
− Beginning WIP inventory	(10,000)	(10,000)	(5,000)
= Current production	30,000	30,000	32,000

STEP 3. COMPUTE COST PER EQUIVALENT UNIT.

The cost per equivalent unit would be computed using the weighted-average method by dividing *total* production costs by *total* equivalent units as follows:

	TI costs	direct materials	conversion costs	Total
Beginning WIP inventory	$18,000	$ 36,500	$ 19,400	$ 73,900
+ Current production costs	60,000	103,500	136,000	299,500
= Total production costs	$78,000	$140,000	$155,400	$373,400
÷ Total equivalent units	40,000	40,000	37,000	
= Cost per equivalent unit	$ 1.95	$ 3.50	$ 4.20	

Notice that a separate cost per equivalent unit is computed for transferred-in costs. Using the weighted-average method, total production costs would be divided by total equivalent units for each category of production costs to find cost per equivalent unit.

STEP 4. ALLOCATE PRODUCTION COSTS.

The costs per equivalent unit would be used to allocate production costs to ending WIP inventory and units completed using the weighted-average method as follows:

	TI costs	direct materials	conversion costs	Total
Ending WIP inventory equivalent units	5,000	5,000	2,000	
× Cost per equivalent unit	$ 1.95	$ 3.50	$ 4.20	
= Total production costs allocated to ending WIP inventory	$ 9,750	$ 17,500	$ 8,400	$ 35,650
Units completed	35,000	35,000	35,000	
× Cost per equivalent unit	$ 1.95	$ 3.50	$ 4.20	
= Total production costs allocated to units completed	$68,250	$122,500	$147,000	$337,750
Total production costs allocated				$373,400

Notice that total production costs allocated equal the total production costs computed in Step 3. Exhibit 4-3 presents a production cost report for the analysis in Example 4-10 using the weighted-average method.

EXHIBIT 4-3

The Clemson Company
Production Cost Report (Weighted-Average Method)
Department B
For the Month Ended June 30, 19X7

Summarize physical units and compute equivalent units.

	PHYSICAL UNITS	EQUIVALENT UNITS		
		TI costs	direct materials	conversion costs
Beginning WIP inventory	10,000	10,000	10,000	5,000
Units started	30,000			
Current production		30,000	30,000	32,000
Total units to account for	40,000	40,000	40,000	37,000
Ending WIP inventory	5,000	5,000	5,000	2,000
Units completed	35,000	35,000	35,000	35,000
Total units accounted for	40,000	40,000	40,000	37,000

Compute cost per equivalent unit.

	TI costs	direct materials	conversion costs	Total
Beginning WIP inventory	$18,000	$ 36,500	$ 19,400	$ 73,900
Current production costs	60,000	103,500	136,000	299,500
Total production costs	$78,000	$140,000	$155,400	$373,400
÷ Total equivalent units	40,000	40,000	37,000	
= Cost per equivalent unit	$ 1.95	$ 3.50	$ 4.20	

Exhibit 4-3 (*Continued*)

Allocate production costs.	TI costs	direct materials	conversion costs	Total
Ending WIP inventory equivalent units	5,000	5,000	2,000	
× Cost per equivalent unit	$ 1.95	$ 3.50	$ 4.20	
Total production costs allocated to ending WIP inventory	$ 9,750	$ 17,500	$ 8,400	$ 35,650
Units completed	35,000	35,000	35,000	
× Cost per equivalent unit	$ 1.95	$ 3.50	$ 4.20	
Total production costs allocated to units completed	$68,250	$122,500	$147,000	$337,750
Total production costs allocated				$373,400

B. Transferred-in costs using the FIFO method

Accounting for transferred-in costs using the FIFO method involves applying the same procedures as presented in Section 4-3. However, Steps 3 and 4 are computed using the FIFO method. In this section, we are using departmental FIFO.

EXAMPLE 4-11: Using the information from Example 4-10, allocate production costs using the FIFO method to ending WIP inventory and units completed in Department B.

STEPS 1 AND 2. SUMMARIZE PHYSICAL UNITS AND COMPUTE EQUIVALENT UNITS.

The physical units would be summarized and equivalent units computed in the same manner as in Example 4-10 as follows:

	PHYSICAL UNITS	EQUIVALENT UNITS		
		TI costs	direct materials	conversion costs
Beginning WIP inventory	10,000	10,000	10,000	5,000
Units started	30,000			
Current production		30,000	30,000	32,000
Total units to account for	40,000	40,000	40,000	37,000
Ending WIP inventory	5,000	5,000	5,000	2,000
Units completed	35,000	35,000	35,000	35,000
Total units accounted for	40,000	40,000	40,000	37,000

STEP 3. COMPUTE COST PER EQUIVALENT UNIT.

The cost per equivalent unit would be computed using the FIFO method by dividing *current* production costs by *current* equivalent units as follows:

	TI costs	direct materials	conversion costs	Total
Total production costs	$78,000	$140,000	$155,400	$373,400
− Beginning WIP inventory costs	18,000	36,500	19,400	73,900
= Current production costs	$60,000	$103,500	$136,000	$299,500
÷ Current production equivalent units	30,000	30,000	32,000	
= Cost per equivalent unit	$ 2.00	$ 3.45	$ 4.25	

Notice that a separate cost per equivalent unit is computed for transferred-in costs.

STEP 4. ALLOCATE PRODUCTION COSTS.

The FIFO cost per equivalent unit would be used to allocate production costs using the FIFO method to ending WIP inventory and units completed as follows:

	TI costs	direct materials	conversion costs	Total
Ending WIP inventory equivalent units	5,000	5,000	2,000	
× FIFO cost per equivalent unit	$ 2.00	$ 3.45	$ 4.25	
= Production costs allocated to ending WIP inventory	$10,000	$ 17,250	$ 8,500	$ 35,750
Total production costs	$78,000	$140,000	$155,400	$373,400
− Production costs allocated to ending WIP inventory	10,000	17,250	8,500	35,750
= Production costs allocated to units completed	$68,000	$122,750	$146,900	$337,650
Total production costs allocated				$373,400

Notice that the total production costs allocated equal the total production costs computed in Step 3. Exhibit 4-4 presents a production cost report for the analysis in Example 4-11 using the FIFO method.

EXHIBIT 4-4

The Clemson Company
Production Cost Report (FIFO Method)
Department B
For the Month Ended June 30, 19X7

Summarize physical units and compute equivalent units.

	PHYSICAL UNITS	EQUIVALENT UNITS		
		TI costs	direct materials	conversion costs
Beginning WIP inventory	10,000	10,000	10,000	5,000
Units started	30,000			
Current production		30,000	30,000	32,000
Total units to account for	40,000	40,000	40,000	37,000
Ending WIP inventory	5,000	5,000	5,000	2,000
Units completed	35,000	35,000	35,000	35,000
Total units accounted for	40,000	40,000	40,000	37,000

Compute cost per equivalent unit.

	TI costs	direct materials	conversion costs	Total
Total production costs	$78,000	$140,000	$155,400	$373,400
− Beginning WIP inventory costs	18,000	36,500	19,400	73,900
= Current production costs	$60,000	$103,500	$136,000	$299,500
÷ Current production equivalent units	30,000	30,000	32,000	
= Cost per equivalent unit	$ 2.00	$ 3.45	$ 4.25	

Allocate production costs.

	TI costs	direct materials	conversion costs	Total
Ending WIP inventory equivalent units	5,000	5,000	2,000	
× FIFO cost per equivalent unit	$ 2.00	$ 3.45	$ 4.25	
= Production costs allocated to ending WIP inventory	$10,000	$ 17,250	$ 8,500	$ 35,750
Total production costs	$78,000	$140,000	$155,400	$373,400
− Production costs allocated to ending WIP inventory	10,000	17,250	8,500	35,750
= Production costs allocated to units completed	$68,000	$122,750	$146,900	$337,650
Total production costs allocated				$373,400

The alternative approach found in some textbooks for allocating production costs to units completed and ending WIP inventory (Step 4) using the FIFO method is summarized below:

	TI costs	direct materials	conversion costs	Total
Beginning WIP inventory	$18,000	$ 36,500	$ 19,400	$ 73,900
Current costs added to complete beginning WIP inventory [(10,000 × 50%) × $4.25]	−0−	−0−	21,250	21,250
Total costs allocated to beginning WIP inventory	$18,000	$ 36,500	$ 40,650	$ 95,150
Costs allocated to units started and completed in current period:				
TI costs (25,000 × $2.00)	50,000			
direct materials (25,000 × $3.45)		86,250		
conversion costs (25,000 × $4.25)			106,250	242,500
Total production costs allocated to units completed	$68,000	$122,750	$146,900	$337,650
Costs allocated to ending WIP inventory:				
TI costs (5,000 × $2.00)	10,000			
direct materials (5,000 × $3.45)		17,250		
conversion costs (2,000 × $4.25)			8,500	35,750
Total production costs allocated	$78,000	$140,000	$155,400	$373,400

4-5. Process Costing and Standard Costs

Chapters 6 and 7 discuss standard costing, which is a system of assigning predetermined costs to production. The use of standard costs avoids the need to compute cost per equivalent unit.

EXAMPLE 4-12: Using the data from Example 4-8, assume that the standard cost per unit for direct materials is $3.55, and that the standard cost per unit for conversion costs is $4.15. Allocating production costs to ending WIP inventory and units completed would be done as follows:

Allocate production costs (standard costs).

	direct materials	conversion costs	Total
Ending WIP inventory equivalent units	5,000	2,000	
× Standard cost per unit	$ 3.55	$ 4.15	
= Total production costs allocated to ending WIP inventory	$ 17,750	$ 8,300	$ 26,050
Units completed	35,000	35,000	
× Standard cost per unit	$ 3.55	$ 4.15	
= Total production costs allocated to units completed	$124,250	$145,250	$269,500
Total standard costs allocated			$295,550

Notice that the total production costs allocated using standard costs were $295,550, and the total production costs allocated using actual costs in Example 4-8 were $295,400. Standard costs are compared to actual costs to compute variances. This topic will be covered in Chapters 6 and 7.

4-6. Spoilage, Waste, and Defective Units

Most production processes involve some degree of spoilage, defective units, waste, and scrap. Some units of production may not meet production quality standards, and some units may be lost or damaged during the production process. This section will explain the concepts of spoilage, defective units, waste, and scrap. In addition, methods of accounting for spoilage in a process costing system will be discussed.

A. Spoilage

Spoilage represents units of production that do not meet production quality standards and cannot be efficiently reworked to meet those standards. The amount for which spoiled units can be sold is the *disposal value*. *Normal spoilage* is spoilage that occurs under efficient production operations. In contrast, *abnormal spoilage* is spoilage that is not expected to occur under efficient production operations. Normal spoilage and abnormal spoilage are accounted for differently.

1. ACCOUNTING FOR NORMAL SPOILAGE

The costs of normal spoilage are considered to be part of the cost of production. There are basically two methods of accounting for normal spoilage under process costing. The first method omits the equivalent units of normal spoilage from the equivalent units of production when computing the cost per equivalent unit. However, the costs associated with these spoiled units are included in total production costs when computing cost per equivalent unit. Using this method, the costs associated with the spoiled units (normal spoilage) would be spread over the equivalent units of unspoiled production.

The second method of accounting for normal spoilage under process costing includes the units of normal spoilage when computing equivalent units of production and includes the costs associated with normal spoilage when computing the cost per equivalent unit. The cost of the normal spoilage (using the cost per equivalent unit) can then be assigned to WIP inventory, Finished Goods Inventory, and Cost of Goods Sold.

2. ACCOUNTING FOR ABNORMAL SPOILAGE

The cost of abnormal spoilage is excluded from the cost of production and is charged (debited) to a loss account for abnormal spoilage. Therefore, the cost of abnormal spoilage is written off as a loss in the current period. With process costing, the equivalent units of abnormal spoilage are included in the computation of equivalent units of production, and the cost of abnormal spoilage is included in the computation of cost per equivalent unit. The cost of abnormal spoilage (based on the cost per equivalent unit) is accounted for by charging that amount as a loss from abnormal spoilage.

B. Defective units, waste, and scrap

Defective units are units of production that do not meet production quality standards but, in contrast to spoilage, can be reworked to meet those standards. *Waste* is residue from the production process that has no measurable value. In contrast, *scrap* is residue from the production process that has measurable, but relatively minor, value.

RAISE YOUR GRADES

Can you explain...?

☑ what equivalent units are
☑ how to compute equivalent units of production
☑ how to compute production costs per equivalent unit
☑ how to summarize physical units and equivalent units of production
☑ how to allocate production costs to ending Work-in-Process and units completed
☑ how to use the weighted-average method of process costing

☑ how to use the FIFO method of process costing
☑ how to use standard costs in process costing
☑ what transferred-in costs are
☑ what normal spoilage and abnormal spoilage are
☑ how to account for normal spoilage
☑ how to account for abnormal spoilage
☑ what defective units are
☑ what waste and scrap are

SUMMARY

1. Process costing is a product costing method that is used to allocate production costs to the units of production.
2. Process costing is used in industries where each unit of production requires approximately the same amounts of direct materials, direct labor, and factory overhead.
3. Equivalent units measure the relative amount of production completed.
4. Average cost per unit is used in both process costing and job-order costing methods.
5. In process costing, production cost per equivalent unit is used to allocate production costs to ending WIP inventory and units completed.
6. Physical units are units of production that have been started and that may or may not be complete—i.e., the degree of completion of the units is ignored.
7. Equivalent units are computed by multiplying physical units by the percentage of completion.
8. If the beginning WIP inventory is assumed to be zero, cost per equivalent unit (CPEU) is completed by dividing production costs by equivalent units.
9. If the beginning WIP inventory is not zero, then the process costing analysis must be done using a cost-flow assumption such as the weighted-average method or the FIFO method.
10. With the weighted-average method, cost per equivalent unit is computed by dividing *total* production costs by *total* equivalent units of production.
11. With the FIFO method, cost per equivalent unit is computed by dividing *current* production costs by *current* production equivalent units.
12. The use of standard costs in process costing avoids the need to compute cost per equivalent unit using the weighted-average or FIFO method.
13. Process costing using standard costs involves allocating standard production costs to ending WIP inventory and units completed.
14. Transferred-in costs are production costs transferred from one production department to another.
15. Spoilage represents units of production that do not meet production quality standards and cannot be efficiently reworked to meet those standards.
16. Normal spoilage is spoilage that occurs under efficient production operations.
17. Abnormal spoilage is spoilage that is not expected to occur under efficient production operations.
18. The cost of normal spoilage is considered to be part of the cost of production.
19. The cost of abnormal spoilage is excluded from the cost of production and charged (debited) to a loss account for abnormal spoilage.
20. Defective units are units of production that do not meet production quality standards but that can be reworked to meet those standards.
21. Waste is residue from the production process that has no measurable value, whereas scrap is residue from the production process that has measurable, but relatively minor, value.

RAPID REVIEW

1. Process costing is used in industries where each unit of production requires approximately the same amounts of direct materials, direct labor, and factory overhead: (**a**) true, (**b**) false. [See Section 4-1.]

2. Conversion costs are the costs of (a) direct materials and direct labor, (b) direct materials and factory overhead, (c) direct labor and factory overhead. [See Section 4-1.]

3. Equivalent units measure the relative amount of production completed: (a) true, (b) false. [See Section 4-2.]

4. Average costs per unit are used in (a) process costing, (b) job-order costing, (c) both process and job-order costing. [See Section 4-1.]

5. The purpose of process costing is to allocate production costs to ending WIP inventory and units completed: (a) true, (b) false. [See Section 4-1.]

6. Equivalent units are computed by multiplying physical units by the percentage of completion: (a) true, (b) false. [See Section 4-2.]

7. For process costing using the weighted-average method, cost per equivalent unit is based on (a) current production costs, (b) total production costs. [See Section 4-3.]

8. For process costing using the FIFO method, cost per equivalent unit is based on (a) current production costs, (b) total production costs. [See Section 4-3.]

9. Transferred-in costs are transferred from one production department to another: (a) true, (b) false. [See Section 4-4.]

10. For process costing using standard costs, production costs are allocated to ending WIP inventory and units completed based on (a) weighted-average cost per equivalent unit, (b) standard cost per unit, (c) current cost per unit. [See Section 4-5.]

11. Spoilage represents units of production that do not meet production quality standards and (a) can be efficiently reworked to meet quality standards, (b) cannot be efficiently reworked to meet quality standards. [See Section 4-6.]

12. Normal spoilage is spoilage that occurs under (a) efficient production operations, (b) inefficient production operations. [See Section 4-6.]

13. The cost of normal spoilage should be (a) included in the cost of production, (b) charged as a loss for normal spoilage. [See Section 4-6.]

14. The cost of abnormal spoilage should be (a) included in the cost of production, (b) charged as a loss for abnormal spoilage. [See Section 4-6.]

15. Defective units are units of production that do not meet production quality standards and (a) can be efficiently reworked to meet quality standards, (b) cannot be efficiently reworked to meet quality standards. [See Section 4-6.]

16. Waste is residue from the production process that has no measurable value, and scrap is residue that has measurable value: (a) true, (b) false. [See Section 4-6.]

Answers:
1. (a)   2. (c)   3. (a)   4. (c)   5. (a)   6. (a)   7. (b)   8. (a)   9. (a)   10. (b)
11. (b)   12. (a)   13. (a)   14. (b)   15. (a)   16. (a)

SOLVED PROBLEMS

Problems 4-1 and 4-2 are based on the following data.

Northern Company uses a process costing system. All direct materials are introduced at the beginning of the production process in Department 1. Conversion costs are applied to units of production uniformly throughout the production process. The following information is available for Department 1 for the month of June 19X4.

	PHYSICAL UNITS
WIP inventory, June 1, 19X4	
(40% complete for conversion costs)	1,000
Units started	9,000
WIP inventory, June 30, 19X4	
(50% complete for conversion costs)	800

PROBLEM 4-1: Summarize physical units.

Solution: Using the format given in Section 4-1, fill in the information that you know.

Beginning WIP inventory	1,000
Units started	9,000
Total units to account for	10,000
Ending WIP inventory	800
Units completed	?
Total units accounted for	10,000

You know that the number of total units to account for must always equal the total units accounted for. Therefore, you now know that the number of units completed equals 9,200.

Total units accounted for	10,000
Ending WIP inventory	800
Units completed	9,200

[See Section 4-1.]

PROBLEM 4-2: Calculate equivalent units.

Solution: Use equation 4.3 to calculate equivalent units for beginning WIP inventory and ending WIP inventory.

$$EU = PU \times \%C$$

Direct Materials

Beginning WIP inventory equivalent units = 1,000 × 100%
= 1,000

Ending WIP inventory equivalent units = 800 × 100%
= 800

Conversion Costs

Beginning WIP inventory equivalent units = 1,000 × 40%
= 400

Ending WIP inventory equivalent units = 800 × 50%
= 400

Units completed were found in Problem 4-1 to be 9,200. These units are 100% complete by definition, and are therefore already expressed in equivalent units.

Current production in equivalent units is computed using equation 4.4:

	EQUIVALENT UNITS	
	direct materials	conversion costs
Ending WIP inventory	800	400
+ Units completed	+ 9,200	+ 9,200
− Beginning WIP inventory	− 1,000	− 400
= Current production	9,000	9,200

The equivalent units of production can be summarized as follows:

	EQUIVALENT UNITS	
	direct materials	conversion costs
Beginning WIP inventory	1,000	400
+ Current production	9,000	9,200
= Total equivalent units	10,000	9,600
Ending WIP inventory	800	400
+ Units completed	9,200	9,200
= Total equivalent units	10,000	9,600

[See Section 4-2.]

Problems 4-3 to 4-6 are based on the following data.

Elfin Manufacturing Company has provided the following information for a particular production department.

	PHYSICAL UNITS	EQUIVALENT UNITS	
		direct materials	conversion costs
Beginning WIP inventory	2,000	2,000	1,000
Percentage completed		100%	50%
Units started	22,000		
Current production		22,000	20,000
Ending WIP inventory	4,000	4,000	1,000
Percentage completed		100%	25%
Units completed	20,000	20,000	20,000

	direct materials	conversion costs
Production costs:		
Beginning WIP inventory costs	$ 6,200	$ 5,000
Current production costs	41,800	79,000
Total production costs	$48,000	$84,000

All direct materials are applied to units of production at the beginning of the production process, and conversion costs are applied on a uniform basis throughout the production process.

PROBLEM 4-3: Using the weighted-average method of process costing, compute the cost per equivalent unit for direct materials and conversion costs.

Solution: In order to solve this problem, you must first compute the total equivalent units for direct materials and conversion costs.

	EQUIVALENT UNITS	
	direct materials	conversion costs
Beginning WIP inventory	2,000	1,000
Current production	22,000	20,000
Total units to account for	24,000	21,000
Ending WIP inventory	4,000	1,000
Units completed	20,000	20,000
Total units accounted for	24,000	21,000

You can now find the cost per equivalent unit for direct materials and conversion costs.

Direct Materials

$$\text{Cost per equivalent unit} = \frac{\text{Total production costs}}{\text{Total equivalent units}}$$

$$= \frac{\$48,000}{24,000}$$

$$= \$2.00$$

Conversion Costs

$$\text{Cost per equivalent unit} = \frac{\text{Total production costs}}{\text{Total equivalent units}}$$

$$= \frac{\$84,000}{21,000}$$

$$= \$4.00$$

[See Sections 4-2 and 4-3.]

PROBLEM 4-4: Using the costs per equivalent unit that you found in Problem 4-3, allocate production costs to ending WIP inventory and units completed using the weighted-average method.

Solution: You would allocate production costs as follows:

	direct materials	conversion costs	Total
Ending WIP inventory equivalent units	4,000	1,000	
Cost per equivalent unit	$ 2.00	$ 4.00	
Total production costs allocated to ending WIP inventory	$ 8,000	$ 4,000	$ 12,000
Units completed	20,000	20,000	
Cost per equivalent unit	$ 2.00	$ 4.00	
Total production costs allocated to units completed	$40,000	$80,000	$120,000
Total production costs allocated			$132,000

Therefore, $12,000 would be allocated to ending WIP inventory, and $120,000 would be allocated to units completed. The total production costs allocated of $132,000 ($12,000 + $120,000) are the same as the total production costs to allocate of $132,000 ($48,000 direct materials and $84,000 conversion costs). [See Section 4-3.]

PROBLEM 4-5: Compute the cost per equivalent unit for direct materials and conversion costs using the FIFO method.

Solution: With the FIFO method, you find the cost per equivalent unit by dividing *current* production costs by *current* production in equivalent units.

Direct Materials

$$\text{Cost per equivalent unit} = \frac{\text{Current production costs}}{\text{Current production}}$$

$$= \frac{\$41,800}{22,000}$$

$$= \$1.90$$

Conversion Costs

$$\text{Cost per equivalent unit} = \frac{\text{Current production costs}}{\text{Current production}}$$

$$= \frac{\$79,000}{20,000}$$

$$= \$3.95$$

[See Section 4-3.]

PROBLEM 4-6: Using the costs per equivalent unit that you found in Problem 4-5, allocate the production costs to ending WIP inventory and to units completed using the FIFO method.

Solution: Using the FIFO method, you would allocate production to ending WIP inventory and to units completed as follows:

	direct materials	conversion costs	Total
Ending WIP inventory equivalent units	4,000	1,000	
× FIFO cost per equivalent unit	$ 1.90	$ 3.95	
= Production costs allocated to ending WIP inventory	$ 7,600	$ 3,950	$ 11,550
Total production costs	$48,000	$84,000	
− Production costs allocated to ending WIP inventory	7,600	3,950	
= Production costs allocated to units completed	$40,400	$80,050	$120,450
Total production costs allocated			$132,000

Therefore, $11,550 would be allocated to ending WIP inventory and $120,450 would be allocated to units completed.

An alternative approach found in some textbooks for allocating production costs to units completed and ending WIP inventory (Step 4) using the FIFO method is summarized below:

	direct materials	conversion costs	Total
Beginning WIP inventory	$ 6,200	$ 5,000	$ 11,200
Current costs added to complete beginning WIP inventory	−0−		
conversion costs (1,000 × $3.95)		3,950	3,950
Total costs allocated to beginning WIP inventory	$ 6,200	$ 8,950	$ 15,150
Costs allocated to units started and completed in current period			
direct materials (18,000* × $1.90)	34,200		
conversion costs (18,000* × $3.95)		71,100	105,300
Total production costs allocated to units completed	$40,400	$80,050	$120,450
Costs allocated to ending WIP inventory			
direct materials (4,000 × $1.90)	7,600		
conversion costs (1,000 × $3.95)		3,950	11,550
Total production costs allocated	$48,000	$84,000	$132,000

* Units started and completed in the current period are found as follows:

Units completed	20,000
− Beginning WIP inventory	2,000
= Units started and completed	18,000

[See Section 4-3.]

PROBLEM 4-7: During the month of May 19X5, Micro Company's production department 2 had costs per equivalent unit, computed under the weighted-average method, as follows:

Direct materials	$2.00
Conversion costs	$3.00
Transferred-in costs	
(from department 1)	$1.00

Direct materials and conversion costs are applied to units of production uniformly throughout the production process in department 2. There were 2,000 physical units (40% complete for both direct materials and conversion costs) in ending WIP inventory on May 31.

Allocate production costs to ending WIP inventory.

Solution: You must first find the number of equivalent units in ending WIP inventory using equation 4.3:

$$EU = PU \times \%C$$
$$= 2,000 \times 40\%$$
$$= 800$$

Allocate production costs to ending WIP inventory as follows:

Direct Materials	
800 equivalent units × $2.00	= $1,600
Conversion Costs	
800 equivalent units × $3.00	= 2,400
Transferred-in costs	
2,000 equivalent units × $1.00	= 2,000
Total production costs allocated to ending WIP inventory	$6,000

Note that the units of production associated with the transferred-in costs are considered 100% complete. [See Sections 4-3 and 4-4.]

PROBLEM 4-8: Assume that Dover Company has two production departments (Department A and Department B). Department A completes the first part of the production process and transfers the units to Department B, where the units are completed. For the month of June, Department A has transferred 15,000 units to Department B with production costs of $60,000. The following information is provided for the month of June for Department B.

Beginning WIP inventory	5,000
(100% complete for direct materials; 50% complete for conversion costs)	
Units started (Transferred-in)	15,000
Units completed	17,500
Ending WIP inventory	2,500
(100% complete for direct materials; 40% complete for conversion costs)	
Transferred-in costs:	
Beginning WIP inventory	$ 18,000
Current production	$ 60,000

Direct materials costs:

Beginning WIP inventory	$ 36,500
Current production	$103,500

Conversion costs:

Beginning WIP inventory	$ 19,400
Current production	$136,000

Assume that 100% of the direct materials are added to all units when they begin production in Department B. Using the weighted-average method, determine the amount of production costs that should be allocated to ending WIP inventory and units completed in Department B.

Solution:

STEPS 1 AND 2. SUMMARIZE PHYSICAL UNITS AND COMPUTE EQUIVALENT UNITS.

The physical units would be summarized and equivalent units would be computed in the same manner as in Section 4-3. However, "TI costs" (transferred-in costs) are added as an additional category for computing equivalent units. Notice that the units of production associated with transferred-in costs are 100% complete when transferred into Department B.

	PHYSICAL UNITS	EQUIVALENT UNITS TI costs	EQUIVALENT UNITS direct materials	EQUIVALENT UNITS conversion costs
Beginning WIP inventory	5,000	5,000	5,000	2,500
Units started	15,000			
Current production		15,000	15,000	16,000
Total units to account for	20,000	20,000	20,000	18,500
Ending WIP inventory	2,500	2,500	2,500	1,000
Units completed	17,500	17,500	17,500	17,500
Total units accounted for	20,000	20,000	20,000	18,500

Remember that you would compute the current production in equivalent units using equation 4.4 as follows:

$$\frac{\text{Current}}{\text{production}} = \frac{\text{Ending WIP inventory}}{\text{equivalent units}} + \frac{\text{Units}}{\text{completed}} - \frac{\text{Beginning WIP inventory}}{\text{equivalent units}}$$

This equation can be used to compute current production for each of the production cost categories (TI costs, direct materials, and conversion costs) as follows:

	EQUIVALENT UNITS TI costs	EQUIVALENT UNITS direct materials	EQUIVALENT UNITS conversion costs
Ending WIP inventory	2,500	2,500	1,000
+ Units completed	17,500	17,500	17,500
− Beginning WIP inventory	(5,000)	(5,000)	(2,500)
= Current production	15,000	15,000	16,000

STEP 3. COMPUTE COST PER EQUIVALENT UNIT.

The cost per equivalent unit would be computed using the weighted-average method by dividing *total* production costs by *total* equivalent units as follows:

	TI costs	direct materials	conversion costs	Total
Beginning WIP inventory	$18,000	$ 36,500	$ 19,400	$ 73,900
+ Current production costs	60,000	103,500	136,000	299,500
= Total production costs	$78,000	$140,000	$155,400	$373,400
÷ Total equivalent units	20,000	20,000	18,500	
= Cost per equivalent unit	$ 3.90	$ 7.00	$ 8.40	

Using the weighted-average method, *total* production costs would be divided by *total* equivalent units for each category of production costs to find cost per equivalent unit. Notice that a separate cost per equivalent unit is computed for transferred-in costs.

STEP 4. ALLOCATE PRODUCTON COSTS.

The cost per equivalent unit would be used to allocate production costs to ending WIP inventory and units completed using the weighted-average method as follows:

	TI costs	direct materials	conversion costs	Total
Ending WIP inventory equivalent units	2,500	2,500	1,000	
× Cost per equivalent unit	$ 3.90	$ 7.00	$ 8.40	
= Total production costs allocated to ending WIP inventory	$ 9,750	$ 17,500	$ 8,400	$ 35,650
Units completed	17,500	17,500	17,500	
× Cost per equivalent unit	$ 3.90	$ 7.00	$ 8.40	
= Total production costs allocated to units completed	$68,250	$122,500	$147,000	337,750
Total production costs allocated				$373,400

Notice that the total production costs allocated equal the total production costs computed in Step 3. [See Section 4-4.]

PROBLEM 4-9: Using the information in Problem 4-8, allocate production costs to ending WIP inventory and units completed in Department B, using the FIFO method.

Solution:

STEPS 1 AND 2. SUMMARIZE PHYSICAL UNITS AND COMPUTE EQUIVALENT UNITS.

The physical units would be summarized and the equivalent units would be computed exactly as they were in Problem 4-8.

	PHYSICAL UNITS	EQUIVALENT UNITS TI costs	direct materials	conversion costs
Beginning WIP inventory	5,000	5,000	5,000	2,500
Units started	15,000			
Current production		15,000	15,000	16,000
Total units to account for	20,000	20,000	20,000	18,500
Ending WIP inventory	2,500	2,500	2,500	1,000
Units completed	17,500	17,500	17,500	17,500
Total units accounted for	20,000	20,000	20,000	18,500

STEP 3. COMPUTE COST PER EQUIVALENT UNIT.

The cost per equivalent unit would be computed using the FIFO method by dividing *current* production costs by *current* equivalent units as follows:

	TI costs	direct materials	conversion costs	Total
Total production costs	$78,000	$140,000	$155,400	$373,400
− Beginning WIP inventory costs	18,000	36,500	19,400	73,900
= Current production costs	$60,000	$103,500	$136,000	$299,500
÷ Current production equivalent units	15,000	15,000	16,000	
= Cost per equivalent unit	$ 4.00	$ 6.90	$ 8.50	

STEP 4. ALLOCATE PRODUCTION COSTS.

The FIFO cost per equivalent unit would be used to allocate production costs using the FIFO method to ending WIP inventory and units completed as follows:

	TI costs	direct materials	conversion costs	Total
Ending WIP inventory equivalent units	2,500	2,500	1,000	
× FIFO cost per equivalent unit	$ 4.00	$ 6.90	$ 8.50	
= Production costs allocated to ending WIP inventory	$10,000	$ 17,250	$ 8,500	$ 35,750
Total production costs	$78,000	$140,000	$155,400	$373,400
− Production costs allocated to ending WIP inventory	10,000	17,250	8,500	35,750
= Production costs allocated to units completed	$68,000	$122,750	$146,900	$337,650
Total production costs allocated				$373,400

Notice that the total production costs allocated equal the total production costs computed in Step 3.

An alternative approach found in some textbooks for allocating production costs to units completed and ending WIP inventory (Step 4) using the FIFO method is summarized below:

	TI costs	direct materials	conversion costs	Total
Beginning WIP inventory	$18,000	$ 36,500	$ 19,400	$ 73,900
Current costs added to complete beginning WIP inventory conversion costs (2,500 × $8.50)	−0−	−0−	21,250	21,250
Total costs allocated to beginning WIP inventory	$18,000	$ 36,500	$ 40,650	$ 95,150
Costs allocated to units started and completed in current period				
TI costs (12,500 × $4.00)	50,000			
direct materials (12,500 × $6.90)		86,250		
conversion costs (12,500 × $8.50)			106,250	242,500
Total production costs allocated to units completed	$68,000	$122,750	$146,900	$337,650
Costs allocated to ending WIP inventory				
TI costs (2,500 × $4.00)	10,000			
direct materials (2,500 × $6.90)		17,250		
conversion costs (1,000 × $8.50)			8,500	37,750
Total production costs allocated	$78,000	$140,000	$155,400	$373,400

[See Section 4-4.]

Problems 4-10 and 4-11 are based on the following data.

The production process begins in department A of Melton Manufacturing Company. The following information is available for department A for August 19X5.

	PHYSICAL UNITS
Work-in-Process, August 1 (60% complete for conversion costs)	20,000
Units started	100,000
Units completed	80,000
Work-in-Process, August 31 (40% complete for conversion costs)	40,000

PROBLEM 4-10: Summarize physical and equivalent units of production for conversion costs for department A for the month of August.

Solution: Use equation 4.3 to compute equivalent units for beginning and ending WIP inventory for conversion costs.

$$EU = PU \times \%C$$

Beginning WIP Inventory

$$= 20,000 \times 60\%$$

$$= 12,000$$

Ending WIP Inventory

$$= 40,000 \times 40\%$$

$$= 16,000$$

Use equation 4.4 to compute current production in equivalent units.

	EQUIVALENT UNITS conversion costs
Ending WIP inventory	16,000
+ Units completed	+ 80,000
− Beginning WIP inventory	− 12,000
= Current production	84,000

Your summary of physical and equivalent units would be as follows:

	PHYSICAL UNITS	EQUIVALENT UNITS conversion costs
Beginning WIP inventory	20,000	12,000
Units started	100,000	
Current production		84,000
Total units to account for	120,000	96,000
Ending WIP inventory	40,000	16,000
Units completed	80,000	80,000
Total units accounted for	120,000	96,000

[See Section 4-2.]

PROBLEM 4-11: Determine the cost per equivalent unit for conversion costs using the FIFO and weighted-average methods. Beginning WIP inventory conversion costs were $20,400, and the conversion costs applied to production during August were $176,400.

Solution: The weighted-average method computes cost per equivalent unit based on *total* production costs and *total* equivalent units. Total production costs equal $20,400 + $176,400 = $196,800. Total equivalent units of 96,000 were found in Problem 4-10.

$$\text{Cost per equivalent unit} = \frac{\text{Total production costs}}{\text{Total equivalent units}}$$

$$= \frac{\$196,800}{96,000}$$

$$= \$2.05$$

The FIFO method computes cost per equivalent unit based on *current* production costs and *current* production in equivalent units. Current production costs equal $176,400. The current production in equivalent units of 84,000 was found in Problem 4-11.

$$\text{Cost per equivalent unit} = \frac{\text{Current production costs}}{\text{Current production in equivalent units}}$$

$$= \frac{\$176,400}{84,000}$$

$$= \$2.10$$

[See Section 4-3.]

PROBLEM 4-12: Alpha Manufacturing Company uses process costing with standard costs as its method of product costing. The standard cost per equivalent unit in department 1 is $3.20 for direct materials and $5.00 for conversion costs. The ending WIP inventory in department 1 was 10,000 units, which were 100% complete for direct materials and 40% complete for conversion costs. Compute the amount of standard costs allocated to ending WIP inventory.

Solution: You must first compute equivalent units using equation 4.3 for direct materials and conversion costs.

$$EU = PU \times \%C$$

Direct Materials

$$= 10,000 \times 100\%$$

$$= \underline{10,000}$$

Conversion Costs

$$= 10,000 \times 40\%$$

$$= \underline{4,000}$$

The standard costs allocated to ending WIP inventory would be computed as follows:

	direct materials	conversion costs	Total
Ending WIP inventory equivalent units	10,000	4,000	
Standard cost per unit	$ 3.20	$ 5.00	
Total production costs allocated to ending WIP inventory	$32,000	$20,000	$52,000

[See Section 4-5.]

5 BUDGETING AND RESPONSIBILITY ACCOUNTING

THIS CHAPTER IS ABOUT

- ☑ **Budgeting Concepts**
- ☑ **Master Budgets**
- ☑ **Operating Budgets**
- ☑ **Financial Budgets**
- ☑ **Responsibility Accounting**

5-1. Budgeting Concepts

A. What is a budget?

A **budget** is a plan expressed in quantitative terms that reflects the objectives of management. A budget encompasses the planned operating and financial activities of an organization.

B. Form and content of a budget.

A budget's form and content are based on the information the accountant wants to convey. Specific types of budgets represent various components of the budgeted income statement and balance sheet.

C. Advantages of a budget

The advantages of a budget include the following:

1. A budget facilitates planning in an organization.
2. A budget improves the coordination of planning in an organization.
3. A budget improves communication of management's objectives throughout an organization.
4. A budget provides the basis for performance evaluation of managers.

D. Features of a budget.

When budgeting an activity, you must determine what the budget's timeframe and specific content will be, whether you will use the static or the flexible approach, and whether you want a continuous budget.

1. TIMEFRAME

The *timeframe* for a budget is usually one year. An annual budget is often divided into quarterly or monthly periods. The annual budget corresponds to the operating cycle and financial reporting periods of most organizations.

2. SPECIFIC CONTENT

The *specific content* of a budget is determined by what you are budgeting: sales dollars, number of units, direct labor hours, direct labor dollars, net income, etc. Section 5-2 presents a description of the master budget.

'3. STATIC VERSUS FLEXIBLE APPROACH

A budget may be classified as either static (fixed) or flexible (variable). A *static budget* is based on a *predetermined* level of activity for production and sales and will not generally reflect the actual level of activity. In contrast, a *flexible budget* can be determined for the *actual* level of activity for production and sales.

4. CONTINUOUS BUDGETS

In a *continuous budget*, as one month or quarter expires, an additional month or quarter is added to the budget, so that there is always one year of budgeted data available. For example, at the end of the first quarter of 19X2, that quarter would be dropped from the budget and an additional quarter–the first quarter of 19X3–would be added. As a result, a continuous budget always extends one full year into the future.

5-2. Master Budgets

The *master budget* is a collection of individual budgets that encompasses the planned operating and financial activities throughout the firm. The two primary components of the master budget are (1) the operating budget and (2) the financial budget.

A. Operating budgets

The *operating budget* is composed of the budgeted income statement and the individual budgets related to the budgeted income statement, as follows:

1. Sales budget
2. Production budget
3. Direct materials budget
4. Direct labor budget
5. Factory overhead budget
6. Cost-of-goods-sold budget
7. Selling expense budget
8. Administrative expense budget

B. Financial budgets

The *financial budget* is composed of the budgeted balance sheet and the budgets related to the budgeted balance sheet, as follows:

1. Budgeted balance sheet
2. Capital budget
3. Cash budget
4. Budgeted statement of changes in financial position

C. Master budget flowchart

The flowchart in Exhibit 5-1 presents the interrelationships between the various components of the master budget.

5-3. Operating Budgets

In this section, an example will be used to demonstrate the preparation of an operating budget. Each component of the operating budget is interrelated with the budget's other parts.

A. Information for preparing an operating budget.

The following information will be used to prepare an operating budget for the Example Company for the year 19X2:

1. PRODUCTION DATA

The management of the Example Company has provided the following budgeted production costs for 19X2:

Direct materials	$3.00 per pound
Direct labor	$9.00 per hour
Factory overhead is applied on the basis of direct labor hours.	
Direct materials per unit of output	4 pounds
Direct labor per unit of output	2 hours

Factory overhead:

Indirect materials (variable)	$ 20,000
Indirect labor wages (variable)	35,000
Indirect labor salaries (fixed)	10,000
Utilities (variable portion)	7,000
Utilities (fixed portion)	3,000
Maintenance (variable portion)	3,000
Maintenance (fixed portion)	7,000
Depreciation (fixed)	20,000
Total	$105,000

(information continued on page 84)

EXHIBIT 5-1

Master Budget Flowchart

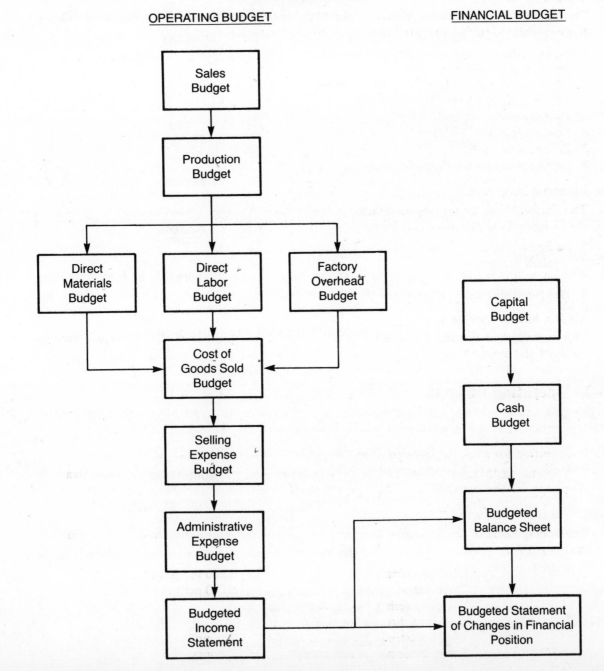

2. INVENTORIES

The management of the Example Company has provided the following inventory information:

	Units	Cost per unit	Total cost
Finished Goods Inventory:			
Beginning balance, January 1, 19X2	150	$45	$ 6,750
Desired ending balance, December 31, 19X2	1,150	$45	51,750
Work-in-Process Inventory:			
Assume that beginning and ending balances are zero.			

	Pounds	Cost
Direct Materials Inventory:		
Beginning balance, January 1, 19X2	1,000	$ 3,000
Desired ending balance, December 31, 19X2	7,000	21,000

3. OTHER INFORMATION

The following budget information is also available for the Example Company for 19X2:

Forecasted sales (in units)	6,000
Budgeted selling price per unit	$ 70
Selling expenses:	
Sales commissions (variable)	$12,000
Advertising (variable)	6,000
Salaries (fixed)	15,000
Miscellaneous (fixed)	3,000
Total	$36,000
Administrative expenses:	
Salaries and wages (fixed)	$40,000
Supplies (fixed)	2,000
Miscellaneous (fixed)	3,000
Total	$45,000

B. Sales budget

A *sales budget* is the starting point in the preparation of an operating budget. The sales budget is based on the forecasted (budgeted) sales volume (in units) and the budgeted sales price per unit.

$$\text{Budgeted sales revenue} = \frac{\text{Forecasted sales volume}}{\text{in units}} \times \frac{\text{Budgeted sales price}}{\text{per unit}}$$

The sales budget for the Example Company in 19X2 is shown in Exhibit 5-2.

EXHIBIT 5-2

Example Company
Sales Budget
For the Year Ended December 31, 19X2

Forecasted sales volume (in units)	Budgeted selling price per unit	Budgeted sales revenue
6,000	$70	$420,000

C. Production budget

The *production budget* is developed on the basis of the sales budget and the Finished Goods Inventory, as follows:

Desired ending Finished Goods Inventory
+ Forecasted sales volume (in units)
− Beginning Finished Goods Inventory
= Budgeted production (in units)

The production budget for the Example Company for 19X2 is shown in Exhibit 5-3.

EXHIBIT 5-3

Example Company
Production Budget
For the Year Ended December 31, 19X2

	Units
Desired ending Finished Goods Inventory	1,150
+ Forecasted sales volume (in units)	6,000
− Beginning Finished Goods Inventory	150
= Budgeted production (in units)	7,000

D. Direct materials budget

The direct materials budget is concerned with the budgeted amount of direct materials purchases. These budgeted purchases are computed as follows:

Desired ending Direct Materials Inventory
+ Budgeted usage of direct materials in 19X2
− Beginning Direct Materials Inventory
= Budgeted direct materials purchases in 19X2

The direct materials budget for the Example Company for 19X2 is shown in Exhibit 5-4.

EXHIBIT 5-4

Example Company
Direct Materials Budget
For the Year Ended December 31, 19X2

	Pounds	Cost per pound	Cost
Desired ending Direct Materials Inventory	7,000	$3.00	$ 21,000
+ Budgeted direct materials usage	28,000 (Note 1)	3.00	84,000
− Beginning Direct Materials Inventory	1,000	3.00	3,000
= Budgeted direct materials purchases	34,000		$102,000

Note 1: 7,000 units of budgeted production (see Exhibit 5-3) times 4 pounds of direct materials per unit equals 28,000 pounds of budgeted direct materials usage.

E. Direct labor budget

The direct labor budget is based on the direct labor rate per hour, the direct labor hours per unit of output, and the budgeted production (in units).

$$\text{Budgeted direct labor costs} = \text{Budgeted production in units} \times \text{Direct labor hours per unit} \times \text{Direct labor rate per hour}$$

The direct labor budget for the Example Company for 19X2 is shown in Exhibit 5-5.

EXHIBIT 5-5

Example Company
Direct Labor Budget
For the Year Ended December 31, 19X2

Budgeted production (in units)	Direct labor hours per unit	Total hours	Direct labor rate per hour	Budgeted direct labor costs
7,000	2	14,000	$9.00	$126,000

F. Factory overhead budget

The factory overhead budget is based on the budgeted variable factory overhead and budgeted fixed factory overhead. The factory overhead budget for the Example Company for 19X2 is shown in Exhibit 5-6.

EXHIBIT 5-6

Example Company
Factory Overhead Budget
For the Year Ended December 31, 19X2
(at the Budgeted Activity Level of 14,000 Direct Labor Hours)

Indirect materials (variable)	$20,000	
Indirect labor wages (variable)	35,000	
Utilities (variable portion)	7,000	
Maintenance (variable portion)	3,000	
Budgeted variable overhead		$ 65,000
Utilities (fixed portion)	$ 3,000	
Indirect labor salaries (fixed)	10,000	
Maintenance (fixed portion)	7,000	
Depreciation (fixed)	20,000	
Budgeted fixed overhead		40,000
Total budgeted factory overhead		$105,000

$$\text{Factory overhead cost per direct labor hour} = \frac{\$105,000}{14,000}$$

$$= \$7.50$$

G. Cost of goods sold budget

The cost of goods sold budget is computed as follows:

Beginning Finished Goods Inventory
+ Budgeted direct materials usage
+ Budgeted direct labor costs
+ Budgeted factory overhead
+ Add the decrease (deduct the increase) in
    Work-in-Process Inventory
− Desired ending Finished Goods Inventory
= Budgeted cost of goods sold

The cost of goods sold budget for the Example Company for 19X2 is shown in Exhibit 5-7.

EXHIBIT 5-7

Example Company
Cost of Goods Sold Budget
For the Year Ended December 31, 19X2

Finished Goods Inventory, January 1		$ 6,750
+ Budgeted direct materials usage		
(Exhibit 5-4)	$ 84,000	
+ Budgeted direct labor costs		
(Exhibit 5-5)	126,000	
+ Budgeted factory overhead		
(Exhibit 5-6)	105,000	
Total production costs		315,000
+ Add the decrease (deduct the increase)		
in Work-in-Process Inventory		−0−
− Desired ending Finished Goods		
Inventory, December 31 ($45.00 × 1,150)		51,750
Budgeted cost of goods sold		$270,000

The production cost per unit would be:

		Cost per unit
Direct materials	$3.00 × 4 lbs./unit	$12.00
Direct labor	$9.00 × 2 hours	18.00
Factory overhead	$7.50 × 2 hours	15.00
Total production cost per unit		$45.00

H. Selling and administrative expense budget

For simplicity, this chapter will combine the selling expense budget and the administrative expense budget. The selling and administrative expense budget for the Example Company for 19X2 is shown in Exhibit 5-8.

EXHIBIT 5-8

Example Company
Selling and Administrative Expense Budget
For the Year Ended December 31, 19X2

Selling expenses:		
Sales commissions	$12,000	
Advertising	6,000	
Salaries	15,000	
Miscellaneous	3,000	
Total budgeted selling expenses		$36,000
Administrative expenses:		
Salaries and wages	$40,000	
Supplies	2,000	
Miscellaneous	3,000	
Total budgeted administrative expenses		45,000
Total budgeted selling and administrative expenses		$81,000

I. Budgeted income statement

The *budgeted income statement* represents a summary of the subcomponent budgets (Exhibits 5-2 to 5-8) of the operating budget. The budgeted income statement for the Example Company for 19X2 is shown in Exhibit 5-9.

EXHIBIT 5-9

Example Company
Budgeted Income Statement
For the Year Ended December 31, 19X2

Budgeted sales revenue (Exhibit 5-2)	$420,000
Budgeted cost of goods sold (Exhibit 5-7)	− 270,000
Gross margin	$150,000
Budgeted selling and administrative expenses (Exhibit 5-8)	− 81,000
Operating income	$69,000

5-4. Financial Budgets

The other major part of the master budget is the financial budget. The financial budget consists of the *capital budget, cash budget, budgeted balance sheet,* and the *budgeted statement of changes in financial position.* The capital budget is covered in Chapter 13 of the outline. The statement of changes in financial position is beyond the scope of this outline; it is covered in most financial accounting textbooks. This section of the outline will provide an example of the cash budget, which is emphasized in most cost accounting textbooks and courses.

A. Information for a cash budget

Development of a cash budget requires the following information: (1) budgeted cash receipts, (2) budgeted cash disbursements, and (3) beginning cash balance, desired minimum balance, and financing activities.

1. BUDGETED CASH RECEIPTS

Budgeted cash receipts would be estimated based on budgeted sales activity. For example, a company can develop estimates of when cash would be collected from customers. The following example demonstrates the process of estimating budgeted cash receipts.

Assume that all sales of Example Company are made on account. Example Company estimates that 80% of the sales made in a quarter are collected in that quarter; 17% of the sales are collected in the next quarter; and 3% of the sales are uncollectible. The following quarterly sales revenue information is provided:

Quarter	19X1 budgeted sales revenue	19X2 budgeted sales revenue
4th quarter 19X1	$120,000	
1st quarter 19X2		$100,000
2nd quarter 19X2		100,000
3rd quarter 19X2		100,000
4th quarter 19X2		120,000
Total Budgeted Sales 19X2		$420,000

Based on the sales revenue and assumptions, cash receipts from sales would be computed as shown in Exhibit 5-10:

EXHIBIT 5-10

Example Company
Budgeted Cash Receipts
For the Year Ended December 31, 19X2

	Quarter			
	1	2	3	4
Cash receipts from sales:				
Current quarter				
(80% of current quarter sales)	$ 80,000	$80,000	$80,000	$ 96,000
Previous quarter				
(17% of previous quarter sales)	20,400	17,000	17,000	17,000
Total collections	$100,400	$97,000	$97,000	$113,000

2. BUDGETED CASH DISBURSEMENTS

Budgeted cash disbursements would be estimated for each quarter (or month) in order to prepare a cash budget. Assume that the Example Company has estimated the following budgeted cash disbursements for each quarter in the year.

EXHIBIT 5-11

Example Company
Budgeted Cash Disbursements
For the Year Ended December 31, 19X2

	Quarter			
	1	2	3	4
Disbursements:				
Direct materials	$ 25,000	$ 25,000	$25,000	$ 27,000
Direct labor	30,000	30,000	30,000	36,000
Factory overhead	20,000	20,000	16,000	25,000
Other expenses	20,000	20,000	16,000	21,000
Income taxes	7,400	5,000	4,000	3,000
Total disbursements	$102,400	$100,000	$91,000	$112,000

3. BEGINNING CASH BALANCE, DESIRED MINIMUM BALANCE, AND FINANCING ACTIVITIES

The cash balance of Example Company on January 1, 19X2, is $20,000. Example Company desires to maintain a $20,000 minimum cash balance at the end of each quarter. The company can borrow or repay cash in multiples of $1,000 during the year at an interest rate of 10% per year. Interest, which is paid at the time the principal is repaid, is based on the time between borrowing (at the beginning of the quarter) and repayment (at the end of the quarter). Assume that Example Company will borrow and repay cash (in multiples of $1,000) in order to maintain the desired minimum balance requirements ($20,000).

On the basis of the information provided, you can construct a cash budget for the Example Company for 19X2.

B. Cash budget

The cash budget summarizes the cash receipts, cash disbursements, and cash position (beginning and ending balances) of the company for the budget period. The general formula for the cash budget follows:

> Beginning cash balance
> + Cash receipts
> ――――――――――――――――
> = Cash available
> − Cash disbursements
> ――――――――――――――――
> = Cash balance before financing
> Financing activities:
> + Financing borrowing
> − Financing repayment
> − Interest
> ――――――――――――――――
> = Ending cash balance

The cash budget for the Example Company for 19X2 is shown in Exhibit 5-12.

EXHIBIT 5-12

Example Company
Cash Budget
For the Year Ended December 31, 19X2

	Quarters			
	1	2	3	4
Beginning cash balance	$ 20,000	$ 20,000	$ 20,000	$ 20,700
Add cash receipts:				
Collection from customers	100,400	97,000	97,000	113,000
Total cash receipts	$120,400	$117,000	$117,000	$133,700
Less cash disbursements:				
Direct materials	25,000	25,000	25,000	27,000
Direct labor	30,000	30,000	30,000	36,000
Factory overhead	20,000	20,000	16,000	25,000
Other expenses	20,000	20,000	16,000	21,000
Income taxes	7,400	5,000	4,000	3,000
Total cash disbursements	$102,400	$100,000	$ 91,000	$112,000
Cash balance before financing	$ 18,000	$ 17,000	$ 26,000	$ 21,700
Financing:				
Borrowing	$ 2,000	$ 3,000	–	–
Repayment	–	–	$ (5,000)	–
Interest	–	–	(300)	–
Total financing	$ 2,000	$ 3,000	$ (5,300)	–
Ending cash balance	$ 20,000	$ 20,000	$ 20,700	$ 21,700

Note that the Example Company cannot begin to repay the cash it borrowed until the third quarter, when the cash balance before financing is greater than the desired minimum balance. The principal of $5,000 would be repaid in the third quarter since the company has the ability to repay that amount and it would be expensive (in terms of interest) to hold excess cash balances. According to the financing assumptions in the example, interest on the repaid principal would also be paid at that time. The interest amount for the third quarter would be computed based on the $2,000 principal at 10% for three quarters and the $3,000 principal at 10% for two quarters as follows:

$$\$2,000 \times 10\% \times 3/4 = \$150$$
$$\$3,000 \times 10\% \times 2/4 = \underline{\ \ 150}$$
$$\text{Total interest} \qquad \underline{\underline{\$300}}$$

C. Budgeted balance sheet

The budgeted balance sheet is based on the beginning balances plus or minus the budgeted changes in each balance sheet item. Many of the items in the budgeted balance sheet are determined from information obtained from subcomponents of the master budget. For example, the budgeted cash balance would be obtained directly from the cash budget. Similarly, the budgeted direct materials disbursements would be obtained directly from the direct materials budget.

5-5. Responsibility Accounting

A *responsibility accounting system* is designed to accumulate and report information about different segments, or responsibility centers, within an organization. *Responsibility centers* are segments within an organization where the manager is held responsible or accountable for expenses, revenues, and/or investment. There are four types of responsibility centers: expense centers, revenue centers, profit centers, and investment centers.

A. Expense centers.

An *expense center* (cost center) is a segment where the manager is held responsible for expenses incurred within the segment. An example of an expense center is a production department, where the manager has responsibility for controlling production expenses (direct materials, direct labor, and factory overhead) incurred in the department.

B. Revenue centers.

A *revenue center* is a segment of an organization where the manager is held responsible for revenues generated by the segment. For example, a sales department of a company may be considered a revenue center because the manager is held responsible for meeting sales revenue targets.

C. Profit centers

A *profit center* is a segment of an organization where the manager is held responsible for both revenues and expenses. Therefore, profit (revenues − expenses) can be computed as a responsibility measure for such a center. For example, a division of a company where the manager has control over revenues and expenses would generally be treated as a profit center.

D. Investment centers

An *investment center* is a segment of an organization where the manager is held responsible for revenues, expenses, and invested funds. The investment center differs from the profit center in that the investment center manager has the additional responsibility for investment in the division. For example, a division of a company where the manager has control over investment (funds invested in the division) as well as over the division's revenues and expenses would generally be classified as an investment center.

E. Responsibility centers and budgets

Budgets are usually prepared for all responsibility centers within an organization. The managers of responsibility centers are evaluated by comparing the budgeted results with actual results. For example, the budget for a profit center would be a budgeted income statement, and the profit center manager would be evaluated by comparing actual profit with budgeted profit.

RAISE YOUR GRADES

Can you explain...?

☑ what determines the form and content of a budget
☑ four advantages of a budget
☑ the timeframe of a budget
☑ the difference between a static budget and a flexible budget
☑ what a continuous budget is
☑ the components of a master budget
☑ how to develop an operating budget ✓
☑ how to prepare a sales budget
☑ how to prepare a production budget
☑ how to prepare a direct materials budget
☑ how to prepare a direct labor budget
☑ how to prepare a factory overhead budget
☑ how to prepare a cost of goods sold budget
☑ how to prepare a selling expense budget
☑ how to prepare an administrative expense budget
☑ how to prepare a budgeted income statement
☑ the four parts of a financial budget
☑ how to prepare a cash budget
☑ the differences between the four types of responsibility centers
☑ the definition of a responsibility accounting system

SUMMARY

1. A budget is a plan expressed in quantitative terms that reflects the objectives of management.
2. The form and content of budgets are generally based on the form and content of financial statements.
3. Budgets are usually developed for a one-year timeframe.
4. Annual budgets are often divided into quarterly or monthly periods.
5. Static budgets are based on predetermined levels of activity for sales and production.
6. Flexible budgets are based on actual levels of activity for production and sales.
7. A continuous budget involves adding a quarter or month to the budget at the end of a quarter or month, so that an entire year of budgeted data is always available.
8. A master budget is a collection of individual budgets that reflects the planned operating and financial activities of the organization.
9. A master budget is composed of an operating budget and a financial budget.
10. The operating budget is composed of the budgeted income statement and the subcomponent budgets of the budgeted income statement.
11. The financial budget is composed of the budgeted balance sheet and the subcomponent budgets of the budgeted balance sheet.
12. The sales budget is the starting point in developing an operating budget.
13. Budgeted production in units equals desired ending Finished Goods Inventory, plus forecasted sales volume (in units), minus beginning Finished Goods Inventory.
14. Budgeted direct materials purchases equals desired ending Direct Materials Inventory, plus budgeted usage of direct materials, minus beginning Direct Materials Inventory.
15. A responsibility accounting system is designed to accumulate and report information about different responsibility centers within an organization.
16. The four types of responsibility centers are expense centers, revenue centers, profit centers, and investment centers.

RAPID REVIEW

1. A budget reflects the planned operating and financial activities of an organization: (a) true, (b) false. [See Section 5-1.]

2. Budgets can improve coordination of planning in an organization: (a) true, (b) false. [See Section 5-1.]

3. Budgets cannot provide the basis for evaluating the performance of managers: (a) true, (b) false. [See Section 5-1.]

4. The timeframe for a budget is usually (a) one year, (b) one quarter, (c) five years. [See Section 5-1.]

5. A master budget includes (a) a budgeted balance sheet, (b) a budgeted income statement, (c) a cash budget, (d) a production budget, (e) all of the above. [See Section 5-2.]

6. The primary components of the master budget are (a) the operating budget and the budgeted income statement, (b) the sales budget and the cash budget, (c) the operating budget and the financial budget. [See Section 5-2.]

7. Investment center managers are held responsible for (a) investment, (b) revenues, (c) expenses, (d) all of the above, (e) none of the above. [See Section 5-5.]

8. Budgeted direct materials purchases equals desired ending direct materials inventory plus budgeted direct materials usage minus beginning direct materials inventory: (a) true, (b) false. [See Section 5-3.]

9. Budgeted production (in units) equals beginning finished goods inventory plus forecasted sales volume (in units) minus desired ending finished goods inventory: (a) true, (b) false. [See Section 5-3.]

10. The preparation of the operating budget usually begins with the preparation of the (a) budgeted income statement, (b) sales budget, (c) cash budget, (d) production budget. [See Section 5-3.]

11. A continuous budget drops the current month or quarter when it expires and adds a future month or quarter: (a) true, (b) false. [See Section 5-1.]

12. Profit center managers are held responsible for (a) revenues only, (b) expenses only, (c) revenues and expenses, (d) none of the above. [See Section 5-5.]

Answers:

1. (a)   2. (a)   3. (b)   4. (a)   5. (e)   6. (c)   7. (d)   8. (a)   9. (b)   10. (b)
11. (a)   12. (c)

SOLVED PROBLEMS

Problems 5-1 to 5-3 are based on the following information.

Northern Company has prepared the following budget information for the year 19X1:

Forecasted sales volume (in units)	48,000
Budgeted selling price per unit	$10.00
Finished Goods Inventory:	
Beginning balance, January 1	15,000 units
Desired ending balance, December 31	14,000 units
Direct Materials Inventory:	
Beginning balance, January 1	58,000 pounds
Desired ending balance, December 31	70,000 pounds

To produce one unit of output, Northern Company uses 4 pounds of direct materials at a cost of $2.00 per pound. Total production costs (including direct materials, direct labor, and factory overhead) are $9.00 per unit. Assume that Northern Company has no Work-in-Process Inventory.

PROBLEM 5-1: Compute the budgeted sales revenue for Northern Company.

Solution: The budgeted sales revenue would be computed as follows:

$$\text{Budgeted sales revenue} = \frac{\text{Forecasted sales volume}}{\text{in units}} \times \frac{\text{Budgeted sales price}}{\text{per unit}}$$

$$= 48{,}000 \text{ units} \times \$10.00 \text{ per unit}$$

$$= \$480{,}000$$

[See Section 5-3.]

PROBLEM 5-2: Prepare a production budget for Northern Company.

Solution: You would prepare the production budget for Northern Company as follows:

Northern Company
Production Budget
For the Year Ended December 31, 19X1

Desired ending Finished Goods Inventory	14,000 units
+ Forecasted sales volume (in units)	48,000 units
− Beginning Finished Goods Inventory	15,000 units
= Budgeted production (in units)	47,000 units

[See Section 5-3.]

PROBLEM 5-3: Prepare a direct materials purchases budget for Northern Company.

Solution: In order to prepare the direct materials budget, you need to find the budgeted direct materials usage. Use the budgeted production in units that you found in Problem 5-2.

$$\text{Budgeted direct materials usage} = \frac{\text{Budgeted production}}{\text{in units}} \times \frac{\text{Direct materials per}}{\text{unit of output}}$$

$$= 47{,}000 \text{ units} \times 4 \text{ pounds}$$

$$= 188{,}000 \text{ pounds}$$

Now you can prepare the direct materials purchases budget for Northern Company.

Northern Company
Direct Materials Budget
For the Year Ended December 31, 19X1

Desired ending Direct Materials Inventory	70,000
+ Budgeted direct materials usage	188,000
− Beginning Direct Materials Inventory	58,000
= Budgeted direct materials purchases	200,000 pounds

[See Section 5-3.]

Problems 5-4 to 5-6 are based on the following data.

ABC Company has prepared the following budget information for the year 19X2.

	Units
Forecasted sales volume	500
Finished Goods Inventory:	
Beginning balance, January 1	100
Desired ending balance, December 31	130

	Pounds
Direct Materials Inventory:	
Beginning balance, January 1	50
Desired ending balance, December 31	40

ABC Company uses 2 direct labor hours and 0.5 pounds of direct materials to produce one unit of output. The direct labor rate per hour is $6.00.

PROBLEM 5-4: Compute the budgeted production in units for the ABC Company.

Solution: You compute the budgeted production in units as follows:

	Units
Desired ending Finished Goods Inventory	130
+ Forecasted sales volume (in units)	500
− Beginning Finished Goods Inventory	100
= Budgeted production (in units)	530

[See Section 5-3.]

PROBLEM 5-5: Prepare the direct labor budget for ABC Company.

Solution: Using the budgeted production found in Problem 5-4, you prepare the direct labor budget for ABC Company as follows:

ABC Company
Direct Labor Budget
For the Year Ended December 31, 19X1

Budgeted production (in units)	Direct labor hours per unit	Total hours	Direct labor rate per hour	Budgeted direct labor costs
530	2	1,060	$6.00	$6,360

[See Section 5-3.]

PROBLEM 5-6: Compute the amount of direct materials that must be purchased by ABC Company in 19X2.

Solution: You must first compute the budgeted usage of direct materials. To do this, you will need to use the budgeted production found in Problem 5-4.

$$\text{Budgeted direct materials usage} = \frac{\text{Budgeted production}}{\text{in units}} \times \frac{\text{Direct materials per}}{\text{unit of output}}$$

$$= 530 \text{ units} \times 0.5 \text{ pounds}$$

$$= 265 \text{ pounds}$$

Now you can compute the budgeted direct materials purchases.

Desired ending Direct Materials Inventory	40
+ Budgeted usage of direct materials	265
− Beginning direct materials inventory	50
− Budgeted direct materials purchases	255 pounds

[See Section 5-3.]

PROBLEM 5-7: Alpha Company had the following budget information for 19X2, which was their first year of operations·

Sales (90% were collected in 19X2)	$1,500,000
Disbursements for costs and expenses	1,200,000
Disbursements for income taxes	90,000

Purchases of fixed assets for cash	400,000
Proceeds from issuance of common stock	500,000
Proceeds from short-term borrowings	100,000
Repayment of short-term borrowings	50,000

On the basis of this information, what would the cash balance be on December 31, 19X2?

Solution: The cash balance for Alpha Company would be computed as follows:

Beginning cash balance		$ –0–
Add cash receipts:		
Collections on sales (90% × $1,500,000)	$1,350,000	
Proceeds–common stock	500,000	
Proceeds–borrowing	100,000	
Total cash receipts		1,950,000
Less cash disbursements:		
Costs and expenses	$1,200,000	
Income taxes	90,000	
Purchases of fixed assets	400,000	
Repayment on borrowing	50,000	
Total cash disbursements		1,740,000
Ending cash balance, December 31, 19X2		$ 210,000

Note that the beginning cash balance is zero because 19X2 is the first year of operations for the company. [See Section 5-4.]

PROBLEM 5-8: Micro Company has provided the following information for preparing the budget for 19X2:

Beginning Finished Goods Inventory	$ 70,000
Desired ending Finished Goods Inventory	85,000
Direct materials costs	123,000
Direct labor costs	145,000
Factory overhead	105,000
Work-in-process inventories (beginning and ending balances)	–0–

On the basis of this information, prepare a cost of goods sold budget for Micro Company.

Solution: The cost of goods sold budget for Micro Company would be prepared as follows:

Micro Company
Cost of Goods Sold Budget
For the Year Ended December 31, 19X2

Beginning Finished Goods Inventory, January 1		$ 70,000
+ Budgeted direct materials usage	$123,000	
+ Budgeted direct labor costs	145,000	
+ Budgeted factory overhead	105,000	
Total production costs		373,000
+ Add the decrease (deduct the increase) in Work-in-Process Inventory		–0–
– Desired ending Finished Goods Inventory		85,000
= Budgeted cost of goods sold		$358,000

[See Section 5-3.]

PROBLEM 5-9: Retail Company is preparing a cash budget for 19X3. The cash budget is based on the following assumptions:

All sales are billed on account at the end of the month.
85% of sales are collected within one month of billing.
9% of the sales are collected the second month after billing.

6% of sales are uncollectible.

June sales are budgeted at 12,500 units at $3.00 per unit.

July sales are budgeted at 12,000 units at $3.00 per unit.

August sales are budgeted at 13,000 units at $3.00 per unit.

Based on these assumptions, what are the budgeted cash receipts from sales during September 19X3?

Solution: The budgeted cash receipts for September 19X3 would be computed as follows:

Cash receipts from August sales	
(13,000 × $3.00 × 85%)	$33,150
Cash receipts from July sales	
(12,000 × $3.00 × 9%)	3,240
Budgeted cash receipts for September	$36,390

[See Section 5-4.]

PROBLEM 5-10: Southeast Company is preparing a cash budget for the month of May. The following budgeted information is available concerning cash for May:

Beginning cash balance, May 1	$ 4,200
Budgeted cash receipts	98,000
Budgeted cash disbursements	97,000
Minimum ending cash balance, May 31	8,000

Based on this information, compute the amount of short-term borrowing that is necessary to provide the minimum ending cash balance of $8,000.

Solution: The amount of short-term borrowing would be computed as follows:

Beginning cash balance	$ 4,200
+ Budgeted cash receipts	98,000
− Budgeted cash disbursements	97,000
− Minimum ending cash balance	8,000
= Short-term borrowing needed	$ 2,800

[See Section 5-4.]

6 STANDARD COSTING AND VARIANCE ANALYSIS: PART I

THIS CHAPTER IS ABOUT

☑ **Standard Costs**
☑ **Standard Costs, Actual Costs, and Variances**
☑ **Direct Materials Variances**
☑ **Direct Labor Variances**
☑ **Investigating the Causes of Variances**

6-1. Standard Costs

Standard costs are predetermined unit production costs used for management planning and control. Standard costs represent what production costs should be under efficient operations. In management planning, standard costs provide the basis for determining budgeted costs (see Chapter 5). For management control purposes, standard costs are compared with actual costs to compute variances. A variance is the difference between actual costs and standard costs in a standard cost system. A variance can be favorable or unfavorable. Variances should be investigated to determine why they occurred.

Standard costs per unit of production are usually determined for direct materials, direct labor, and factory overhead. Standard direct materials costs and standard direct labor costs are discussed in this chapter. Standard factory overhead costs are the subject of Chapter 7.

A. Standard cost for direct materials

The standard direct materials cost per unit of production is determined by multiplying:

1. the standard quantity of direct materials needed to produce one unit of production *by*
2. the standard price per unit of direct materials

Equation 6.1 is used to determine the standard cost for direct materials.

$$\text{Standard direct materials cost per unit of production} = \text{Standard quantity of direct materials to produce one unit} \times \text{Standard price per unit of direct material} \qquad (6.1)$$

$$\boxed{\text{SDMC} = \text{SQDM} \times \text{SPDM}}$$

EXAMPLE 6-1: The standard quantity of direct materials for Sail Company is 4 yards of cloth to produce one unit of Product A. The standard cost per yard is $2.00. Using equation 6.1, the standard direct materials cost per unit of Product A is $8.00.

$$\text{Standard direct materials cost per unit of production} = 4 \text{ yards} \times \$2.00$$
$$= \$8.00$$

B. Standard cost for direct labor

The standard direct labor cost per unit of production is determined by multiplying:

1. the standard number of direct labor hours needed to produce one unit of production *by*
2. the standard rate per direct labor hour

Equation 6.2 is used to determine the standard cost per direct labor hour.

$$\text{Standard direct labor cost per unit of production} = \text{Standard number of direct labor hours to produce one unit} \times \text{Standard rate per direct labor hour} \qquad (6.2)$$

$$\boxed{\text{SDLC} = \text{SHDL} \times \text{SRDL}}$$

EXAMPLE 6-2: Sail Company determined that the standard number of direct labor hours to produce one unit of Product A is 1.5. The standard rate per direct labor hour is $12.00. Using equation 6.2, the standard direct labor cost per unit of Product A is $18.00.

$$\begin{aligned}\text{Standard direct labor cost per unit of production} &= 1.5 \times \$12.00 \\ &= \$18.00\end{aligned}$$

6-2. Standard Costs, Actual Costs, and Variances

Standard costs are compared with actual costs to compute variances. In general, a cost variance can be represented by the following equation:

$$\text{Cost variance} = \text{Actual costs} - \text{Standard costs} \qquad (6.3)$$

This general cost variance equation can also be stated as follows:

$$\text{Cost variance} = \left(\begin{array}{c}\text{Actual} \\ \text{price}\end{array} \times \begin{array}{c}\text{Actual} \\ \text{quantity}\end{array}\right) - \left(\begin{array}{c}\text{Standard} \\ \text{price}\end{array} \times \begin{array}{c}\text{Standard} \\ \text{quantity}\end{array}\right) \qquad (6.3)$$

A cost variance is favorable if actual costs are less than standard costs. A cost variance is unfavorable if actual costs are greater than standard costs. Expression 6.4 restates these relationships:

$$\begin{aligned}\text{Actual costs} &< \text{Standard costs} \rightarrow \text{Favorable variance} \\ \text{Actual costs} &> \text{Standard costs} \rightarrow \text{Unfavorable variance}\end{aligned} \qquad (6.4)$$

Variances can be computed for:

1. price
2. quantity

A. Price variance.

A price variance is computed as follows:

$$\text{Price variance} = \left(\begin{array}{c}\text{Actual} \\ \text{price}\end{array} \times \begin{array}{c}\text{Actual} \\ \text{quantity}\end{array}\right) - \left(\begin{array}{c}\text{Standard} \\ \text{price}\end{array} \times \begin{array}{c}\text{Actual} \\ \text{quantity}\end{array}\right) \qquad (6.5)$$

This equation can be restated:

$$\text{Price variance} = (\text{Actual price} - \text{Standard price}) \times \text{Actual quantity} \qquad (6.5)$$

Expression 6.4 can be used to determine whether the price variance is favorable or unfavorable:

$$\begin{aligned}\text{Actual price} &< \text{Standard price} \rightarrow \text{Favorable variance} \\ \text{Actual price} &> \text{Standard price} \rightarrow \text{Unfavorable variance}\end{aligned} \qquad (6.4)$$

NOTE: In this outline, to compute the price variance, we subtract the standard price from the actual price. Using this method, a negative price variance means a favorable price variance (actual price was less than standard price). A positive price variance means an unfavorable price variance (actual price was greater than standard price).

Other textbooks may subtract actual price from standard price to compute variances. Use expression 6.4 to verify a favorable or unfavorable variance.

The sames rules for determining a favorable or unfavorable variance apply to the quantity variance.

EXAMPLE 6-3: Mandel Company incurred an actual price of $600. The standard price was $500. The actual quantity was 200. Using equation 6.5, the price variance is $20,000:

$$\text{Price variance} = (\$600 - \$500) \times 200$$
$$= \$100 \times 200$$
$$= \$20{,}000 \text{ price variance}$$

Using expression 6.4, we can determine that the price variance was unfavorable because the actual price incurred was more than the standard price allowed.

$$\$600 > \$500 \rightarrow \text{Unfavorable variance}$$

Therefore, Mandel Company had an unfavorable price variance of $20,000.

Price variances are computed for:

1. direct materials
2. direct labor rate

B. Quantity variance

A quantity variance is computed as follows:

$$\text{Quantity variance} = \left(\begin{array}{c}\text{Actual} \\ \text{quantity}\end{array} \times \begin{array}{c}\text{Standard} \\ \text{price}\end{array}\right) - \left(\begin{array}{c}\text{Standard} \\ \text{quantity}\end{array} \times \begin{array}{c}\text{Standard} \\ \text{price}\end{array}\right) \qquad \textbf{(6.6)}$$

This equation can be restated:

$$\text{Quantity variance} = (\text{Actual quantity} - \text{Standard quantity}) \times \text{Standard price} \qquad \textbf{(6.6)}$$

Expression 6.4 can be used to determine whether the quantity variance is favorable or unfavorable. (Because we are calculating a quantity variance, we substitute the word *quantity* for *price* in expression 6.4.)

$$\text{Actual quantity} < \text{Standard quantity} \rightarrow \text{Favorable variance}$$
$$\text{Actual quantity} > \text{Standard quantity} \rightarrow \text{Unfavorable variance}$$

(6.4)

EXAMPLE 6-4: The actual quantity of direct materials used by Switch Company was 200 pounds. The standard quantity of direct materials was 210 pounds. The standard price per pound of direct materials was $1.50 per pound. Using equation 6.6, the quantity variance is $15.

$$\text{Quantity variance} = (200 - 210) \times \$1.50$$
$$= (-10) \times \$1.50$$
$$= -\$15 \text{ quantity variance}$$

Using expression 6.4, we can determine that the quantity variance was favorable because the actual quantity used was less then the standard quantity allowed.

$$200 < 210 \rightarrow \text{Favorable variance}$$

Therefore, Switch Company had a favorable quantity variance of $15.

Quantity variances are computed for:

1. direct materials
2. direct labor hours

6-3. Direct Materials Variances

The cost accountant must compute direct materials variances, interpret these variances, and make the journal entries to record these variances.

A. Computation of direct materials variances.

There are two direct materials variances to compute:

1. direct materials price variance
2. direct materials quantity variance

EXAMPLE 6-5: The following information will be used to illustrate the computation of direct materials variances:

> Standard cost per unit: 4 gallons @ $6.00 per gallon
> Gallons purchased: 5,680 @ $5.90 per gallon
> Gallons used in production: 5,600
> Units finished: 1,350

1. DIRECT MATERIALS PRICE VARIANCE

The direct materials price variance can be computed either on the basis of materials purchased or materials used.

(a) materials price variance (*quantity purchased*)

Equation 6.7 is used to compute the direct materials price variance when materials are purchased.

$$\text{Direct materials price variance} = \left(\begin{array}{c}\text{Actual price per}\\ \text{unit of direct}\\ \text{materials}\end{array} - \begin{array}{c}\text{Standard price per}\\ \text{unit of direct}\\ \text{materials}\end{array}\right) \times \begin{array}{c}\text{Actual quantity of}\\ \text{direct materials}\\ \text{purchased}\end{array} \quad (6.7)$$

$$\boxed{\text{MPV} = (\text{APDM} - \text{SPDM}) \times \text{ADMP}}$$

$$\text{MPV} = (\$5.90 - \$6.00) \times 5,680$$
$$= -\$568 \text{ favorable* purchase price variance}$$

(b) Materials price variance (*quantity used*)

Equation 6.8 is used to compute the direct materials price variance when the material is issued to production. In this outline, we are assuming that the quantity of direct materials issued to production equals the quantity used in production.

$$\text{Direct materials price variance} = \left(\begin{array}{c}\text{Actual price per}\\ \text{unit of direct}\\ \text{materials}\end{array} - \begin{array}{c}\text{Standard price per}\\ \text{unit of direct}\\ \text{materials}\end{array}\right) \times \begin{array}{c}\text{Actual quantity of}\\ \text{direct materials}\\ \text{used}\end{array} \quad (6.8)$$

$$\boxed{\text{MPV} = (\text{APDM} - \text{SPDM}) \times \text{ADMU}}$$

$$\text{MPV} = (\$5.90 - \$6.00) \times 5,600$$
$$= -\$560 \text{ favorable* usage price variance}$$

* The variance is favorable in both computations because the actual price is less than the standard price.

2. DIRECT MATERIALS QUANTITY VARIANCE

This variance can also be referred to as the usage or efficiency variance. Use equation 6.9 to calculate the direct materials quantity variance.

$$\text{Direct materials quantity variance} = \left(\begin{array}{c}\text{Actual quantity of}\\ \text{direct materials}\\ \text{used}\end{array} - \begin{array}{c}\text{Standard direct}\\ \text{materials quantity}\\ \text{allowed}\end{array}\right) \times \begin{array}{c}\text{Standard price}\\ \text{per unit of}\\ \text{direct materials}\end{array} \quad (6.9)$$

$$\boxed{\text{MQV} = (\text{ADMU} - \text{SDM}) \times \text{SPDM}}$$

To find SDM, the standard quantity of direct materials per unit of production (SQDM) must be multiplied by the number of units of production. There were 1,350 units finished, and the standard allows 4 gallons per unit. The standard material quantity allowed must be 5,400 (1,350 units × 4 gallons).

$$\text{MQV} = (5,600 - 5,400) \times \$6.00$$
$$= \$1,200 \text{ unfavorable* material quantity variance}$$

* The variance is unfavorable because the actual quantity used is greater than the standard quantity allowed.

B. Interpretation of direct materials variances

To be sure that you have correctly interpreted the direct materials variances as favorable or unfavorable, always remember these general rules:

If *actual is greater than standard*, the variance is *unfavorable*.
If *actual is less than standard*, the variance is *favorable*.

C. Journal entries for direct materials variances

Journal entries are made to record the purchase of direct materials and the issuance of direct materials to production. The direct materials price variance is recognized either at the time of purchase or at the time the direct materials are issued to production.

The direct materials quantity variance is recorded when direct materials are issued to production. In this outline, we assume that the quantity of direct materials issued to production equals the quantity of direct materials used in production. We also assume that the number of units produced during the period is known when the direct materials are issued to production.

EXAMPLE 6-6: Using the same information found in Example 6-5, we will illustrate the journal entries for direct materials variances.

Standard cost per unit: 4 gallons @ $6.00 per gallon
Gallons purchased: 5,680 @ $5.90 per gallon
Gallons used in production: 5,600
Units finished: 1,350

METHOD 1

Direct Materials Price Variance Recorded at Time of Purchase

1. PURCHASE OF DIRECT MATERIALS

The preferable procedure is to record the direct materials price variance at the time of purchase. This means that the Materials Control account is kept at standard price per unit times the actual quantity of direct materials purchased ($6.00 × 5,680 = $34,080). Accounts Payable is credited for the actual amount paid for the direct materials (5,680 × $5.90 = $33,512). The direct materials purchase price variance is $568 favorable, as computed in Example 6-5, equation 6.7. A favorable direct materials price variance (quantity purchased) is a credit entry.

The journal entry for a direct materials price variance recognized at the time of purchase is as follows:

Materials Control (Direct Materials)		
(5,680 × $6.00)	$34,080	
Direct Materials Purchase Price Variance		
(5,680 × $.10)		$ 568
Accounts Payable (5,680 × $5.90)		33,512

2. ISSUANCE OF DIRECT MATERIALS TO PRODUCTION

The price variance was recorded when direct materials were purchased. Therefore, when direct materials are issued to production, the Work-in-Process (WIP) Control account is debited for the standard price per unit of direct materials times the standard quantity allowed ($6.00 × 5,400 = $32,400). The Materials Control account is credited for the standard price per unit of direct materials times the actual quantity of direct materials used in (issued to) production ($6.00 × 5,600 = $33,600). The $1,200 unfavorable direct materials quantity variance that was found in Example 6-5, equation 6.9, is debited.

WIP Control (Direct Materials) ($6.00 × 5,400)	$32,400	
Direct Materials Quantity Variance (200 × $6.00)	1,200	
Materials Control (Direct Materials)		
($6.00 × 5,600)		$33,600

METHOD 2

Direct Materials Price Variance Recorded at Time of Issuance to Production

1. PURCHASE OF DIRECT MATERIALS

Because the direct materials price variance is recorded when direct materials are issued to production, the purchase of direct materials is recorded at actual cost, not standard. The debit and credit entry are found by multiplying the actual price per unit of direct material by the actual quantity of direct materials purchased ($5.90 × 5,680 = $33,512).

Materials Control (Direct Materials)		
($5.90 × 5,680)	$33,512	
Accounts Payable		$33,512

2. ISSUANCE OF DIRECT MATERIALS TO PRODUCTION

To record the materials price variance, the amount debited to WIP Control is found by multiplying the standard quantity of materials allowed in production by the standard price per unit (5,400 × $6.00 = $32,400). The Materials Control account is credited for the actual quantity of material issued to (used in) production multiplied by the actual price per unit of direct materials (5,600 × $5.90 = $33,040).

The $560 favorable direct materials price variance that was found in Example 6-5, equation 6.8, is credited. The $1,200 unfavorable direct materials quantity variance that was found in Example 6-5, equation 6.9, is debited.

WIP Control (Direct Materials) (5,400 × $6.00)	$32,400	
Direct Materials Quantity Variance		
(200 × $6.00)	1,200	
Direct Materials Price Variance		
(5,600 × $0.10)		$ 560
Materials Control (Direct Materials)		
(5,600 × $5.90)		33,040

EXAMPLE 6-7: The following information is available for ABC Company's production activities during the month of October 19X5.

Units of production	1,000 units
Direct materials purchased	5,000 lb
Direct materials used in production	4,200 lb
Standard price of direct materials	$2.00/lb
Actual price of direct materials	$1.90/lb
Standard quantity of direct materials per unit of production	4 lb/unit

ABC Company records the direct materials price variance when direct materials are purchased. On the basis of the information provided, compute the direct materials price variance and the direct materials quantity variance, and prepare the appropriate journal entries for the purchase of direct materials and the issuance of direct materials to production.

VARIANCES
PRICE

You compute the direct materials price variance (quantity purchased) using equation 6.7.

$$\text{Direct materials price variance} = (\text{APDM} - \text{SPDM}) \times \text{ADMP}$$
$$= (\$1.90 - \$2.00) \times 5,000$$
$$= \$500 \text{ favorable}$$

QUANTITY

You compute the direct materials quantity variance using equation 6.9.

$$\text{Direct materials quantity variance} = (\text{ADMU} - \text{SDM}) \times \text{SPDM}$$

SDM equals the standard quantity of direct materials per unit of production multiplied by the number of units of production, or

$$4 \text{ lb./unit} \times 1,000 \text{ units} = 4,000 \text{ SDM}$$

$$\text{Direct materials quantity variance} = (4,200 - 4,000) \times \$2.00$$
$$= \$400 \text{ unfavorable}$$

JOURNAL ENTRIES

1. PURCHASE OF DIRECT MATERIALS

Because the direct materials price variance is recorded at the time of purchase, Method 1 should be used.

The debit to Materials Control equals SPDM × ADMP ($2.00 × 5,000). The credit to Accounts Payable equals APDM × ADMP ($1.90 × 5,000). The $500 favorable direct materials price variance (quantity purchased) was found using equation 6.7 and is credited because it is favorable.

Materials Control (Direct Materials)		
(5,000 × $2.00)	$10,000	
Direct Materials Price Variance (5,000 × $.10)		$ 500
Accounts Payable (5,000 × $1.90)		9,500

2. ISSUANCE OF DIRECT MATERIALS TO PRODUCTION

The price variance was recorded when direct materials were purchased. The debit to WIP Control equals SPDM × SDM ($2.00 × 4,000). The credit to Materials Control equals SPDM × ADMU ($2.00 × 4,200). The $400 unfavorable quantity variance was found using equation 6.9 and is debited because it is unfavorable.

WIP Control (Direct Materials) (4,000 × $2.00)	$8,000	
Direct Materials Quantity Variance (200 × $2.00)	400	
Materials Control (Direct Materials)		
(4,200 × $2.00)		$8,400

EXAMPLE 6-8: Use the same information as in Example 6-7, but assume that ABC Company records the direct materials price variance when direct materials are issued to production (Method 2). Compute the price and quantity variances, and prepare the appropriate journal entries for the purchase of direct materials and the issuance of direct materials to production.

VARIANCES

PRICE

You compute the direct materials price variance (quantity used) using equation 6.8.

$$\begin{aligned} \text{Direct materials price variance} &= (\text{APDM} - \text{SPDM}) \times \text{ADMU} \\ &= (\$1.90 - \$2.00) \times 4,200 \\ &= \$420 \text{ favorable} \end{aligned}$$

QUANTITY

You compute the direct materials quantity variance using equation 6.9. (The quantity variance is the same whether you record the price variance at time of purchase or at time of use.)

$$\text{Direct materials quantity variance} = (\text{ADMU} - \text{SDM}) \times \text{SPDM}$$

SDM equals the standard quantity of direct materials per unit of production multiplied by the number of units of production, or

$$4 \text{ lb./unit} \times 1,000 \text{ units} = 4,000 \text{ SDM}$$

$$\begin{aligned} \text{Direct materials quantity variance} &= (4,200 - 4,000) \times \$2.00 \\ &= \$400 \text{ unfavorable} \end{aligned}$$

JOURNAL ENTRIES

1. PURCHASE OF DIRECT MATERIALS

Because the direct materials price variance is recorded when materials are issued to production, the debit to the Materials Control account is equal to APDM × ADMP ($1.90 × 5,000).

Materials Control (Direct Materials)		
(5,000 × $1.90)	$9,500	
Accounts Payable		$9,500

2. ISSUANCE OF DIRECT MATERIALS TO PRODUCTION

The debit to WIP Control equals SPDM × SDM ($2.00 × 4,000). The credit to Materials Control equals APDM × ADMU ($1.90 × 4,200). The $420 favorable usage price variance was calculated using equation 6.8 and is credited because it is favorable. The $400 unfavorable quantity variance was found using equation 6.9 and is debited because it is unfavorable.

WIP Control (Direct Materials) (4,000 × $2.00)	$8,000	
Direct Materials Quantity Variance (200 × $2.00)	400	
Direct Materials Price Variance (4,200 × $.10)		$ 420
Materials Control (Direct Materials) (4,200 × $1.90)		7,980

6-4. Direct Labor Variances

The cost accountant must compute direct labor variances, interpret these variances, and make journal entries to record these variances.

A. Computation of direct labor variances

There are two direct labor variances to compute:

1. direct labor rate variance
2. direct labor efficiency variance

EXAMPLE 6-9: The following information will be used to illustrate the computation of direct labor variances:

> Standard cost per unit: 3 hours @ $4.20 per hour
> Actual labor hours and cost: 1,500 hours @ $5.00 per hour
> Units: 600 units produced

1. DIRECT LABOR RATE VARIANCE

The direct labor rate variance compares the rate that is actually paid to the standard rate. Equation 6.10 is used to compute the direct labor rate variance.

$$\begin{matrix} \text{Direct labor} \\ \text{rate variance} \end{matrix} = \left(\begin{matrix} \text{Actual rate per} \\ \text{direct labor hour} \end{matrix} - \begin{matrix} \text{Standard rate per} \\ \text{direct labor hour} \end{matrix} \right) \times \begin{matrix} \text{Actual number} \\ \text{of direct labor} \\ \text{hours} \end{matrix} \quad \text{(6.10)}$$

$$\boxed{\text{LRV} = (\text{ARDL} - \text{SRDL}) \times \text{AHDL}}$$

$$\text{LRV} = (\$5.00 - \$4.20) \times 1,500$$
$$= \$1,200 \text{ unfavorable rate variance}$$

This variance is unfavorable because the actual rate is greater than the standard rate.

2. DIRECT LABOR EFFICIENCY VARIANCE

The direct labor efficiency variance compares the actual number of direct labor hours used in production to the standard number of direct labor hours allowed for the number of units produced. The total standard number of direct labor hours allowed is found by multiplying the standard direct labor hours allowed for 1 unit of production by the actual number of units produced. There are 600 units finished, and the standard allows 3 hours per unit. The standard direct labor hours allowed must be 1,800 (600 units × 3 hours). Equation 6.11 is used to compute the direct labor efficiency variance.

$$\begin{matrix} \text{Direct labor} \\ \text{efficiency variance} \end{matrix} = \left(\begin{matrix} \text{Actual number of} \\ \text{direct labor hours} \end{matrix} - \begin{matrix} \text{Total standard number of} \\ \text{direct labor hours} \end{matrix} \right) \times \begin{matrix} \text{Standard rate} \\ \text{per direct} \\ \text{labor hour} \end{matrix} \quad \text{(6.11)}$$

$$\boxed{\text{LEV} = (\text{AHDL} - \text{TSHDL}) \times \text{SRDL}}$$

$$\text{LEV} = (1,500 - 1,800) \times \$4.20$$
$$= \$1,260 \text{ favorable efficiency variance}$$

The variance is favorable because the actual hours are less than the standard hours.

B. Interpretation of direct labor variances

To be sure that you have correctly interpreted the direct labor variances as favorable or unfavorable, always remember these general rules:

> If *actual is greater than standard*, the variance is *unfavorable*.
> If *actual is less than standard*, the variance is *favorable*.

C. Journal entries for direct labor variances

The WIP Control account is debited for the total standard number of direct labor hours allowed multiplied by the standard rate per direct labor hour ($1,800 \times \$4.20 = \$7,560$). The Accrued Payroll account is credited for the actual number of direct labor hours used in production multiplied by the actual rate per direct labor hour ($1,500 \times \$5.00 = \$7,500$). The Direct Labor Rate Variance account is debited for the $1,200 unfavorable rate variance. The Direct Labor Efficiency Variance account is credited for the $1,260 favorable efficiency variance.

WIP Control (Direct Labor) (1,800 × $4.20)	$7,560	
Direct Labor Rate Variance ($.80 × 1,500)	1,200	
Direct Labor Efficiency Variance (300 × $4.20)		$1,260
Accrued Payroll (1,500 × $5.00)		7,500

EXAMPLE 6-10: The following information is available for ABC Company's production activities during the month of October 19X5:

Units of production	1,000 units
Actual direct labor hours used	2,100 hours
Standard direct labor hours per unit of production	2 hours/unit
Actual rate per direct labor hour	$10.00/hour
Standard rate per direct labor hour	$12.00/hour

On the basis of this information, compute the direct labor rate variance and the direct labor efficiency variance, and prepare the appropriate journal entry.

VARIANCES

RATE

You compute the direct labor rate variance using equation 6.10.

$$\text{Direct labor rate variance} = (\text{ARDL} - \text{SRDL}) \times \text{AHDL}$$
$$= (\$10.00 - \$12.00) \times 2,100$$
$$= \$4,200 \text{ favorable rate variance}$$

EFFICIENCY

You compute the direct labor efficiency variance using equation 6.11:

$$\text{Direct labor efficiency variance} = (\text{AHDL} - \text{TSHDL}) \times \text{SRDL}$$
$$= (2,100 - 2,000) \times \$12.00$$
$$= \$1,200 \text{ unfavorable efficiency variance}$$

Remember that the total standard number of direct labor hours allowed for production (TSHDL) must be determined before equation 6.11 can be computed. The TSHDL is found by multiplying the standard direct labor hours allowed per unit of production by the number of production units (2 hours × 1,000 units = 2,000 hours).

JOURNAL ENTRY

The WIP Control account is debited for the total standard number of direct labor hours allowed multiplied by the standard rate per direct labor hour ($2,000 \times \$12.00 = \$24,000$). The Accrued Payroll account is credited for the actual number of direct labor hours used in production multiplied by the actual rate per direct labor hour ($2,100 \times \$10.00 = \$21,000$). The Direct Labor Efficiency Variance account is debited for the $1,200 unfavorable efficiency variance. The Direct Labor Rate Variance account is credited for the $4,200 favorable rate variance. iance.

WIP Control (Direct Labor) (2,000 × $12.00)	$24,000	
Direct Labor Efficiency Variance (100 × $12.00)	1,200	
Direct Labor Rate Variance ($2.00 × 2,100)		$ 4,200
Accrued Payroll (2,100 × $10.00)		21,000

6-5. Investigating the Causes of Variances

It is important to determine the causes of unfavorable variances in order to assign responsibility and take corrective action. It is also important to understand the interrelationships between variances.

A. Assigning responsibility for variances

The assignment of responsibility for variances is an important part of measuring managerial performance. For example, responsibility for the direct materials price variance generally would be assigned to the purchasing department manager, while responsibility for the direct materials quantity variance would be assigned to the production department manager.

B. Taking corrective action

Knowing the cause of an unfavorable variance can lead to the proper course of action to correct the problem. For example, if an unfavorable direct materials quantity variance is caused by ineffective materials handling, improved procedures for materials handling can be developed. Similarly, if an unfavorable direct materials price variance is caused by ineffective purchasing practices, the development of improved purchasing procedures would be the appropriate corrective action.

C. Interrelationships between variances

You should also consider the possible interrelationships between direct materials and direct labor variances when interpreting variances. For example, a favorable direct labor rate variance may be the result of using workers with relatively less skill and experience, and thus a lower wage rate, than the standards require. The use of less skilled workers might then result in an unfavorable direct labor efficiency variance if the workers were less productive than more experienced workers. In this case, a favorable direct labor rate variance would be related to an unfavorable direct labor efficiency variance. Therefore, it is important to consider the effect one variance might have on another.

RAISE YOUR GRADES

Can you explain...?

☑ what standard costs are
☑ the two components of standard direct materials cost per unit
☑ the two components of standard direct labor cost per unit
☑ how to compute the direct materials purchase price variance
☑ how to compute the direct materials usage price variance
☑ how to interpret a variance as favorable or unfavorable
☑ how to prepare the two different journal entries to record the direct materials price variance
☑ how to compute the direct materials quantity variance
☑ how to prepare the journal entry to record the direct materials quantity variance
☑ how to compute the direct labor rate and efficiency variances
☑ how to prepare the journal entry to record the direct labor rate and efficiency variances
☑ why it is important to determine the causes of unfavorable variances

SUMMARY

1. Standard costs are predetermined unit costs.
2. Standard costs are determined for direct materials, direct labor, and factory overhead.
3. Standard direct materials costs per unit equal the standard quantity of direct materials needed to produce one unit of output (SQDM) times the standard price per unit of direct materials (SPDM).
4. Standard direct labor costs per unit equal the standard number of direct labor hours needed to produce one unit of output (SHDL) times the standard rate per direct labor hour (SRDL).
5. A cost variance is computed as the difference between actual costs and standard costs.
6. If actual costs are less than standard costs, the cost variance is favorable.
7. If actual costs are greater than standard costs, the cost variance is unfavorable.
8. The direct materials price variance (quantity purchased) is equal to the difference between the actual price and the standard price per unit of direct materials times the actual quantity of direct materials purchased [(APDM − SPDM) × ADMP].
9. The direct materials price variance (quantity used) is equal to the difference between the actual price and standard price per unit of direct materials times the actual quantity of direct materials used [(APDM − SPDM) × ADMU].
10. The direct materials price variance is favorable if the actual price of direct materials is less than the standard price and unfavorable if the actual price is greater than the standard price.
11. You can compute and record the direct materials price variance either when direct materials are purchased or when they are issued to production.
12. A favorable variance is a credit entry and an unfavorable variance is a debit entry.
13. The direct materials quantity variance is equal to the difference between the actual quantity used and the standard quantity allowed in production times the standard price per unit of direct materials [(ADMU − SDM) × SPDM].
14. The direct materials quantity variance is favorable if the actual quantity of direct materials issued to production is less than the standard quantity of direct materials allowed and unfavorable if the actual quantity is greater.
15. You compute the direct labor rate variance as the difference between the actual rate per direct labor hour and the standard rate per direct labor hour times the actual direct labor hours used in production [(ARDL − SRDL) × AHDL)].
16. The direct labor efficiency variance is the difference between the actual number of direct labor hours used in production and the total standard number of direct labor hours allowed times the standard rate per direct labor hour [(AHDL − TSHDL) × SRDL].
17. The direct labor efficiency variance is favorable if the actual number of direct labor hours used in production is less than the standard number of direct labor hours and unfavorable if the actual number is greater.
18. The direct labor rate variance and direct labor efficiency variance are recorded when direct labor is used in production.
19. By determining the cause of an unfavorable variance, responsibility for the variance can be assigned and corrective action taken.
20. Since relationships exist between direct materials variances and direct labor variances, an unfavorable materials variance could be caused by a favorable labor variance and vice versa.

RAPID REVIEW

1. Standard costs per unit of production are usually determined for **(a)** direct materials, **(b)** direct labor, **(c)** factory overhead, **(d)** all of the above. [See Section 6-1.]
2. The standard direct materials cost per unit of production equals the standard quantity of direct materials needed to produce one unit times **(a)** the actual price per unit of direct materials, **(b)** the standard price per unit of direct materials, **(c)** the actual quantity of direct materials. [See Section 6-1.]
3. The direct materials price variance is favorable if the actual price per unit of direct materials is greater than the standard price: **(a)** true, **(b)** false. [See Section 6-3.]

4. The direct materials quantity variance is favorable if the actual quantity of direct materials used in production is greater than the standard quantity allowed: **(a)** true, **(b)** false. [See Section 6-3.]

5. A cost variance is the difference between actual costs and **(a)** actual quantity, **(b)** standard quantity, **(c)** standard costs. [See Section 6-2.]

6. The standard direct labor cost per unit equals the standard number of direct labor hours needed to produce one unit of production times **(a)** the actual rate per direct labor hour, **(b)** the standard rate per direct labor hour, **(c)** the actual number of direct labor hours. [See Section 6-1.]

7. The direct labor rate variance is favorable if the actual rate per direct labor hour is less than the standard rate per direct labor hour: **(a)** true, **(b)** false. [See Section 6-4.]

8. The direct labor efficiency variance is favorable if the total standard number of direct labor hours allowed for production is greater than the actual number of direct labor hours used: **(a)** true, **(b)** false. [See Section 6-4.]

9. The journal entry to record the direct materials price variance may be recorded **(a)** only when direct materials are purchased, **(b)** only when direct materials are issued to production, **(c)** either when direct materials are purchased or when they are issued to production. [See Section 6-3.]

10. The journal entry to record the direct materials quantity variance may be recorded **(a)** only when direct materials are purchased, **(b)** only when direct materials are issued to production, **(c)** either when direct materials are purchased or when they are issued to production. [See Section 6-3.]

11. The journal entry to record the direct labor rate and efficiency variances includes a credit to Accrued Payroll and a debit to **(a)** Materials Control, **(b)** WIP Control, **(c)** Standard direct labor rate. [See Section 6-4.]

12. A favorable variance is a **(a)** credit entry, **(b)** debit entry. [See Section 6-3.]

13. An unfavorable variance is a **(a)** credit entry, **(b)** debit entry. [See Section 6-3.]

Answers
1. (d)   2. (b)   3. (b)   4. (b)   5. (c)   6. (b)   7. (a)   8. (a)   9. (c)   10. (b)
11. (b)   12. (a)   13. (b)

SOLVED PROBLEMS

Problems 6-1 to 6-4 are based on the following data.

Frankfort Company uses a standard costing system. The following information is available for the November production.

Standard price per unit of direct materials	$3.00/gallon
Actual price per unit of direct materials	$2.80/gallon
Standard quantity of direct materials per unit of production	5 gallons/unit
Actual quantity of direct materials used in production	5,200 gallons
Actual quantity of direct materials purchased	4,000 gallons
Actual production	1,000 units

PROBLEM 6-1: Assuming that the direct materials price variance is computed when materials are purchased, compute the price variance.

Solution: Compute the direct materials price variance (quantity purchased) using equation 6.7.

$$\text{Direct materials price variance} = (\text{APDM} - \text{SPDM}) \times \text{ADMP}$$
$$= (\$2.80 - \$3.00) \times 4,000$$
$$= \$800 \text{ favorable}$$

The actual price ($2.80) is less than the standard price ($3.00), which results in a favorable direct materials price variance. [See Section 6-3.]

PROBLEM 6-2: Prepare the journal entry to record Frankfort Company's purchase of direct materials in November. Assume that the company computes and records the direct materials price variance when materials are purchased.

Solution: In order to prepare the journal entry, you must first determine the amounts to enter for the Materials Control and Accounts Payable accounts. The debit to Materials Control is equal to the actual quantity of direct materials purchased times the standard price per unit of direct materials (4,000 × $3.00). The credit to Accounts Payable is equal to the actual quantity of direct materials purchased times the actual price per unit of direct materials (4,000 × $2.80). The $800 favorable direct materials price variance found in Problem 6-1 is credited.

Materials Control (Direct Materials)	$12,000	
Direct Materials Price Variance		$ 800
Accounts Payable		11,200

[See Section 6-3.]

PROBLEM 6-3: Compute the direct materials quantity variance for Frankfort Company.

Solution: You compute the direct materials quantity variance using equation 6.9. To use this equation, you must first determine the standard quantity of direct materials allowed for production (SDM). SDM equals the standard quantity of direct materials per unit of production times the number of units of production (5 × 1,000 = 5,000 gallons).

$$\text{Direct materials quantity variance} = (\text{ADMU} - \text{SDM}) \times \text{SPDM}$$
$$= (5,200 - 5,000) \times \$3.00$$
$$= \$600 \text{ unfavorable}$$

The unfavorable direct materials quantity variance reflects the fact that the actual quantity of direct materials used in production was greater than the standard quantity of direct materials allowed for production. [See Section 6-3.]

PROBLEM 6-4: Assume that Frankfort Company records the direct materials price variance when materials are issued to production. On the basis of this assumption, prepare the journal entries to record the purchase of direct materials and the issuance of direct materials to production.

Solution: To record the purchase of direct materials when the direct materials price variance is recorded at the time direct materials are issued to production, both the debit to Materials Control and the credit to Accounts Payable equal the actual price per unit of direct materials times the actual quantity of direct materials purchased ($2.80 × 4,000).

Materials Control (Direct Materials)	$11,200	
Accounts Payable		$11,200

The journal entry to record the issuance of direct materials to production will include both the price and quantity variances. In Problem 6-3, you computed a $600 unfavorable quantity variance. Remember that the quantity variance is not affected by when you record the price variance.

Use equation 6.8 to compute the direct materials price variance (quantity used).

$$\begin{aligned}\text{Direct materials price variance} &= (\text{APDM} - \text{SPDM}) \times \text{ADMU} \\ &= (\$2.80 - \$3.00) \times 5,200 \\ &= \$1,040 \text{ favorable}\end{aligned}$$

The WIP Control account is debited for the standard quantity of direct materials allowed for production times the standard price per unit of direct materials (5,000 × $3.00). The credit to Materials Control equals the actual price per unit of direct materials times the actual quantity of direct materials used in production ($2.80 × 5,200). The $1,040 favorable materials price variance is credited. The $600 unfavorable materials quantity variance is debited.

WIP Control (Direct Materials)	$15,000	
Direct Materials Quantity Variance	600	
Direct Materials Price Variance		$ 1,040
Materials Control (Direct Materials)		14,560

[See Section 6-3.]

Problems 6-5 and 6-6 are based on the following data.

The following information is available for the Jackson Company:

Standard rate per direct labor hour	$5.00/hour
Actual rate per direct labor hour	$5.50/hour
Standard direct labor hours per unit	2 hours/unit
Actual direct labor hours used	600 hours
Actual production	350 units

PROBLEM 6-5: Compute the direct labor rate variance and the direct labor efficiency variance.

Solution: Use equation 6.10 to compute the direct labor rate variance.

$$\begin{aligned}\text{Direct labor rate variance} &= (\text{ARDL} - \text{SRDL}) \times \text{AHDL} \\ &= (\$5.50 - \$5.00) \times 600 \\ &= \$300 \text{ unfavorable}\end{aligned}$$

The variance is unfavorable because the actual direct labor rate per hour is greater than the standard direct labor rate per hour.

Use equation 6.11 to compute the direct labor efficiency variance.

$$\begin{aligned}\text{Direct labor efficiency variance} &= (\text{AHDL} - \text{TSHDL}) \times \text{SRDL} \\ &= (600 - 700) \times \$5.00 \\ &= \$500 \text{ favorable}\end{aligned}$$

Remember that TSHDL is found by multiplying the actual number of units produced by the standard direct labor hours allowed per unit (350 × 2 = 700). The favorable direct labor efficiency variance reflects the fact that the actual direct labor hours used are less than the total standard direct labor hours allowed. [See Section 6-4.]

PROBLEM 6-6: Prepare the journal entry to record the direct labor rate and efficiency variances.

Solution: Besides the direct labor variances determined in Problem 6-5, the journal entry also must include amounts for WIP Control and Accrued Payroll accounts. The debit to WIP Control equals the total standard direct labor hours allowed for production times the standard rate per direct labor hour (700 × $5.00 = $3,500). The credit to Accrued Payroll equals the actual direct labor hours used in production times the actual rate per direct labor hour (600 × $5.50 =

$3,300). The $300 unfavorable direct labor rate variance found in Problem 6-5 is debited. The $500 favorable direct labor efficiency variance is credited.

WIP Control (Direct Labor)	$3,500	
Direct Labor Rate Variance	300	
Direct Labor Efficiency Variance		$ 500
Accrued Payroll		3,300

[See Section 6-4.]

PROBLEM 6-7: The following information is available for Wabash Company:

Standard direct labor rate	$10/hour
Actual direct labor rate	$11/hour
Total standard direct labor hours allowed for production	5,000/hour
Direct labor efficiency variance	$9,000 favorable

On the basis of this information, compute the actual number of direct labor hours used in production.

Solution: With the given information, you can determine the actual number of direct labor hours (AHDL) by using equation 6.11.

$$\text{Direct labor efficiency variance} = (\text{AHDL} - \text{TSHDL}) \times \text{SRDL}$$
$$-\$\,9,000 = (\text{AHDL} - 5,000) \times \$10$$
$$-\$\,9,000 = \$10\,\text{AHDL} - \$50,000$$
$$\$41,000 = \$10\,\text{AHDL}$$
$$4,100 = \text{AHDL}$$

Note that we put a negative sign before the $9,000 favorable direct labor efficiency variance. We know that in this outline a favorable variance is a negative variance. Therefore, you know before you do any calculations that the actual number of direct labor hours used in production is less than the total number of standard hours allowed for production. [See Section 6-4.]

PROBLEM 6-8: The following information is available for Capital Manufacturing Company:

Standard price per pound of direct materials	$4.00/lb
Standard quantity of direct materials needed to produce one unit of production	3 lb/unit
Actual production	2,000 units

On the basis of this information, compute the standard direct materials cost per unit of production and the standard direct materials cost applied to production.

Solution: Compute the standard direct materials cost per unit of production using equation 6.1:

$$\text{Standard direct materials cost per unit of production} = \text{SQDM} \times \text{SPDM}$$
$$= 3\,\text{lb/unit} \times \$4/\text{lb}$$
$$= \$12/\text{unit}$$

The standard direct materials cost applied to production is equal to the standard cost per unit times the number of units of production:

$$\text{Standard direct materials cost applied to production} = \$12/\text{unit} \times 2,000\,\text{units}$$
$$= \$24,000$$

[See Section 6-1.]

PROBLEM 6-9: During the month of August, Micro Company's direct materials costs for the manufacture of product X were as follows:

Actual price per unit of direct materials	$6.50/lb
Standard quantity of direct materials allowed for production	2,100 lb
Actual quantity of direct materials used in production	2,300 lb
Standard price per unit of direct materials	$6.25/lb

On the basis of this information, compute the direct materials quantity variance for the month of August.

Solution: You compute the direct materials quantity variance using equation 6.9:

$$\text{Direct materials quantity variance} = (\text{ADMU} - \text{SDM}) \times \text{SPDM}$$
$$= (2{,}300 - 2{,}100) \times \$6.25$$
$$= \$1{,}250 \text{ unfavorable}$$

The quantity variance is unfavorable because the actual quantity of direct materials used in production exceeded the standard quantity allowed for production. [See Section 6-3.]

PROBLEM 6-10: DePaul Company has provided the following information relating to direct labor costs during the month of May:

Standard direct labor cost applied to production during May	$210,000
Actual direct labor cost incurred during May	$225,000
Direct labor rate variance	$25,000 unfavorable
Direct labor efficiency variance	$10,000 favorable

On the basis of this information, prepare the journal entry to record the direct labor variances.

Solution: For this journal entry, the debit to WIP Control is equal to the total standard direct labor hours allowed for production times the standard rate per direct labor hour. Since this amount is the standard direct labor cost applied to production, the debit to WIP Control is $210,000. Similarly, the credit to Accrued Payroll equals AHDL × ARDL, which equals the actual direct labor cost incurred, or $225,000. Thus, the journal entry to record the direct labor variances would be:

WIP Control (Direct Labor)	$210,000	
Direct Labor Rate Variance	25,000	
Direct Labor Efficiency Variance		$ 10,000
Accrued Payroll		225,000

[See Section 6-4.]

PROBLEM 6-11: The following information is provided about the direct materials cost during the month of December:

Actual cost of direct materials purchased	$380,000
Standard cost of direct materials purchased	$355,000

Assume that the direct materials price variance is recorded when the materials are purchased. Compute the direct materials price variance.

Solution: You compute the direct materials price variance using equation 6.3.

$$\text{Price variance} = \text{Actual costs} - \text{Standard costs}$$
$$= \$380{,}000 - \$355{,}000$$
$$= \$25{,}000 \text{ unfavorable}$$

The price variance is unfavorable since the actual cost of direct materials is greater than the standard cost. [See Section 6-1.]

PROBLEM 6-12: The following information is available for Michigan Manufacturing Company for the month of April:

Total standard direct labor hours allowed	21,000 hours
Actual direct labor hours used in production	20,000 hours
Direct labor rate variance	$8,400 unfavorable
Standard rate per direct labor hour	$6.30 hour

On the basis of this information, compute the actual rate per direct labor hour.

Solution: With the information that is given, you can compute the actual rate per direct labor hour (ARDL) by using equation 6.10.

$$\text{Direct labor rate variance} = (\text{ARDL} - \text{SRDL}) \times \text{AHDL}$$

$$\$8,400 = (\text{ARDL} - \$6.30) \times 20,000$$

$$\$8,400 = 20,000\ \text{ARDL} - \$126,000$$

$$\$134,400 = 20,000\ \text{ARDL}$$

$$\$6.72 = \text{ARDL}$$

[See Section 6-4.]

7 STANDARD COSTING AND VARIANCE ANALYSIS: PART II

THIS CHAPTER IS ABOUT

- ☑ **Factory Overhead Costs**
- ☑ **Standard Factory-Overhead Rates**
- ☑ **Variable Overhead Variances**
- ☑ **Fixed Overhead Variances**
- ☑ **Journal Entries for Standard Overhead Costs**
- ☑ **Analysis of Overhead Variances**

7-1. Factory Overhead Costs

Factory overhead includes manufacturing costs other than direct labor and direct materials. Factory overhead costs are generally classified into two categories: (1) variable overhead costs and (2) fixed overhead costs. Standard costs and variances are usually computed separately for these two categories of costs. Chapter 2 covers variable costs and fixed costs in detail.

A. Variable overhead costs

Variable overhead costs in *total* change in direct proportion to changes in production activity. Variable overhead costs would generally include such items as utility costs and indirect labor costs.

B. Fixed overhead costs

Fixed overhead costs in *total* remain unchanged when significant changes in production activity occur. Fixed overhead costs would generally include depreciation, factory insurance, and factory rent.

7-2. Standard Factory-Overhead Rates

Standard factory-overhead rates are predetermined rates used to apply factory overhead costs to production. Rates are generally determined separately for variable overhead and fixed overhead. Total overhead costs can be estimated (budgeted) for the budgeted production activity level. Total budgeted overhead costs must be broken down into budgeted fixed-overhead costs and budgeted variable-overhead costs.

A. Standard rates for variable overhead

Standard variable-overhead rates are based on budgeted variable-overhead costs at the budgeted level of production activity. The standard variable-overhead rate is usually expressed in terms of some measure of production activity, such as direct labor hours, direct labor dollars, or machine hours. This chapter will use direct labor hours as the measure of production activity.

The standard variable-overhead rate per direct labor hour is computed as follows:

$$\text{Standard variable-overhead rate} = \frac{\text{Budgeted variable overhead}}{\text{Budgeted direct labor hours}} \qquad (7.1)$$

$$\boxed{\text{SVOR} = \frac{\text{BVO}}{\text{BHDL}}}$$

It important here to distinguish between total standard direct labor hours (TSHDL) and budgeted direct labor hours (BHDL).

$$\text{TSHDL} = \begin{array}{c}\text{Standard direct labor}\\ \text{hours allowed per unit}\\ \text{of production}\end{array} \times \begin{array}{c}\textit{actual} \text{ number}\\ \text{of}\\ \text{units produced}\end{array}$$

$$\text{BHDL} = \begin{array}{c}\text{Standard direct labor}\\ \text{hours allowed per unit}\\ \text{of production}\end{array} \times \begin{array}{c}\textit{budgeted} \text{ number}\\ \text{of}\\ \text{units to be produced}\end{array}$$

Total standard direct labor hours (TSHDL) represent the number of standard direct labor hours allowed for the actual production. In contrast, budgeted direct labor hours (BHDL) represent the number of standard direct labor hours allowed for the budgeted production.

EXAMPLE 7-1: A company has budgeted variable overhead to be $450,000. It allows 2 direct labor hours per unit of production, and budgets 25,000 units to be produced. To find the variable overhead rate, you must first determine budgeted direct labor hours.

$$\text{BHDL} = 2 \text{ standard hours} \times 25,000 \text{ budgeted units}$$
$$= 50,000$$

Use equation 7.1 to compute SVOR.

$$\text{SVOR} = \frac{\text{BVO}}{\text{BHDL}}$$
$$= \frac{\$450,000}{50,000}$$
$$= \$9.00$$

The SVOR is $9.00 per direct labor hour. The SVOR is used to apply standard variable-overhead costs to units of production.

The standard variable-overhead rate remains the same, regardless of changes in the budgeted production activity. This is true because the numerator of equation 7.1, budgeted variable overhead, and the denominator of equation 7.1, budgeted direct labor hours, both change in direct proportion to the budgeted production level.

B. Standard rates for fixed overhead

Standard fixed-overhead rates are based on budgeted fixed-overhead costs at the budgeted level of production activity. You would compute the standard fixed-overhead rate per direct labor hour as follows:

$$\begin{array}{c}\text{Standard fixed-}\\ \text{overhead rate}\end{array} = \frac{\text{Budgeted fixed overhead}}{\text{Budgeted direct labor hours}} \qquad (7.2)$$

$$\boxed{\text{SFOR} = \frac{\text{BFO}}{\text{BHDL}}}$$

EXAMPLE 7-2: A company has budgeted fixed factory overhead to be $150,000. It allows 50,000 standard direct-labor hours for the budgeted level of production. To compute the standard fixed-overhead rate, you would use equation 7.2:

$$\text{SFOR} = \frac{\text{BFO}}{\text{BHDL}}$$
$$= \frac{\$150,000}{50,000}$$
$$= \$3.00$$

The SFOR is $3.00 per direct labor hour.

Total fixed overhead costs remain constant regardless of changes in the production activity. Therefore, the standard fixed-overhead rate decreases as the budgeted production activity increases. The standard fixed-overhead rate increases as the budgeted production activity decreases.

EXAMPLE 7-3: The following information is available for the Weston Company's 19X8 budget:

Budgeted variable overhead	$120,000
Budgeted fixed overhead	$ 80,000
Budgeted production level	10,000 units
Standard direct-labor hours	2 hrs./unit

On the basis of this information, compute the standard rate for variable overhead and fixed overhead in terms of direct labor hours.

You must first compute BHDL—standard direct-labor hours allowed per unit × budgeted production activity:

$$BHDL = 2 \text{ hours} \times 10,000 \text{ units}$$
$$= 20,000 \text{ budgeted direct labor hours}$$

You can now use equation 7.1 to compute the standard variable-overhead rate per direct labor hour:

$$SVOR = \frac{BVO}{BHDL}$$
$$= \frac{\$120,000}{20,000}$$
$$= \$6.00 \text{ per direct labor hour}$$

You would compute the standard fixed-overhead rate per direct labor hour using equation 7.2:

$$SFOR = \frac{BFO}{BHDL}$$
$$= \frac{\$80,000}{20,000}$$
$$= \$4.00 \text{ per direct labor hour}$$

C. Uses of standard overhead rates

Standard overhead rates are used for three purposes: product costing, management planning, and management control. For management control purposes, standard overhead rates are used to compute overhead cost variances. The computation of overhead cost variances will be covered in Sections 7-3 and 7-4.

1. PRODUCT COSTING

Standard overhead rates are used to apply factory overhead costs to units of production. You apply standard variable-overhead costs to production using equation 7.3:

$$\begin{array}{ccc} \text{Standard variable-} \\ \text{overhead applied} \end{array} = \begin{array}{c} \text{Total standard direct labor} \\ \text{hours allowed for} \\ \text{actual production} \end{array} \times \begin{array}{c} \text{Standard variable-} \\ \text{overhead rate per} \\ \text{direct labor hour} \end{array} \qquad \textbf{(7.3)}$$

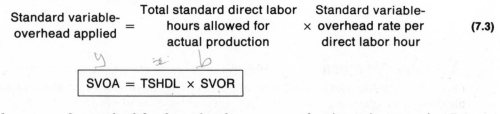

$$\boxed{SVOA = TSHDL \times SVOR}$$

Similarly, you apply standard fixed-overhead costs to production using equation 7.4:

$$\begin{array}{ccc} \text{Standard fixed-} \\ \text{overhead applied} \end{array} = \begin{array}{c} \text{Total standard direct labor} \\ \text{hours allowed for} \\ \text{actual production} \end{array} \times \begin{array}{c} \text{Standard fixed-} \\ \text{overhead rate per} \\ \text{direct labor hour} \end{array} \qquad \textbf{(7.4)}$$

$$\boxed{SFOA = TSHDL \times SFOR}$$

EXAMPLE 7-4: Using the information in Example 7-3, determine the overhead costs applied to production of 8,000 units in 19X8.

Before overhead rates can be applied, total standard direct labor hours allowed for actual production must be determined.

$$\text{TSHDL} = 8{,}000 \text{ actual units of production} \times 2 \text{ hrs./unit}$$
$$= 16{,}000$$

The variable and fixed overhead rates of $6.00 and $4.00, respectively, were found in Example 7-3.

To compute applied overhead costs, use equations 7.3 and 7.4:

$$\overset{y}{\text{SVOA}} = \overset{b}{\text{TSHDL}} \times \overset{x}{\text{SVOR}}$$
$$= 16{,}000 \times \$6.00$$
$$= \$96{,}000$$

$$\text{SFOA} = \text{TSHDL} \times \text{SFOR}$$
$$= 16{,}000 \times \$4.00$$
$$= \$64{,}000$$

Total standard overhead applied equals $160,000 ($96,000 + $64,000).

2. MANAGEMENT PLANNING

For planning purposes, standard overhead rates are used to develop flexible budgets for overhead costs. Remember from Chapter 5 that flexible budgets can be adjusted to reflect the actual level of production activity. Use equation 7.5 to compute the flexible budget for overhead costs:

$$\overset{y}{\text{Flexible budget for overhead costs}} = \overset{a}{\text{Budgeted fixed overhead}} + \overset{+ b(x)}{(\text{TSHDL} \times \text{SVOR})} \qquad (7.5)$$

$$\boxed{\text{FBOC} = \text{BFO} + (\text{TSHDL} \times \text{SVOR})}$$

In a flexible budget, the budgeted fixed overhead does not change (i.e., vary) in response to a change in production activity. Nor does the standard variable-overhead rate vary in response to a change in production activity. What does vary is the TSHDL, which is based on the *actual* number of units of production times the standard direct labor hours allowed per unit of production.

EXAMPLE 7-5: Using the information from Example 7-3, compute the flexible budget for overhead costs at an actual output level of 8,000 units.

To use equation 7.5 to compute the flexible budget for overhead costs, you must first determine the TSHDL, which would equal 16,000 (8,000 actual units of production × 2 hrs./unit). The budgeted fixed overhead of $80,000 remains unchanged.

$$\text{FBOC} = \text{BFO} + (\text{TSHDL} \times \text{SVOR})$$
$$= \$80{,}000 + (16{,}000 \times \$6.00)$$
$$= \$176{,}000$$

7-3. Variable Overhead Variances

There are two variable overhead variances: the variable-overhead efficiency variance, and the variable-overhead spending variance. The variable-overhead efficiency variance is similar to the quantity variance computed for direct materials and the efficiency variance computed for direct labor in Chapter 6. The variable-overhead spending variance is similar to the price variance computed for direct materials and the rate variance computed for direct labor in Chapter 6.

A. Variable-overhead efficiency variance

Like the direct-labor efficiency variance, the variable-overhead efficiency variance reflects the difference between the actual use of direct labor hours in production and the standard direct labor hours allowed for production. Remember that although direct labor is not part of variable overhead, in this chapter we are using direct labor hours as the measure of production activity in which standard variable-overhead rates are expressed. Use equation 7.6 to compute the variable-overhead efficiency variance:

$$\text{Variable-overhead efficiency variance} = (\text{AHDL} \times \text{SVOR}) - (\text{TSHDL} \times \text{SVOR}) \qquad \textbf{(7.6)}$$

This equation can also be expressed as follows:

$$\boxed{\text{VOEV} = (\text{AHDL} - \text{TSHDL}) \times \text{SVOR}}$$

The variance is interpreted as follows:

If actual hours used are greater than standard hours allowed, the variance is unfavorable.

If actual hours used are less than standard hours allowed, the variance is favorable.

When direct labor is inefficiently used—that is, when actual direct-labor hours used exceed total standard direct-labor hours allowed—you can assume that variable overhead costs will also be inefficiently used. Remember that, in general, a favorable direct-labor efficiency variance implies a favorable variable-overhead efficiency variance when standard overhead rates are based on direct labor hours. An unfavorable direct-labor efficiency variance implies an unfavorable variable-overhead efficiency variance when standard overhead rates are based on direct labor hours.

B. Variable-overhead spending variance

Like the direct-materials price variance and the direct-labor rate variance, the variable-overhead spending variance reflects the difference between actual costs and standard costs. You would compute the variable-overhead spending variance using equation 7.7:

$$\text{Variable-overhead spending variance} = (\text{AHDL} \times \text{SVOR}) - \text{AVO} \qquad \textbf{(7.7)}$$

$$\boxed{\text{VOSV} = (\text{AHDL} \times \text{SVOR}) - \text{AVO}}$$

You would interpret the variance as follows: If the actual variable overhead (AVO) is less than the standard variable overhead based on direct labor hours (AHDL × SVOR), the variable-overhead spending variance is favorable. If the actual variable overhead is greater than the standard variable overhead, the variance is unfavorable.

EXAMPLE 7-6: The following information is available for Zeldon Company for 19X8:

Total standard direct labor hours allowed for production	16,000
Actual direct labor hours used	18,000
Standard variable-overhead rate per direct labor hour	$ 6.00
Actual variable-overhead costs	$98,000

On the basis of this information, compute the variable-overhead efficiency variance and the variable-overhead spending variance.

You would compute the variable-overhead efficiency variance using equation 7.6:

$$\text{VOEV} = (\text{AHDL} - \text{TSHDL}) \times \text{SVOR}$$
$$= (18,000 - 16,000) \times \$6.00$$
$$= 2,000 \times \$6.00$$
$$= \$12,000 \text{ unfavorable}$$

The variance is unfavorable because actual direct labor hours used in production exceeded the total standard direct labor hours allowed for production.

You would compute the variable-overhead spending variance using equation 7.7:

$$VOSV = (AHDL \times SVOR) - AVO$$
$$= (18{,}000 \times \$6.00) - \$98{,}000$$
$$= 108{,}000 - \$98{,}000$$
$$= \$10{,}000 \text{ favorable}$$

The variance is favorable because the actual variable overhead is less than the standard variable overhead based on direct labor hours.

7-4. Fixed Overhead Variances

There are two fixed overhead variances: the fixed-overhead budget variance, and the fixed-overhead production-volume variance. These variances are completely different from the variances for variable production costs, such as variable overhead, direct materials, and direct labor.

A. Fixed-overhead budget variance

The fixed-overhead budget variance is a spending variance that measures the difference between actual fixed-overhead costs and budgeted fixed-overhead costs. You would compute the fixed-overhead budget variance using equation 7.8:

$$\frac{\text{Fixed-overhead}}{\text{budget variance}} = \frac{\text{Budgeted fixed}}{\text{overhead}} - \frac{\text{Actual fixed}}{\text{overhead}} \qquad \textbf{(7.8)}$$

$$\boxed{FOBV = BFO - AFO}$$

If actual fixed-overhead costs are less than budgeted fixed-overhead costs, the fixed-overhead budget variance is favorable; if the actual fixed overhead is greater, the variance is unfavorable.

B. Fixed-overhead production-volume variance

The fixed-overhead production-volume variance measures the difference between budgeted fixed overhead and standard fixed-overhead applied. You would compute the fixed-overhead production-volume variance using equation 7.9:

$$\frac{\text{Fixed-overhead production-}}{\text{volume variance}} = \text{Budgeted fixed overhead} - (TSHDL \times SFOR) \qquad \textbf{(7.9)}$$

$$\boxed{FOPVV = BFO - (TSHDL \times SFOR)}$$

Because TSHDL × SFOR = SFOA = Standard fixed overhead applied (see equation 7.4), equation 7.9 can be restated as follows:

$$\boxed{FOPVV = BFO - SFOA} \qquad \textbf{(7.9)}$$

You would interpret the variance as follows: If the budgeted fixed overhead is less than the standard fixed-overhead applied (TSHDL × SFOR), the variance is favorable. If the budgeted fixed overhead is greater than the standard fixed-overhead applied (TSHDL × SFOR), the variance is unfavorable.

Remember that budgeted fixed overhead is used in computing the standard fixed-overhead rate per direct labor hour in equation 7.2:

$$\boxed{SFOR = \frac{BFO}{BHDL}} \qquad \textbf{(7.2)}$$

By rearranging this equation, you can solve for the budgeted fixed overhead:

$$BFO = BHDL \times SFOR$$

And from equation 7.4:

$$SFOA = TSHDL \times SFOR$$

(7.4)

Notice that the difference between budgeted fixed overhead (BFO) and standard fixed overhead applied (SFOA) reflects the difference between BHDL, which are based on *budgeted* production volume, and TSHDL, which are based on *actual* production volume. Therefore, the fixed-overhead production-volume variance reflects the difference between the *budgeted* production volume and the *actual* production volume. In this sense, a favorable fixed-overhead production-volume variance means that the actual utilization of production capacity is greater than the budgeted utilization of production capacity.

EXAMPLE 7-7: The following information is available for Winchester Company for 19X8:

Total standard direct-labor hours allowed for production	16,000
Standard fixed-overhead rate per direct labor hour	$ 4.00
Actual fixed-overhead costs	$67,000
Budgeted fixed overhead	$80,000

On the basis of this information, compute the fixed overhead variances.
   You would use equation 7.8 to compute the fixed-overhead budget variance:

$$FOBV = BFO - AFO$$
$$= \$80,000 - \$67,000$$
$$= \$13,000 \text{ favorable}$$

The fixed-overhead production-volume variance would be computed using equation 7.9:

$$FOPVV = BFO - (TSHDL \times SFOR)$$
$$= \$80,000 - (16,000 \times \$4.00)$$
$$= \$80,000 - \$64,000$$
$$= \$16,000 \text{ unfavorable}$$

7-5. Journal Entries for Standard Overhead Costs

The journal entries to record factory overhead costs involve recording actual overhead costs and recording standard overhead costs applied to production. (These journal entries are very similar to those described in Chapter 3 for recording factory overhead incurred and factory overhead applied.) Journal entries for standard factory-overhead costs are generally segregated by the variable overhead and fixed overhead components.

A. Journal entries for variable overhead costs

There are two journal entries for variable overhead costs: one records the actual variable-overhead costs, and the other records the standard variable-overhead costs applied to production:
   The following journal entry records the *actual* variable-overhead costs incurred:

	Debit	Credit
Variable Factory Overhead Control	$XX,XXX	
Accounts Payable, and other accounts		$XX,XXX

The debit to the Variable Factory Overhead Control account represents the *actual* variable-overhead costs incurred.
   The journal entry to record the standard variable-overhead costs *applied* to production

would be as follows:

	Debit	Credit
Work-in-Process Control	$XX,XXX	
Variable Factory Overhead Applied		$XX,XXX

The credit to the Variable Factory Overhead Applied account represents the standard variable-overhead *applied* (SVOA), as computed using equation 7.3:

$$SVOA = TSHDL \times SVOR$$

Note that when using standard costing, standard overhead costs are credited to the overhead "applied" accounts, and actual overhead costs are debited to the overhead "control" accounts.

The difference between actual variable-overhead incurred (debit balance in the Variable Factory Overhead Control account) and standard variable-overhead applied (credit balance in the Variable Factory Overhead Applied account) represents the total underapplied or overapplied variable factory overhead. You would compute the underapplied or overapplied variable overhead using equation 7.10:

$$\text{Total underapplied or overapplied variable overhead} = \text{Actual variable overhead incurred} - \text{Standard variable overhead applied} \quad (7.10)$$

Total underapplied variable factory overhead occurs when actual variable-overhead costs incurred are greater than the standard variable-overhead costs applied. Total overapplied variable factory overhead occurs when the actual variable overhead costs incurred are less than the standard variable factory overhead costs applied.

The amount of total underapplied or overapplied variable overhead represents the total difference between actual variable overhead incurred and standard variable overhead applied. Total *underapplied* variable overhead indicates that either the variable-overhead efficiency variance or the variable-overhead spending variance is unfavorable or both of them are unfavorable. Total *overapplied* variable overhead indicates that either the variable-overhead efficiency variance or the variable-overhead spending variance is favorable or both of them are favorable.

However, we can't tell from the *total* underapplied or *total* overapplied variable-overhead variance what combination of favorable or unfavorable variances exist. Therefore, total underapplied or overapplied variable-overhead variance is not a very exact analysis of variance. More exact analyses of variance will be shown in Section 7-6.

B. Journal entries for fixed overhead costs

There are two journal entries for fixed overhead costs: one to record the actual fixed-overhead costs, and one to record the standard fixed-overhead costs applied to production.

The journal entry to record the actual fixed-overhead costs incurred would be as follows:

	Debit	Credit
Fixed Factory Overhead Control	$XX,XXX	
Accounts Payable, and other accounts		$XX,XXX

The debit to the Fixed Factory Overhead Control account represents the actual fixed-overhead costs incurred.

The following journal entry records the standard fixed-overhead costs applied to production:

	Debit	Credit
Work-in-Process Control	$XX,XXX	
Fixed Factory Overhead Applied		$XX,XXX

The credit to the Fixed Factory Overhead Applied account represents the standard fixed-overhead applied (SFOA), as computed in equation 7.4:

$$SFOA = TSHDL \times SFOR$$

The difference between actual fixed-overhead incurred (debit balance in the Fixed Factory Overhead Control account) and standard fixed-overhead applied (credit balance in the Fixed Factory Overhead Applied account) represents the total underapplied or overapplied fixed factory overhead. You would compute the total underapplied or overapplied fixed overhead as follows:

$$\begin{array}{c}\text{Total underapplied}\\\text{or overapplied}\\\text{fixed overhead}\end{array} = \begin{array}{c}\text{Actual fixed}\\\text{overhead incurred}\end{array} - \begin{array}{c}\text{Standard fixed}\\\text{overhead applied}\end{array} \qquad \textbf{(7.11)}$$

Total underapplied fixed overhead means that the combination of the fixed-overhead budget variance and the fixed-overhead production-volume variance is unfavorable. (Either one or both of the overhead variances must be unfavorable for the total fixed overhead variance to be unfavorable.)

Total overapplied fixed overhead means that the combination of the fixed-overhead budget variance and the fixed-overhead production volume variance is favorable. (Either one or both of the overhead variances must be favorable for the total fixed overhead variance to be favorable.)

However, we can't tell from the *total* underapplied or *total* overapplied fixed overhead variance what combination of favorable or unfavorable variances exist. Therefore, total underapplied or overapplied fixed overhead variance is not a very exact analysis of variance. More exact analyses of variance will be shown in Section 7-6.

C. Journal entries for overhead variances

Remember that actual variable and fixed overhead costs are debited to a "control" account and that the standard variable and fixed overhead costs are credited to an "applied" account. After these journal entries have been made, the overhead costs variances can be isolated in the ledger accounts.

A combined journal entry is made to record the overhead cost variances and to close the factory overhead applied account (a debit entry) and to close the factory overhead control account (a credit entry). This journal entry would be made at the end of the year based on the accumulated year-end balances in the overhead applied account and the overhead control account.

1. VARIABLE OVERHEAD VARIANCES

The journal entry to record the variable overhead variances at the end of the year would be:

Variable Factory Overhead Applied	$XX,XXX		
Variable Factory Overhead Spending Variance	XX,XXX	or	$XX,XXX
Variable Factory Overhead Efficiency Variance	XX,XXX	or	XX,XXX
Variable Factory Overhead Control			XX,XXX
To close variable factory overhead accounts and to record variable overhead variances.			

The debit to the Variable Factory Overhead Applied account would be the year-end balance in that account. Similarly, the credit to the Variable Factory Overhead Control account would be the amount of the year-end balance in that account. These accounts would be closed for the year. The variable overhead variance accounts would be debited if their variances are unfavorable and credited if their variances are favorable.

2. FIXED OVERHEAD VARIANCES

The journal entry to record the fixed overhead variances at the end of the year would be:

Fixed Factory Overhead Applied	$XX,XXX		
Fixed Factory-Overhead Budget Variance	XX,XXX	or	$XX,XXX
Fixed Factory-Overhead Production-Volume Variance	XX,XXX	or	XX,XXX
Fixed Factory Overhead Control			XX,XXX
To close fixed factory overhead accounts and to record fixed overhead variances.			

The debit to the Fixed Factory Overhead Applied account and the credit to the Fixed Factory Overhead Control account would be for the year-end balances in those accounts. These accounts would be closed for the year. The fixed overhead variance accounts would be debited if their variances are unfavorable and credited if their variances are favorable.

EXAMPLE 7-8: The following information is available for Cannes Company for the year 19X1:

Budgeted fixed overhead (at 10,000 direct labor hours)	$50,000
Standard fixed overhead rate per direct labor hour	$5.00
Standard variable overhead rate per direct labor hour	$8.00
Actual fixed overhead costs	$60,000
Actual variable overhead costs	$70,000
Actual direct labor hours	9,000
Total standard direct labor hours allowed for production	8,500

Cannes Company applied overhead costs to production based on direct labor hours. Before you can record the year-end journal entries, you must first compute the overhead variances as follows:

Variable-Overhead Spending Variance

$$VOSV = (AHDL \times SVOR) - AVO$$
$$= (9,000 \times \$8.00) - \$70,000$$
$$= \$72,000 - \$70,000$$
$$= \$2,000 \text{ favorable}$$

Variable-Overhead Efficiency Variance

$$VOEV = (AHDL - TSHDL) \times SVOR$$
$$= (9,000 - 8,500) \times \$8.00$$
$$= \$4,000 \text{ unfavorable}$$

Fixed-Overhead Budget Variance

$$FOBV = BFO - AFO$$
$$= \$50,000 - \$60,000$$
$$= \$10,000 \text{ unfavorable}$$

Fixed-Overhead Production-Volume Variance

$$FOPPV = BFO - (TSHDL \times SFOR)$$
$$= \$50,000 - (8,500 \times \$5.00)$$
$$= \$50,000 - \$42,500$$
$$= \$7,500 \text{ unfavorable}$$

Based on the information given and the variances computed for the Cannes Company, the following journal entries can be made:

Variable Factory Overhead Applied		
(8,500 × $8.00)	$68,000	
Variable Overhead Efficiency Variance	4,000	
Variable Overhead Spending Variance		$ 2,000
Variable Factory Overhead Control		70,000

The Variable Overhead Efficiency Variance account is debited for the $4,000 unfavorable variance and the Variable Overhead Spending Variance account is credited for the $2,000 favorable variance.

The journal entry to record the fixed overhead variances at the end of the year would be:

Fixed Factory Overhead Applied (8,500 × $5.00)	$42,500	
Fixed-Overhead Budget Variance	10,000	
Fixed-Overhead Production-Volume Variance	7,500	
Fixed Factory Overhead Control		$60,000

Because both fixed overhead variances are unfavorable, both fixed overhead variance accounts are debited for the amount of the variance.

7-6. Analysis of Overhead Variances

The overhead variances discussed in this chapter can be analyzed at four levels, which are summarized in Exhibit 7-1. Columns 1–4 summarize the figures we will use in our variance analysis.

Column 1 sums the actual variable and fixed overhead costs.

Column 2 computes a flexible budget based on actual direct labor hours (AHDL × SVOR). Although we have never computed a flexible budget based on AHDL, we have used AHDL × SVOR to find the variable-overhead efficiency variance [VOEV = (AHDL × SVOR) − (TSHDL × SVOR)].

Column 3 computes a flexible budget based on total standard direct labor hours allowed (TSHDL × SVOR). Note that the budgeted fixed overhead in columns 2 and 3 will be the same figure.

Column 4 computes the total overhead costs applied to production.

EXHIBIT 7-1

Analysis of Overhead Variance

	(1) Actual overhead costs	(2) Flexible budget based on AHDL	(3) Flexible budget based on TSHDL	(4) Applied overhead costs
Variable Fixed	+ Actual variable overhead Actual fixed overhead	+ AHDL × SVOR Budgeted fixed overhead	+ TSHDL × SVOR Budgeted fixed overhead	+ TSHDL × SVOR TSHDL × SFOR
Total	Actual overhead costs	Flexible budget based on AHDL	Flexible budget based on TSHDL	Overhead costs applied

FOUR-VARIANCE METHOD

Variable overhead:	←Variable-overhead spending variance→	←Variable-overhead efficiency variance→	← −0− →
Fixed overhead:	←Fixed-overhead budget variance→	← −0− →	←Fixed-overhead production-volume variance→

THREE-VARIANCE METHOD

←Overhead spending variance→	←Variable-overhead efficiency variance→	←Fixed-overhead production-volume variance→

TWO-VARIANCE METHOD

←Overhead flexible-budget variance→	←Fixed-overhead production-volume variance→

ONE-VARIANCE METHOD

←Underapplied or Overapplied Overhead→

A. Four-variance method of overhead analysis

The four variance method of overhead analysis computes all four of the variances you have studied in this chapter:

1. Variable-overhead spending variance
2. Variable-overhead efficiency variance

3. Fixed-overhead budget variance
4. Fixed-overhead production-volume variance

B. Three-variance method of overhead analysis

The three-variance method of overhead analysis is composed of the overhead spending variance, the variable-overhead efficiency variance, and the fixed-overhead production-volume variance. The overhead spending variance is the combination of the variable-overhead spending variance and the fixed-overhead budget variance. Another way to compute the overhead spending variance is to subtract the Column 2 total of Exhibit 7-1 from the Column 1 total.

C. Two-variance method of overhead analysis

The two-variance method of overhead analysis is composed of the overhead flexible-budget variance and the fixed-overhead production-volume variance. The overhead flexible-budget variance is the combination of three variances: the variable-overhead spending variance, the fixed-overhead budget variance, and the variable-overhead efficiency variance. Another way to compute the overhead flexible-budget variance is to subtract the Column 3 total of Exhibit 7-1 from the Column 1 total.

D. One-variance method of overhead analysis

The one-variance method of overhead analysis combines all four overhead variances. The underapplied or overapplied overhead represents the net amount of the four overhead variances. Another way to compute the underapplied or overapplied overhead is to subtract the Column 4 total of Exhibit 7-1 from the Column 1 total (total actual overhead costs − total overhead costs applied). Underapplied overhead means that the net amount of the four overhead variances is unfavorable. Overapplied overhead means that the net amount of the overhead variances is favorable.

EXAMPLE 7-9: Using the information in Example 7-8, the overhead variances can be analyzed using the format in Exhibit 7-1.

The four-variance method presents the four overhead variances computed in Example 7-8.

The three-variance method computes the unfavorable overhead spending variance of $8,000 as follows:

Variable-overhead spending variance	$ 2,000 F
Fixed-overhead budget variance	10,000 U
Overhead spending variance	$ 8,000 U

The two-variance method computes the unfavorable overhead flexible-budget variance of $12,000 as follows:

Variable-overhead spending variance	$ 2,000 F
Fixed-overhead budget variance	10,000 U
Variable-overhead efficiency variance	4,000 U
Overhead flexible-budget variance	$12,000 U

The one-variance method is computed as follows:

Actual overhead costs	$130,000
Applied overhead costs	110,500
Underapplied overhead	$ 19,500 U

The one-variance method can also be thought of as a combination of all four overhead variances.

Variable-overhead spending variance	$ 2,000 F
Variable-overhead efficiency variance	4,000 U
Fixed-overhead budget variance	10,000 U
Fixed-overhead production-volume variance	7,500 U
Underapplied overhead	$19,500 U

EXHIBIT 7-2

Analysis of Overhead Variance

	(1) Actual overhead costs	(2) Flexible budget based on AHDL	(3) Flexible budget based on TSHDL	(4) Applied overhead costs
Variable	$ 70,000	$ 72,000	$ 68,000	$ 68,000
Fixed	60,000	50,000	50,000	42,500
Total	$130,000	$122,000	$118,000	$110,500

FOUR-VARIANCE METHOD

Variable overhead:

$70,000 $72,000 $68,000 $68,000

   $2,000 F $4,000 U   –0–

   Variable-overhead spending variance   Variable-overhead efficiency variance

Fixed overhead:

$60,000 $50,000 $50,000 $42,500

   $10,000 U   –0– $7,500 U

   Fixed-overhead budget variance   Fixed-overhead production-volume variance

THREE-VARIANCE METHOD

$130,000 $122,000 $118,000 $110,500

   $8,000 U $4,000 U $7,500 U

   Overhead spending variance   Variable-overhead efficiency variance   Fixed-overhead production-volume variance

TWO-VARIANCE METHOD

$130,000 $118,000 $110,500

   $12,000 U $7,500 U

   Overhead flexible-budget variance   Fixed-overhead production-volume variance

ONE-VARIANCE METHOD

$130,000 $110,500

   $19,500 U

   Underapplied or Overapplied Overhead

Notes: F = Favorable; U = Unfavorable

RAISE YOUR GRADES

Can you explain...?

☑ what variable overhead costs are

☑ what fixed overhead costs are

☑ how standard variable-overhead rates are computed

☑ how standard fixed-overhead rates are computed
☑ the uses of standard overhead rates
☑ how to compute and interpret the variable-overhead efficiency variance
☑ how to compute and interpret the variable-overhead spending variance
☑ how to compute and interpret the fixed-overhead budget variance
☑ how to compute and interpret the fixed-overhead production-volume variance
☑ how to prepare the journal entries to record variable overhead costs
☑ how to prepare the journal entries to record fixed overhead costs
☑ the components of four-way analysis of overhead variances
☑ the components of three-way analysis of overhead variances
☑ the components of two-way analysis of overhead variances
☑ the components of one-way analysis of overhead variances

SUMMARY

1. Factory overhead costs can be classified as either variable overhead costs or fixed overhead costs.
2. Standard overhead costs are usually segregated by variable overhead and fixed overhead components.
3. Standard variable-overhead rates are computed by dividing budgeted variable-overhead costs by the standard direct-labor hours allowed for the budgeted production volume.

$$SVOR = \frac{BVO}{BHDL}$$

4. Standard fixed-overhead rates are computed by dividing budgeted fixed-overhead costs by the standard direct-labor hours allowed for the budgeted production volume.

$$SFOR = \frac{BFO}{BHDL}$$

5. The standard variable overhead applied (SVOA) is determined by multiplying the standard variable-overhead rate per direct labor hour (SVOR) times the total standard direct-labor hours allowed for actual production (TSHDL). $\boxed{SVOA = TSHDL \times SVOR}$

6. The standard fixed overhead applied (SFOA) is determined by multiplying the standard fixed-overhead rate per direct labor hour (SFOR) times the total standard direct-labor hours allowed for actual production (TSHDL). $\boxed{SFOA = TSHDL \times SFOR}$

7. Standard overhead costs are used for management planning, management control, and product costing purposes.

8. The variable-overhead efficiency variance is computed as the difference between actual direct-labor hours times the standard variable-overhead rate per direct labor hour, minus total standard direct-labor hours times the standard variable-overhead rate per direct labor hour. $\boxed{VOEV = (AHDL \times SVOR) - (TSHDL \times SVOR)}$ or

$$\boxed{VOEV = (AHDL - TSHDL) \times SVOR}$$

9. The variable-overhead efficiency variance is favorable if actual direct-labor hours used in production are less than the standard direct-labor hours allowed for production; it is unfavorable if the actual direct-labor hours used in production are greater than the standard direct-labor hours allowed for production.

10. The variable-overhead spending variance is computed as the difference between actual direct-labor hours times the standard variable-overhead rate per direct labor hour minus the actual variable overhead.

$$\boxed{VOSV = (AHDL \times SVOR) - AVO}$$

11. The variable-overhead spending variance is favorable if the actual variable overhead is less than the standard variable overhead based on actual direct-labor hours; it is unfavorable if the actual variable overhead is greater than the standard variable overhead.

12. The fixed-overhead budget variance is computed as the difference between the budgeted fixed overhead and the actual fixed overhead.

$$\boxed{FOBV = BFO - AFO}$$

13. The fixed-overhead budget variance is favorable if the actual fixed overhead is less than the budgeted fixed overhead; it is unfavorable if the actual fixed overhead is greater.

14. The fixed-overhead production-volume variance is computed as the difference between the budgeted fixed overhead and the standard fixed overhead applied.

$$\boxed{FOPVV = BFO - (TSHDL \times SFOR)} \text{ or } \boxed{FOPVV = BFO - SFOA}$$

15. The fixed-overhead production-volume variance is favorable if the budgeted fixed-overhead is less than the standard fixed-overhead applied; it is unfavorable if the budgeted fixed-overhead is greater.

16. When using standard costing, *standard* overhead costs applied are credited to overhead "*applied*" accounts.

17. When using standard costing, *actual* overhead costs incurred are debited to overhead "*control*" accounts.

18. The journal entry to record the actual variable-overhead costs incurred debits the Variable Factory Overhead Control account and credits the Accounts Payable account and other accounts.

19. The journal entry to record the standard variable-overhead costs applied to production debits the Work-in-Process Control account and credits the Variable Factory Overhead Applied account.

20. The journal entry to record the actual fixed-overhead costs incurred debits the Fixed Factory Overhead Control account and credits the Accounts Payable account and other accounts.

21. The journal entry to record the standard fixed-overhead costs applied to production debits the Work-in-Process Control account and credits the Fixed Factory Overhead Applied account.

22. In one-way analysis of overhead variances, the underapplied or overapplied overhead represents the net amount of all four overhead variances.

23. A two-way analysis of overhead variances involves the overhead flexible-budget variance and the fixed-overhead production-volume variance.

24. A three-way analysis of overhead variances involves the overhead spending variance, the variable-overhead efficiency variance, and the fixed-overhead production-volume variance.

25. A four way analysis of overhead variances involves the variable-overhead spending variance, the variable-overhead efficiency variance, the fixed-overhead budget variance, and the fixed-overhead production-volume variance.

RAPID REVIEW

1. Standard costs for variable overhead and fixed overhead are generally determined separately: (a) true, (b) false. [See Section 7-1.]

2. The standard variable-overhead rate is computed by dividing budgeted variable-overhead costs by (a) actual direct-labor hours, (b) standard direct-labor hours allowed for budgeted production, (c) standard direct-labor hours allowed for actual production. [See Section 7-2.]

3. The standard fixed-overhead rate is computed by dividing budgeted fixed-overhead costs by (a) actual direct-labor hours, (b) standard direct-labor hours allowed for budgeted production, (c) standard direct-labor hours allowed for actual production. [See Section 7-2.]

4. Standard overhead costs are used for (**a**) product costing purposes, (**b**) management planning purposes, (**c**) management control purposes, (**d**) all of the above. [See Section 7-2.]

5. The variable-overhead efficiency variance is equal to the difference between the actual direct-labor hours and total standard direct-labor hours, times (**a**) the standard variable-overhead rate, (**b**) the actual variable-overhead rate, (**c**) the standard direct-labor rate, (**d**) the standard fixed-overhead rate. [See Section 7-3.]

6. The variable-overhead efficiency variance is favorable if total standard direct-labor hours allowed for production are (**a**) less than actual direct-labor hours, (**b**) greater than actual direct-labor hours, (**c**) less than budgeted direct-labor hours, (**d**) greater than budgeted direct-labor hours. [See Section 7-3.]

7. The variable-overhead spending variance is equal to the actual direct-labor hours times the standard variable-overhead rate per direct labor hour, minus (**a**) actual variable-overhead costs incurred, (**b**) standard variable-overhead costs, (**c**) budgeted variable-overhead costs, (**d**) none of the above. [See Section 7-3.]

8. The variable-overhead spending variance is favorable if the standard variable-overhead rate times the actual direct-labor hours is (**a**) less than actual variable-overhead costs, (**b**) greater than actual variable-overhead costs, (**c**) less than budgeted variable-overhead costs, (**d**) greater than budgeted variable-overhead costs. [See Section 7-3.]

9. The fixed-overhead budget variance is computed as the difference between actual fixed-overhead costs and (**a**) budgeted fixed-overhead costs, (**b**) applied fixed-overhead costs, (**c**) standard fixed-overhead costs. [See Section 7-4.]

10. The fixed-overhead budget variance is favorable if actual fixed-overhead costs are (**a**) less than budgeted fixed overhead, (**b**) greater than budgeted fixed overhead, (**c**) less than standard fixed-overhead applied, (**d**) greater than standard fixed-overhead applied. [See Section 7-4.]

11. The fixed-overhead production-volume variance is computed as the difference between budgeted fixed-overhead costs and (**a**) actual fixed-overhead costs, (**b**) standard fixed-overhead applied, (**c**) standard fixed-overhead costs. [See Section 7-4.]

12. The fixed-overhead production-volume variance is favorable if budgeted fixed-overhead is (**a**) less than standard fixed-overhead applied, (**b**) greater than standard fixed-overhead applied, (**c**) less than actual fixed overhead, (**d**) greater than actual fixed overhead. [See Section 7-4.]

13. The journal entry to record the actual variable-overhead costs incurred involves a debit to (**a**) Work-in-Process Control, (**b**) Variable Factory Overhead Control, (**c**) Variable Factory Overhead Applied. [See Section 7-5.]

14. The journal entry to record the standard variable-overhead costs applied to production involves (**a**) a debit to Variable Factory Overhead Applied, (**b**) a credit to Variable Factory Overhead Applied, (**c**) a debit to Variable Factory Overhead Control, (**d**) a credit to Work-in-Process Control. [See Section 7-5.]

15. The journal entry to record the standard fixed-overhead costs applied to production involves a debit to (**a**) Fixed Factory Overhead Control, (**b**) Fixed Factory Overhead Applied, (**c**) Work-in-Process Control. [See Section 7-5.]

16. In the three-way analysis of overhead variances, the variable-overhead spending variance is combined with the (**a**) fixed-overhead budget variance, (**b**) fixed-overhead production-volume variance, (**c**) variable-overhead efficiency variance. [See Section 7-6.]

17. The two-way analysis of overhead variances involves the overhead flexible-budget variance and the fixed-overhead production-volume variance: (**a**) true, (**b**) false. [See Section 7-6.]

18. Underapplied overhead implies that the net amount of all overhead variances is (**a**) favorable, (**b**) unfavorable. [See Section 7-6.]

Answers:

1. (a)　2. (b)　3. (b)　4. (d)　5. (a)　6. (b)　7. (a)　8. (b)　9. (a)　10. (a)
11. (b)　12. (a)　13. (b)　14. (b)　15. (c)　16. (a)　17. (a)　18. (b)

SOLVED PROBLEMS

Problems 7-1 to 7-3 are based on the following data.

Horizon Company has developed the following budgeted information for 19X4:

Budgeted variable overhead:		
Indirect labor	$260,000	
Supplies	35,000	
Utilities	85,000	
		$380,000
Budgeted fixed overhead:		
Depreciation	$150,000	
Insurance	75,000	
Property taxes	85,000	
		310,000
Total budgeted overhead		$690,000

Budgeted production in units	100,000 units
Standard direct-labor hours per unit	2 hrs./unit

PROBLEM 7-1: Compute the standard variable-overhead rate and standard fixed-overhead rate per direct labor hour.

Solution: In order to solve this problem, you must first compute the standard direct-labor hours allowed for budgeted production (BHDL):

$$\text{BHDL} = \frac{\text{Budgeted production}}{\text{in units}} \times \frac{\text{Standard direct-labor}}{\text{hours per unit}}$$

$$= 100,000 \text{ units} \times 2 \text{ hrs./unit}$$

$$= 200,000 \text{ direct labor hours}$$

You can now compute the standard variable-overhead rate (SVOR) using equation 7.1.

$$\text{SVOR} = \frac{\text{BVO}}{\text{BHDL}}$$

$$= \frac{\$380,000}{200,000 \text{ hrs.}}$$

$$= \$1.90/\text{direct labor hour}$$

The standard fixed-overhead rate (SFOR) would be computed using equation 7.2.

$$\text{SFOR} = \frac{\text{BFO}}{\text{BHDL}}$$

$$= \frac{\$310,000}{200,000 \text{ hrs.}}$$

$$= \$1.55/\text{direct labor hour}$$

[See Section 7-2.]

PROBLEM 7-2: Compute the standard variable-overhead and standard fixed-overhead costs applied to actual production of 120,000 units.

Solution: The standard overhead costs applied to production are based on the standard rates for variable overhead and for fixed overhead (SVOR) and (SFOR), as computed in Problem 7-1. In order to solve this problem, you must first compute the total standard direct-labor hours allowed for actual production (TSHDL):

$$TSHDL = \frac{\text{Actual production}}{\text{in units}} \times \frac{\text{Standard direct-labor}}{\text{hours per unit}}$$

$$= 120{,}000 \text{ units} \times 2 \text{ hrs./unit}$$

$$= 240{,}000 \text{ direct labor hours}$$

You would compute the standard variable-overhead costs applied to production (SVOA) using equation 7.3.

$$SVOA = TSHDL \times SVOR$$

$$= 240{,}000 \times \$1.90$$

$$= \$456{,}000$$

Similarly, you would compute the standard fixed-overhead applied to production (SFOA) using equation 7.4.

$$SFOA = TSHDL \times SFOR$$

$$= 240{,}000 \times \$1.55$$

$$= \$372{,}000$$

[See Section 7-2.]

PROBLEM 7-3: Prepare the journal entries to record the standard variable- and fixed-overhead costs applied to production, which you computed in Problem 7-2.

Solution: The journal entry to record the standard variable-overhead costs applied to production would be as follows:

Work-in-Process Control	$456,000	
Variable Factory Overhead Applied		$456,000

You would prepare the following journal entry to record the standard fixed-overhead costs applied to production:

Work-in-Process Control	$372,000	
Fixed Factory Overhead Applied		$372,000

[See Section 7-5.]

Problems 7-4 and 7-5 are based on the following data.

Micro Manufacturing Company has summarized the following information about its overhead costs for 19X7:

Standard variable-overhead applied	$450,000
Standard fixed-overhead applied	$230,000
Actual variable-overhead costs incurred	$475,000
Actual fixed-overhead costs incurred	$215,000

PROBLEM 7-4: Prepare the journal entries to record the actual variable-overhead costs incurred and the standard variable-overhead costs applied. Also, compute total underapplied or overapplied variable overhead.

Solution: You would make the following journal entry to record the actual variable-overhead costs.

Variable Factory Overhead Control	$475,000	
Accounts Payable, and other accounts		$475,000

The following journal entry records the standard variable-overhead costs applied to production.

Work-in-Process Control	$450,000	
Variable Factory Overhead Applied		$450,000

The difference between the actual variable-overhead costs incurred (debit balance in the Variable Factory Overhead Control account) and the standard variable-overhead applied (credit balance in the Variable Factory Overhead Applied account) represents the underapplied or overapplied variable factory overhead. You would compute the underapplied or overapplied variable overhead using equation 7.10.

$$\begin{array}{rcl}\text{Total underapplied or} \atop \text{overapplied variable overhead} & = & \text{Actual variable} \atop \text{overhead incurred} - \text{Standard variable} \atop \text{overhead applied}\end{array}$$

$$= \$475{,}000 - \$450{,}000$$

$$= \$25{,}000 \text{ underapplied}$$

The overhead is underapplied because the actual variable-overhead incurred is greater than the standard variable overhead applied. The fact that the overhead is underapplied means that the total variance is unfavorable. [See Section 7-5.]

PROBLEM 7-5: Prepare the journal entries to record the actual fixed-overhead costs incurred and the standard fixed-overhead costs applied to production. Also, compute the underapplied or overapplied fixed overhead and compute total under- or overapplied overhead.

Solution: You would prepare the following journal entry to record the actual fixed-overhead costs incurred.

Fixed Factory Overhead Control	$215,000	
Accounts Payable, and other accounts		$215,000

The journal entry to record the standard fixed-overhead costs applied to production would be as follows:

Work-in-Process Control	$230,000	
Fixed Factory Overhead Applied		$230,000

The difference between the actual fixed-overhead costs incurred (debit balance in the Fixed Factory Overhead Control account) and the standard fixed-overhead applied (credit balance in the Fixed Factory Overhead Applied account) represents the underapplied or overapplied fixed overhead. You compute the underapplied or overapplied fixed overhead using equation 7.11.

$$\begin{array}{rcl}\text{Total underapplied or} \atop \text{overapplied fixed overhead} & = & \text{Actual fixed} \atop \text{overhead incurred} - \text{Standard fixed} \atop \text{overhead applied}\end{array}$$

$$= \$215{,}000 - \$230{,}000$$

$$= \$15{,}000 \text{ overapplied}$$

The fixed overhead is overapplied because actual fixed overhead incurred is less than standard fixed overhead applied. Overapplied overhead indicates a favorable variance.

You would compute the total underapplied or overapplied overhead as follows:

Total actual overhead costs:		
Variable overhead	$475,000	
Fixed overhead	215,000	
		$690,000
Total applied overhead costs:		
Variable overhead	$450,000	
Fixed overhead	230,000	
		− 680,000
Total underapplied overhead		$ 10,000

The total underapplied overhead means that the net amount of the overhead variances is unfavorable. [See Section 7-5.]

Problems 7-6 to 7-8 are based on the following data.

On the basis of 90,000 units of production and 180,000 direct labor hours (2 direct labor hours per unit), PC Manufacturing Company has developed the following standard overhead rates for

June 19X4:

Standard variable-overhead rate per direct labor hour	$3.00
Standard fixed-overhead rate per direct labor hour	5.00
Total	$8.00

During the month of June, 80,000 units were produced. The following additional information is available for the month of June:

Budgeted fixed overhead	$ 900,000
Actual variable overhead	$ 518,000
Actual fixed overhead	$ 860,000
Total overhead incurred	$1,378,000
Actual direct labor hours	165,000 hours

PROBLEM 7-6: Compute the variable-overhead efficiency and spending variances.

Solution: In order to solve this problem, you must first compute the total standard direct labor hours allowed for production (TSHDL).

$$\text{TSHDL} = \frac{\text{Standard direct labor}}{\text{hours per unit}} \times \frac{\text{Actual production}}{\text{in units}}$$

$$= 2 \text{ hours per unit} \times 80,000 \text{ units}$$

$$= 160,000 \text{ standard direct labor hours}$$

You would compute the variable-overhead efficiency variance using equation 7.6:

$$\text{VOEV} = (\text{AHDL} \times \text{SVOR}) - (\text{TSHDL} \times \text{SVOR})$$

$$= (165,000 \times \$3.00) - (160,000 \times \$3.00)$$

$$= \$495,000 - \$480,000$$

$$= \$15,000 \text{ unfavorable}$$

The variable-overhead efficiency variance is unfavorable because the actual direct labor hours used are greater than the standard direct labor hours allowed for production.

You would compute the variable-overhead spending variance using equation 7.7:

$$\text{VOSV} = (\text{AHDL} \times \text{SVOR}) - \text{AVO}$$

$$= (165,000 \times \$3.00) - \$518,000$$

$$= \$495,000 - \$518,000$$

$$= \$23,000 \text{ unfavorable}$$

The variable-overhead spending variance is unfavorable because the actual variable-overhead costs incurred are greater than the standard variable overhead based on actual direct labor hours. [See Section 7-3.]

PROBLEM 7-7: Compute the fixed-overhead budget and production-volume variances.

Solution: You would use equation 7.8 to compute the fixed-overhead budget variance.

$$\text{FOBV} = \text{BFO} - \text{AFO}$$

$$= \$900,000 - \$860,000$$

$$= \$40,000 \text{ favorable}$$

This variance is favorable because actual fixed overhead is less than budgeted fixed overhead.

The fixed-overhead production-volume variance would be computed using equation 7.9. From Problem 7-6, you know that TSHDL = 160,000.

$$\text{FOPVV} = \text{BFO} - (\text{TSHDL} \times \text{SFOR})$$

$$= \$900,000 - (160,000 \times \$5.00)$$

$$= \$900,000 - \$800,000$$

$$= \$100,000 \text{ unfavorable}$$

The fixed-overhead production-volume variance is unfavorable because the standard fixed-overhead applied is less than the budgeted fixed overhead. Remember that the budgeted fixed overhead is based on a budgeted production of 90,000 units (90,000 × 2 SHDL = 180,000 BHDL × $5.00 SFOR = $900,000 BFO). In contrast, the applied fixed overhead is based on an actual production of 80,000 units (80,000 × 2 SHDL = 160,000 TSHDL). The unfavorable fixed-overhead production-volume variance reflects the fact that the actual production volume was less than the budgeted production volume. [See Section 7-4.]

PROBLEM 7-8: Present the four analyses of overhead variances for PC Manufacturing Company.

Solution: Using the variable and fixed overhead variances found in Problems 7-6 and 7-7, you would arrive at the following four-way analysis of overhead variances.

Variable-overhead efficiency variance	$ 15,000 Unfavorable
Variable-overhead spending variance	23,000 Unfavorable
Fixed-overhead budget variance	40,000 Favorable
Fixed-overhead production-volume variance	100,000 Unfavorable
Net overhead variance	$ 98,000 Unfavorable

The overhead spending variance needed for the three-way analysis is simply the sum of the variable-overhead spending variance ($23,000 unfavorable) and the fixed-overhead budget variance ($40,000 favorable). Thus, the three-way analysis of overhead variances would be as follows:

Overhead spending variance	$ 17,000 Favorable
Variable-overhead efficiency variance	15,000 Unfavorable
Fixed-overhead production-volume variance	100,000 Unfavorable
Net overhead variance	$ 98,000 Unfavorable

The overhead flexible-budget variance used in two-way analysis is the sum of the following variances:

Variable-overhead efficiency variance	$ 15,000 Unfavorable
Variable-overhead spending variance	23,000 Unfavorable
Fixed-overhead budget variance	40,000 Favorable
Overhead flexible-budget variance	$ 2,000 Favorable

Therefore, you have the following two-way analysis of overhead variances:

Overhead flexible-budget variance	$ 2,000 Favorable
Fixed-overhead production-volume variance	100,000 Unfavorable
Net overhead variance	$ 98,000 Unfavorable

The one-way analysis of overhead variances simply reflects the difference between actual overhead costs and applied overhead costs. Actual overhead costs of $1,378,000 were given in the problem. Standard variable-overhead applied is found using equation 7.3:

$$SVOA = TSHDL \times SVOR$$
$$= 160,000 \times \$3.00$$
$$= \$480,000$$

Use equation 7.4 to find standard fixed overhead applied.

$$SFOA = TSHDL \times SFOR$$
$$= 160,000 \times \$5.00$$
$$= \$800,000$$

Total overhead applied equals $480,000 + $800,000 = $1,280,000.

Actual overhead costs	$1,378,000
Applied overhead costs	1,280,000
Underapplied overhead variance	$ 98,000 Unfavorable

The overhead variance is underapplied and unfavorable because actual overhead costs were greater than applied overhead costs. [See Section 7-6.]

PROBLEM 7-9: Northern Company has prepared the following summary of overhead costs for May 19X2:

Actual variable-overhead costs	$73,000
Actual fixed-overhead costs	$17,000
Total standard direct labor hours allowed for production	32,000
Standard variable-overhead rate per direct labor hour	$ 2.50
Standard fixed-overhead rate per direct labor hour	$ 0.50

On the basis of this information, compute the total underapplied or overapplied overhead for Northern Company.

Solution: To find the total underapplied or overapplied overhead, you must know the total actual overhead costs and total overhead costs applied. From the given information, you would compute the total overhead costs applied as follows:

Actual variable-overhead costs	$73,000
Actual fixed-overhead costs	17,000
Actual total overhead incurred	$90,000

Standard variable-overhead applied:	
TSHDL × SVOR = 32,000 × $2.50 =	$80,000
Standard fixed-overhead applied:	
TSHDL × SFOR = 32,000 × $0.50 =	16,000
Total overhead costs applied	$96,000

You can now compute the total underapplied or overapplied overhead costs.

Actual total overhead incurred	$90,000
Standard total overhead applied	96,000
Overapplied overhead	$ 6,000

Overhead is overapplied because actual overhead is less than applied overhead. The $6,000 represents a net favorable overhead variance when using a one-way analysis of overhead variances. [See Sections 7-2 and 7-5.]

Problems 7-10 and 7-11 are based on the following data.

The following information is available for Tadich Company for the month of September 19X1:

Total actual overhead costs	$32,000
Budgeted fixed overhead	$ 9,000
Standard direct-labor hours for budgeted production	12,000
Total standard direct-labor hours for actual production	15,000
Actual direct-labor hours used	14,500
Standard fixed-overhead rate per direct labor hour	$ 0.75
Standard variable-overhead rate per direct labor hour	$ 1.50

PROBLEM 7-10: Tadich Company uses a two-way analysis of overhead variances. Compute the overhead flexible-budget variance for the month of September.

Solution: In order to solve this problem, we must first use equation 7.5 to compute the flexible budget overhead costs based on total standard direct labor hours allowed for actual production (see Exhibit 7-1).

$$\text{FBOC} = \text{BFO} + (\text{TSHDL} \times \text{SVOR})$$
$$= \$9{,}000 + (15{,}000 \times \$1.50)$$
$$= \$31{,}500$$

The overhead flexible-budget variance would be computed as follows:

$$\begin{array}{ccc} \text{Overhead flexible-} \\ \text{budget variance} \end{array} = \begin{array}{c} \text{Total actual} \\ \text{overhead} \end{array} - \begin{array}{c} \text{Flexible budget for total} \\ \text{overhead based on standard} \\ \text{direct labor hours allowed} \\ \text{for actual production} \end{array}$$

$$\boxed{\text{OFBV} = \text{TAO} - \text{FBOC}}$$

$$= \$32{,}000 - \$31{,}500$$
$$= \$500 \text{ unfavorable}$$

The overhead flexible-budget variance is unfavorable because the actual overhead costs are greater than the flexible budget for overhead costs based on standard direct labor hours for actual production. [See Section 7-6.]

PROBLEM 7-11: Compute the fixed-overhead production-volume variance for the month of September.

Solution: You would solve this problem using equation 7.9:

$$\text{FOPVV} = \text{BFO} - \text{SFOA}$$

We must first compute SFOA, using equation 7.4:

$$\text{SFOA} = \text{TSHDL} \times \text{SFOR}$$
$$= 15{,}000 \times \$0.75$$
$$= \$11{,}250$$

You can now compute the fixed-overhead production-volume variance:

$$\text{FOPVV} = \text{BFO} - \text{SFOA}$$
$$= \$9{,}000 - \$11{,}250$$
$$= \$2{,}250 \text{ favorable}$$

The variance is favorable because budgeted fixed-overhead costs are less than applied fixed-overhead costs. [See Sections 7-2 and 7-4.]

PROBLEM 7-12: Grant Company, which uses a standard costing system, has provided the following information for the month of December:

Actual fixed-overhead costs	$340,000
Budgeted fixed-overhead costs	$355,000
Standard fixed-overhead costs applied to production	$330,000

On the basis of this information, compute the fixed-overhead budget variance and the fixed-overhead production-volume variance.

Solution: You would compute the fixed-overhead budget variance using equation 7.8:

$$\text{FOBV} = \text{BFO} - \text{AFO}$$
$$= \$355{,}000 - \$340{,}000$$
$$= \$15{,}000 \text{ favorable}$$

The fixed-overhead budget variance is favorable because the actual fixed-overhead costs are less than the budgeted fixed-overhead costs.

You would use equation 7.9 to compute the fixed-overhead production-volume variance:

$$FOPVV = BFO - SFOA$$
$$= \$355,000 - \$330,000$$
$$= \$25,000 \text{ unfavorable}$$

This variance is unfavorable because budgeted fixed overhead is greater than applied fixed overhead, which implies that budgeted production volume was greater than actual production volume. [See Section 7-4.]

MIDTERM EXAMINATION

Chapters 1–7

DIRECTIONS: This examination consists of two parts worth a total of **100 points**. Part I contains multiple-choice questions that cover basic concepts from chapters 1–7. Part II contains multiple-choice problems that involve numerical calculations. You should be able to complete the examination in approximately **90 minutes**. The answers to the examination questions and problems are included at the end of the examination.

Part I: Multiple-Choice Questions (30 points)

1. The primary purpose of cost and management accounting is to provide information to
   - **(a)** stockholders
   - **(b)** creditors
   - **(c)** external decision makers
   - **(d)** internal decision makers

2. The accounting position within an organization that is responsible for general accounting, planning and control, tax administration, and internal auditing is the
   - **(a)** treasurer
   - **(b)** president
   - **(c)** controller
   - **(d)** none of the above

3. Prime costs consist of direct materials costs and
   - **(a)** factory overhead costs
   - **(b)** direct labor costs
   - **(c)** selling and administration costs

4. Conversion costs consist of direct labor costs and
   - **(a)** direct materials costs
   - **(b)** factory overhead costs
   - **(c)** selling and administration costs

5. The production costing system that is used by organizations whose products can be identified by individual jobs or batches is
   - **(a)** process costing
   - **(b)** job-order costing

6. The production costing system that is used by organizations whose products are mass-produced through a continuous series of production steps is
   - **(a)** process costing
   - **(b)** job-order costing

7. Average costs per unit are used in
   - **(a)** process costing
   - **(b)** job-order costing
   - **(c)** both process costing and job-order costing

8. Equivalent units of production are computed by multiplying physical units by the percentage of completion.
   - **(a)** true
   - **(b)** false

9. A master budget usually includes the following:
   - **(a)** budgeted balance sheet
   - **(b)** budgeted income statement
   - **(c)** cash budget
   - **(d)** production budget
   - **(e)** all of the above

10. Preparation of the operating budget usually begins with the preparation of the
    - **(a)** production budget
    - **(b)** sales budget
    - **(c)** cash budget
    - **(d)** none of the above

11. The direct materials price variance is favorable if the actual price per unit of direct materials is

(a) greater than the standard price per unit of direct materials
(b) less than the standard price per unit of direct materials
(c) equal to the standard price per unit of direct materials

12. The direct labor efficiency variance is favorable if the standard number of direct labor hours allowed for production is
    (a) greater than the actual number of direct labor hours used
    (b) less than the actual number of direct labor hours used
    (c) equal to the actual number of direct labor hours used

13. The direct labor rate variance is favorable if the standard rate per direct labor hour is
    (a) greater than the actual rate per direct labor hour
    (b) less than the actual rate per direct labor hour
    (c) equal to the actual rate per direct labor hour

14. The variable overhead spending variance is favorable if the standard variable overhead rate times the actual direct labor hours used in production is
    (a) less than the actual variable overhead costs
    (b) equal to the actual variable overhead costs
    (c) greater than the actual variable overhead costs

15. The fixed overhead budget variance is computed as the difference between budgeted fixed overhead costs and
    (a) applied fixed overhead costs
    (b) actual fixed overhead costs
    (c) standard fixed overhead costs

Part II: Multiple-Choice Problems (70 points)

Problems 1–6 are based on the following data:

	Ending balance	Beginning balance
Finished Goods Inventory	$ 90,000	$110,000
Work-in-Process Inventory	80,000	70,000
Direct Materials Inventory	100,000	90,000

Costs incurred during the period:

Direct materials used	$200,000
Factory overhead costs	$150,000
Total production costs	$575,000

1. Direct materials purchased during the period were
   (a) $200,000   (b) $210,000   (c) $190,000   (d) $100,000   (e) none of the above

2. Direct labor costs incurred during the period were
   (a) $225,000   (b) $200,000   (c) $150,000   (d) $250,000   (e) none of the above

3. The cost of goods manufactured for the period was
   (a) $575,000   (b) $475,000   (c) $425,000   (d) $565,000   (e) none of the above

4. The cost of goods sold during the period was
   (a) $585,000   (b) $600,000   (c) $575,000   (d) $425,000   (e) none of the above

5. The prime costs transferred to Work-in-Process Inventory during the period were
   (a) $575,000   (b) $450,000   (c) $475,000   (d) $425,000   (e) none of the above

6. The conversion costs incurred during the period were
   (a) $375,000   (b) $575,000   (c) $425,000   (d) $475,000   (e) none of the above

Problems 7–12 are based on the following data for the XYZ Company:

Direct materials purchased on account	$100,000
Direct materials issued to production	$150,000
Direct labor costs incurred	
(10,000 direct labor hours)	$ 92,000
Factory overhead costs incurred	$ 92,000
Budgeted factory overhead costs	
(at 8,000 budgeted direct-labor hours)	$ 72,000

The XYZ Company uses a job-order costing system. Assume that factory overhead costs are applied to production based on direct labor hours.

7. The predetermined overhead rate per direct labor hour is
   (a) $8.00   (b) $9.00   (c) $7.20   (d) $9.20   (e) none of the above

8. The factory overhead costs applied are
   (a) $90,000   (b) $92,000   (c) $80,000   (d) $82,000   (e) none of the above

9. Which of the following journal entries records the purchase of direct materials?
(a)	Materials Control	$ 92,000	
	Work-in-Process Control		$ 92,000
(b)	Materials Control	$110,000	
	Accounts Payable		$110,000
(c)	Materials Control	$100,000	
	Work-in-Process Control		$100,000
(d)	Materials Control	$100,000	
	Accounts Payable		$100,000
(e)	none of the above		

10. Which of the following journal entries records the direct labor costs incurred?
(a)	Accrued Payroll	$92,000	
	Work-in-Process Control		$92,000
(b)	Work-in-Process Control	$92,000	
	Accrued Payroll		$92,000
(c)	Work-in-Process Control	$92,000	
	Finished Goods Inventory		$92,000
(d)	Finished Goods Inventory	$92,000	
	Accrued Payroll		$92,000
(e)	none of the above		

11. Which of the following journal entries records the factory overhead costs applied?
(a)	Factory Overhead Applied	$90,000	
	Factory Overhead Control		$90,000
(b)	Factory Overhead Applied	$90,000	
	Work-in-Process Inventory		$90,000
(c)	Work-in-Process Inventory	$90,000	
	Factory Overhead Control		$90,000
(d)	Work-in-Process Inventory	$90,000	
	Factory Overhead Applied		$90,000
(e)	none of the above		

12. The factory overhead costs for the XYZ Company were
   (a) $2,000 underapplied   (d) $4,000 overapplied
   (b) $2,000 overapplied   (e) none of the above
   (c) $4,000 underapplied

Problems 13–18 are based on the following information for ABC Company.

	PHYSICAL UNITS	EQUIVALENT UNITS direct materials	EQUIVALENT UNITS conversion costs
Beginning WIP inventory	10,000	10,000	4,000
Percentage completed		100%	40%
Units started	40,000		
Current production		40,000	42,000
Ending WIP inventory	8,000	8,000	4,000
Percentage completed		100%	50%
Units completed	42,000	42,000	42,000

Production costs:	direct materials	conversion costs
Beginning WIP inventory	$10,000	$ 6,200
Current production costs	50,000	113,400
Total production costs	$60,000	$119,600

The ABC Company uses a process costing system. Assume that direct materials are applied to units of production at the beginning of the production process and that conversion costs are applied to units of production uniformly throughout the production process.

13. Using the weighted-average method, the cost per equivalent unit for direct materials is
    (a) $1.25   (b) $1.20   (c) $1.50   (d) $1.00   (e) none of the above

14. Using the weighted-average method, the cost per equivalent unit for conversion costs is
    (a) $2.60   (b) $2.65   (c) $2.50   (d) $2.55   (e) none of the above

15. Using the FIFO method, the cost per equivalent unit for direct materials is
    (a) $1.00   (b) $1.20   (c) $1.25   (d) $1.30   (e) none of the above

16. Using the FIFO method, the cost per equivalent unit for conversion costs is
    (a) $2.70   (b) $2.60   (c) $2.65   (d) $2.55   (e) none of the above

17. Assume that the cost per equivalent unit using the weighted-average method is $1.00 for direct materials and $2.00 for conversion costs. The amount of production costs allocated to ending Work-in-Process Inventory is
    (a) $8,000   (b) $16,000   (c) $24,000   (d) $12,000   (e) none of the above

18. Assume that the cost per equivalent unit using the FIFO method is $1.20 for direct materials and $2.20 for conversion costs. The amount of production costs allocated to ending WIP Inventory is
    (a) $16,000   (b) $18,000   (c) $18,400   (d) $24,000   (e) none of the above

Problems 19–24 are based on the following information:

	Budgeted beginning balance	Budgeted ending balance
Direct Materials Inventory (pounds)	20,000	30,000
Work-in-Process Inventory (units)	–0–	–0–
Finished Goods Inventory (units)	50,000	40,000

Budgeted sales in units	100,000
Selling price per unit	$5.00
Budgeted total production costs per unit	$3.00
Budgeted direct materials per unit	1 pound

19. The budgeted sales revenue is
(a) $300,000   (b) $500,000   (c) $200,000   (d) $350,000   (e) none of the above

20. The budgeted production in units is
(a) 100,000 units
(b) 90,000 units
(c) 80,000 units
(d) 120,000 units
(e) none of the above

21. The budgeted direct materials usage (in pounds) is
(a) 100,000 pounds
(b) 90,000 pounds
(c) 80,000 pounds
(d) 120,000 pounds
(e) none of the above

22. The budgeted direct materials purchased are
(a) 100,000 pounds
(b) 110,000 pounds
(c) 80,000 pounds
(d) 120,000 pounds
(e) none of the above

23. The budgeted cost of goods sold is
(a) $500,000   (b) $300,000   (c) $200,000   (d) $350,000   (e) none of the above

24. The budgeted cost of goods manufactured is
(a) $270,000   (b) $300,000   (c) $500,000   (d) $450,000   (e) none of the above

Problems 25–30 are based on the following information:

Standard price per pound of direct materials	$5.00/lb
Standard quantity of direct materials needed per unit of production	10 lbs
Actual price per pound of direct materials	$6.00/lb
Actual quantity of direct materials used in production	42,000 lbs
Quantity of direct materials purchased	50,000 lbs
Actual production in units	4,000 units
Standard rate per direct labor hour	$10.00/hr
Actual rate per direct labor hour	$9.00/hr
Standard direct labor hours per unit	2 hrs/unit
Actual direct labor hours used	9,000 hrs

25. The direct materials price variance (recorded when direct materials are purchased) is
(a) $50,000 favorable
(b) $50,000 unfavorable
(c) $40,000 favorable
(d) $40,000 unfavorable
(e) none of the above

26. The direct materials quantity variance is
(a) $10,000 favorable
(b) $10,000 unfavorable
(c) $20,000 favorable
(d) $20,000 unfavorable
(e) none of the above

27. The direct labor rate variance is
(a) $9,000 favorable
(b) $9,000 unfavorable
(c) $10,000 favorable
(d) $10,000 unfavorable
(e) none of the above

28. The direct labor efficiency variance is
(a) $9,000 favorable
(b) $9,000 unfavorable
(c) $10,000 favorable
(d) $10,000 unfavorable
(e) none of the above

29. Which of the following journal entries records the issuance of direct materials to production (direct materials price variance is recorded when direct materials are purchased)?

  (a) Work-in-Process Control $200,000

          Direct Materials Quantity Variance   10,000

              Materials Control $210,000

  (b) Work-in-Process Control $210,000

          Direct Materials Quantity Variance $ 10,000

          Materials Control   200,000

  (c) Work-in-Process Control $200,000

          Materials Control $200,000

  (d) Work-in-Process Control $210,000

          Materials Control $210,000

  (e) none of the above

30. Which of the following journal entries records the direct labor variances?

  (a) Work-in-Process Control $80,000

          Accrued Payroll $80,000

  (b) Work-in-Process Control $80,000

          Direct Labor Efficiency Variance   10,000

              Direct Labor Rate Variance $ 9,000

              Accrued Payroll   81,000

  (c) Work-in-Process Control $80,000

          Direct Labor Rate Variance   10,000

              Direct Labor Efficiency Variance $ 9,000

              Accrued Payroll   81,000

  (d) Work-in-Process Control $90,000

          Accrued Payroll $90,000

  (e) none of the above

Problems 31–35 are based on the following information:

Budgeted fixed overhead	
(at 10,000 budgeted direct labor hours)	$60,000
Standard fixed-overhead rate per direct labor hour	$6.00/hr
Standard variable-overhead rate per direct labor hour	$8.00/hr
Actual fixed overhead	$50,000
Actual variable overhead	$70,000
Actual direct labor hours	9,500
Standard direct labor hours allowed for production	9,000

Assume that overhead costs are applied to production based on direct labor hours.

31. The variable-overhead spending variance is

  (a) $6,000 favorable   **(d)** $4,000 unfavorable

  (b) $6,000 unfavorable   **(e)** none of the above

  (c) $4,000 favorable

32. The variable-overhead efficiency variance is

  (a) $6,000 favorable   **(d)** $4,000 unfavorable

  (b) $6,000 unfavorable   **(e)** none of the above

  (c) $4,000 favorable

33. The fixed-overhead budget variance is

  (a) $10,000 favorable   **(d)** $6,000 unfavorable

  (b) $10,000 unfavorable   **(e)** none of the above

  (c) $6,000 favorable

34. The fixed-overhead production-volume variance is

(a) $10,000 favorable

(b) $10,000 unfavorable

(c) $6,000 favorable

(d) $6,000 unfavorable

(e) none of the above

35. The total underapplied or overapplied overhead is

(a) $6,000 underapplied

(b) $6,000 overapplied

(c) $10,000 underapplied

(d) $10,000 overapplied

(e) none of the above

Answers

DIRECTIONS: Score your examination as follows: In Part 1, score 2 points for each of the 15 items that you answered correctly. In Part 2, score 2 points for each of the 35 items that you answered correctly. **Total possible points: 100.**

Part I: Multiple-Choice Questions

1. (d)	2. (c)	3. (b)	4. (b)	5. (b)
6. (a)	7. (c)	8. (a)	9. (e)	10. (b)
11. (b)	12. (a)	13. (a)	14. (c)	15. (b)

Part II: Multiple-Choice Problems

1. (b)	2. (a)	3. (d)	4. (a)	5. (d)
6. (a)	7. (b)	8. (a)	9. (d)	10. (b)
11. (d)	12. (a)	13. (b)	14. (a)	15. (c)
16. (a)	17. (b)	18. (c)	19. (b)	20. (b)
21. (a)	22. (b)	23. (b)	24. (a)	25. (b)
26. (b)	27. (a)	28. (d)	29. (a)	30. (b)
31. (a)	32. (d)	33. (a)	34. (d)	35. (b)

8 COST ALLOCATIONS: SERVICE DEPARTMENTS AND JOINT PRODUCTS

THIS CHAPTER IS ABOUT

☑ Cost Allocation Concepts
☑ Service Department Cost Allocation
☑ Joint-Product Cost Allocation
☑ Accounting for Byproducts

8-1. Cost Allocation Concepts

Cost allocation is the process of assigning costs to cost objectives within a firm. Cost objectives are the objects (e.g., departments or products) for which a separate measurement of cost is desired. For example, service department cost allocation involves the assignment of service department costs to production departments (the cost objectives) within a factory. A cost allocation base is a systematic measure used to allocate costs to cost objectives. For example, the number of employees in a production department may be used as the cost allocation base for allocating service department costs to the production department.

Costs are allocated for a variety of reasons. In product costing, costs are allocated to units of production to determine the value of inventory and the cost of goods sold. Costs are allocated to departments within an organization to measure departmental performance and to motivate managers to use resources efficiently.

This chapter will discuss two types of cost allocation: the allocation of service department costs and the allocation of joint product costs.

8-2. Service Department Cost Allocation

Service departments within a factory provide services to production departments as well as to other service departments, but are not directly involved in the production process. Cafeterias and maintenance departments within a factory are examples of service departments. Production departments are directly involved in the production process. An example of a production department is an assembly department.

The process of cost allocation initially involves two decisions: choosing the cost objectives and choosing a cost allocation base. The purpose of service department cost allocation is to assign service department costs to the production departments (i.e., the cost objectives). The service department costs that are allocated to production departments are classified as factory overhead costs, and within a production department, all factory overhead costs are applied to units of production. Exhibit 8-1 illustrates the allocation of service department costs to production departments and the subsequent application of factory overhead costs to units of production.

The cost allocation base for a service department should reflect the type of service provided to other departments and should be relatively easy to measure. Note that the cost allocation base does not have to be the same for all service departments. Following is a list of some types of service departments and their possible cost allocation bases.

Factory Service Department	Possible Cost Allocation Base
Administration	Total labor hours
Maintenance	Square footage, machine hours, or total labor hours
Cafeteria	Number of employees
Personnel	Number of employees
Engineering	Direct labor hours

EXHIBIT 8-1

Direct Method of Service Department Cost
Allocation and Application of Factory Overhead
Costs

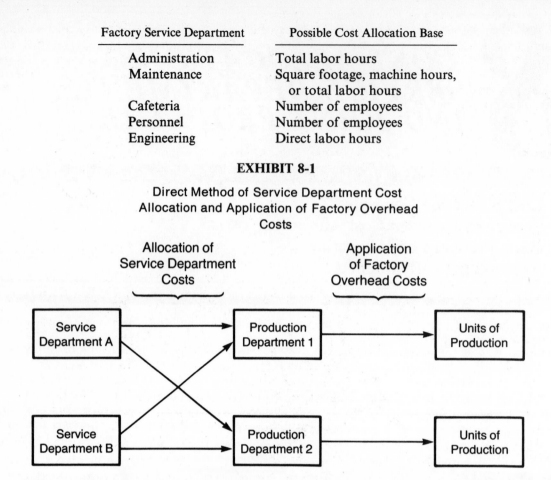

There are two methods of service department cost allocation: the direct method and the step method.

A. The direct method

Under the direct method, each service department's cost is allocated directly to the production departments, with no cost allocation from one service department to another. The cost allocation bases would be chosen based on the type of services provided to each production department. For example, the cost allocation base for factory cafeteria costs could be the number of employees in all production departments while the cost allocation base for the administration costs could be the total labor hours for all production departments.

The following three steps are used to allocate service department costs using the direct method.

DIRECT METHOD

STEP 1. FIND THE TOTAL COST ALLOCATION BASE FOR ALL PRODUCTION DEPARTMENTS THAT RECEIVED SERVICES.

Add together each production department's base to find the total cost allocation base. For example, if number of employees was chosen as the cost allocation base, the total cost allocation base would be found by adding together the number of employees in each production department that received services.

STEP 2. FIND EACH PRODUCTION DEPARTMENT'S PROPORTION OF THE TOTAL COST ALLOCATION BASE.

Do this by developing a fraction for each production department—the numerator is the production department's cost allocation base and the denominator is the total cost allocation base. Convert each fraction to a percentage.

STEP 3. ALLOCATE THE SERVICE DEPARTMENT COST TO THE PRODUCTION DEPARTMENTS.

To do this, multiply the service department cost by the percentages that you found in Step 2.

EXAMPLE 8-1: Northern Manufacturing Company has two service departments—factory administration and factory maintenance—and two production departments—machining and assembly. The company uses the direct method of service department cost allocation. Factory administration costs are allocated to other departments based on the total labor hours, and factory maintenance costs are allocated based on square footage.

The following information is available for the month of June:

	Service Department		Production Department	
	Factory Administration	Factory Maintenance	Machining	Assembly
Department overhead costs	$12,000	$10,000	$800,000	$600,000
Total labor hours	1,000	2,220	8,000	12,000
Square footage	800	1,000	3,000	1,000

Assume that the service departments provide services to each other. On the basis of the information provided, allocate service department costs using the direct method.

Under the direct method, service department costs are allocated directly to the production departments. Therefore, even if the service departments provide service to one another, the cost allocation base is restricted to the production departments.

Use the three steps presented above to allocate service department costs. Remember that each service department's cost is allocated separately.

Factory Administration

STEP 1. FIND THE TOTAL COST ALLOCATION BASE FOR ALL PRODUCTION DEPARTMENTS THAT RECEIVED SERVICES.

Both the machining and assembly departments received services from the factory administration department. Factory administration costs are allocated based on total labor hours. Total labor hours for the machining and assembly departments are 8,000 and 12,000, respectively. Therefore, the total cost allocation base is 8,000 + 12,000 = 20,000 total labor hours.

STEP 2. FIND EACH PRODUCTION DEPARTMENT'S PROPORTION OF THE TOTAL COST ALLOCATION BASE.

Develop a fraction for both the machining and assembly departments. The numerator is the production department's cost allocation base and the denominator is the total cost allocation base. Convert each fraction to a percentage.

$$\text{Machining} \qquad \text{Assembly}$$
$$\frac{8,000}{20,000} = 40\% \qquad \frac{12,000}{20,000} = 60\%$$

STEP 3. ALLOCATE THE SERVICE DEPARTMENT COST TO THE PRODUCTION DEPARTMENTS.

The factory administration cost is $12,000. Multiply this cost by the percentages that you found in Step 2.

$$\text{Machining} \qquad\qquad \text{Assembly}$$
$$\$12,000 \times 40\% = \$4,800 \qquad \$12,000 \times 60\% = \$7,200$$

Factory Maintenance

STEP 1. FIND THE TOTAL COST ALLOCATION BASE FOR ALL PRODUCTION DEPARTMENTS THAT RECEIVED SERVICES.

Both the machining and assembly departments received services from the factory maintenance department. Factory maintenance costs are allocated based on square footage. Total square footage for the machining and assembly departments are 3,000 and 1,000, respectively. Therefore, the total cost allocation base is 3,000 + 1,000 = 4,000 square feet.

STEP 2. FIND EACH PRODUCTION DEPARTMENT'S PROPORTION OF THE TOTAL COST ALLOCATION BASE.

Develop a fraction for both the machining and assembly departments. The numerator is the production department's cost allocation base and the denominator is the total cost allocation base. Convert each fraction to a percentage.

$$\text{Machining} \qquad \text{Assembly}$$
$$\frac{3,000}{4,000} = 75\% \qquad \frac{1,000}{4,000} = 25\%$$

STEP 3. ALLOCATE THE SERVICE DEPARTMENT COST TO THE PRODUCTION DEPARTMENTS.

The factory maintenance cost is $10,000. Multiply this cost by the percentages that you found in Step 2.

Machining	Assembly
$10,000 × 75% = $7,500	$10,000 × 25% = $2,500

The following table summarizes the preceding three steps of cost allocation for the direct method.

	Service Department		Production Department		
	Factory Administration	Factory Maintenance	Machining	Assembly	Total
Department overhead costs	$12,000	$10,000			
Factory administration:					
Total labor hours			8,000	12,000	20,000
Proportion of total labor hours			$\frac{8,000}{20,000}$ = 40%	$\frac{12,000}{20,000}$ = 60%	
Allocation of factory administration costs:					
($12,000 × 40%)			$ 4,800		
($12,000 × 60%)				$ 7,200	$12,000
Factory maintenance:					
Square footage			3,000	1,000	4,000
Proportion of total square footage			$\frac{3,000}{4,000}$ = 75%	$\frac{1,000}{4,000}$ = 25%	
Allocation of factory maintenance costs:					
($10,000 × 75%)			$ 7,500		
($10,000 × 25%)				$ 2,500	$10,000

Exhibit 8-2 illustrates the allocation of overhead costs to the production departments using the direct method.

EXHIBIT 8-2

Direct Method of Service Department Cost Allocation

	Service Department		Production Department		
	Factory Administration	Factory Maintenance	Machining	Assembly	Total
Department overhead costs	$12,000	$10,000	$800,000	$600,000	$1,422,000
Allocation of costs:					
Factory administration:					
($12,000 × 40%)			4,800		
($12,000 × 60%)				7,200	
Factory maintenance:					
($10,000 × 75%)			7,500		
($10,000 × 25%)				2,500	
Total overhead of production departments			$812,300	$609,700	$1,422,000

B. The step method

The step method (also known as the step-down or sequential method) of service department cost allocation involves the allocation of service department costs from one service department to another in a particular sequence or order. The total costs that are allocated to each service department are included with that department's costs, and the total is then allocated to the remaining service and production departments. The step method partially recognizes that services are rendered by one service department to another.

The following four steps are used to allocate service department costs using the step method.

STEP METHOD

STEP 1. DETERMINE THE SEQUENCE OF SERVICE DEPARTMENT COST ALLOCATION.

Begin with the service department that provides services to the greatest number of other service departments. If two or more departments provide services to the same number of other service departments, assign the first position in the sequence to the department with the largest total costs.

STEP 2. FIND THE TOTAL COST ALLOCATION BASE FOR *ALL* DEPARTMENTS TO WHICH COSTS WILL BE ALLOCATED.

Add together each department's base to find the total cost allocation base.

STEP 3. FIND EACH DEPARTMENT'S PROPORTION OF THE TOTAL COST ALLOCATION BASE.

Do this by developing a fraction for each department—the numerator is the department's cost allocation base and the denominator is the total cost allocation base. Convert each fraction to a percentage.

STEP 4. ALLOCATE THE SERVICE DEPARTMENT COSTS.

Multiply the service department cost by the percentages that you found in Step 3.

EXAMPLE 8-2: From the information in Example 8-1, use the step method to allocate service department costs to the other departments. The cost allocation bases are given in Example 8-1.

Use the four steps outlined above to allocate the service department costs under the step method.

STEP 1. DETERMINE THE SEQUENCE OF SERVICE DEPARTMENT COST ALLOCATION.

Note that both service departments provide services to each other. Therefore, because factory administration has the largest total costs, the sequence of departments for cost allocation begins with factory administration. Exhibit 8-3 illustrates the sequence of cost allocation under the step method.

<u>Factory Administration</u>

STEP 2. FIND THE TOTAL COST ALLOCATION BASE FOR ALL DEPARTMENTS TO WHICH COSTS WILL BE ALLOCATED.

Factory administration costs must be allocated to the factory maintenance department and the machining and assembly departments. Factory administration costs are allocated based on total labor hours. Total labor hours for factory maintenance, machining and assembly are 2,220, 8,000, and 12,000, respectively. Therefore, the total cost allocation base is 2,220 + 8,000 + 12,000 = 22,220 total labor hours.

STEP 3. FIND EACH DEPARTMENT'S PROPORTION OF THE TOTAL COST ALLOCATION BASE.

Develop a fraction for each department that received services. The numerator is the department's cost allocation base and the denominator is the total cost allocation base. Convert each fraction to a percentage.

Factory Maintenance	Machining	Assembly
$\dfrac{2,220}{22,220} = 10\%\,^*$	$\dfrac{8,000}{22,220} = 36\%\,^*$	$\dfrac{12,000}{22,220} = 54\%\,^*$

* rounded

EXHIBIT 8-3

Step Method: Sequence of Departments for Cost
Allocation for Northern Manufacturing Company

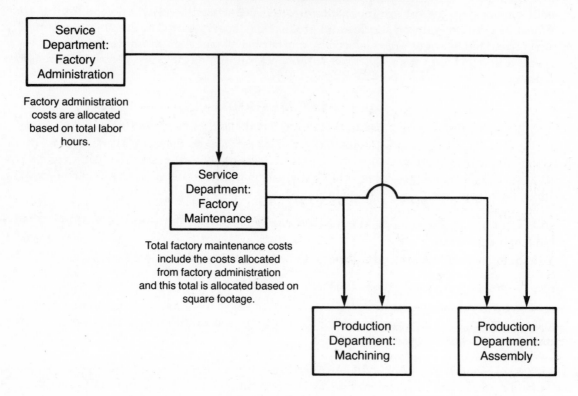

STEP 4. ALLOCATE THE SERVICE DEPARTMENT COSTS.

Multiply the factory administration cost by the percentages that you found in Step 3.

Factory Maintenance	Machining	Assembly
$12,000 × 10% = $1,200	$12,000 × 36% = $4,320	$12,000 × 54% = $6,480

Factory Maintenance

STEP 2. FIND THE TOTAL COST ALLOCATION BASE FOR ALL DEPARTMENTS TO WHICH COSTS WILL BE ALLOCATED.

Factory maintenance costs must be allocated to the machining and assembly departments. Factory maintenance costs are allocated based on square footage. Total square footage for machining and assembly is 3,000 and 1,000, respectively. Therefore, the total cost allocation base is 3,000 + 1,000 = 4,000 square feet.

STEP 3. FIND EACH DEPARTMENT'S PROPORTION OF THE TOTAL COST ALLOCATION BASE.

Develop a fraction for each department that received services. The numerator is the department's cost allocation base and the denominator is the total cost allocation base. Convert each fraction to a percentage.

Machining	Assembly
$\dfrac{3,000}{4,000} = 75\%$	$\dfrac{1,000}{4,000} = 25\%$

STEP 4. ALLOCATE THE SERVICE DEPARTMENT COSTS.

Factory maintenance costs were $10,000. When we allocated the factory administration costs, we allocated $1,200 of those costs to factory maintenance. Therefore, we now have $10,000 + $1,200 = $11,200 of total factory maintenance costs to allocate. Multiply total factory maintenance costs by the percentages that you found in Step 3.

Machining	Assembly
$11,200 × 75% = $8,400	$11,200 × 25% = $2,800

The following table summarizes the preceding four steps of cost allocation for the step method.

	Service Department		Production Department		
	Factory Administration	Factory Maintenance	Machining	Assembly	Total
Department overhead costs	$12,000	$10,000			
Factory administration: Total labor hours		2,220	8,000	12,000	22,220
Proportion of total labor hours		$\frac{2,220}{22,220}$ = 10%	$\frac{8,000}{22,220}$ = 36%	$\frac{12,000}{22,220}$ = 54%	
Allocation of factory administration costs: ($12,000 × 10%) ($12,000 × 36%) ($12,000 × 54%)		$ 1,200	$ 4,320	$ 6,480	$12,000
Factory maintenance costs		10,000			
Total factory maintenance costs to allocate		$11,200			
Square footage			3,000	1,000	4,000
Proportion of total square footage			$\frac{3,000}{4,000}$ = 75%	$\frac{1,000}{4,000}$ = 25%	
Allocation of factory maintenance costs: ($11,200 × 75%) ($11,200 × 25%)			$ 8,400	$ 2,800	$11,200

Exhibit 8-4 illustrates the allocation of overhead costs to the production departments using the step method.

EXHIBIT 8-4

Step Method of Service Department Cost Allocation

	Service Department		Production Department		
	Factory Administration	Factory Maintenance	Machining	Assembly	Total
Department overhead costs	$12,000	$10,000	$800,000	$600,000	$1,422,000
Allocation of costs: Factory administration: ($12,000 × 10%) ($12,000 × 36%) ($12,000 × 54%)		1,200 $11,200	4,320	6,480	
Factory maintenance: ($11,200 × 75%) ($11,200 × 25%)			8,400	2,800	
Total overhead of production departments			$812,720	$609,280	$1,422,000

8-3. Joint-Product Cost Allocation

Joint products are products that are produced together and are not readily identifiable as individual products until a certain point in the production process. The *split-off point* is the point in the production process where joint products become separately identifiable. *Joint costs* (or joint-product costs) are the costs of producing joint products before the split-off point. *Separable costs* are the costs of producing joint products after the split-off point. Joint costs and separable costs generally include direct materials, direct labor, and factory overhead costs. Exhibit 8-5 presents an illustration of the production of two joint products.

The purpose of joint-product cost allocation is to allocate joint costs to the joint products, which are the cost objectives. The cost allocation base is determined by the joint-product cost allocation method used. There are three methods of joint-production cost allocation: (1) the physical units method, (2) the sales value method, and (3) the net realizable value method.

A. Physical units method

The physical units method uses some physical measure, such as pounds, gallons, or units of production, as the base for allocating joint costs to joint products. For example, if two joint products can be measured in terms of gallons, you can use the proportion of gallons for each product to allocate joint costs to the two products. To allocate the costs, you would multiply the proportion of the total base for each product by the joint costs.

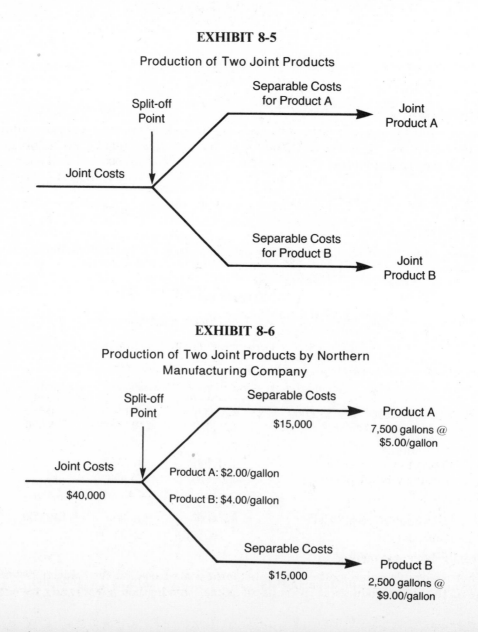

EXHIBIT 8-5

Production of Two Joint Products

EXHIBIT 8-6

Production of Two Joint Products by Northern
Manufacturing Company

EXAMPLE 8-3: Northern Manufacturing Company produces two joint products in its factory. The following information is available:

	Product A	Product B	Total
Joint costs			$40,000
Production in gallons	7,500	2,500	10,000
Separable costs	$15,000	$15,000	$30,000
Sales price per gallon at the split-off point	$2.00	$4.00	
Sales price per gallon at completion	$5.00	$9.00	

Exhibit 8-6 is an illustration of the production of the two joint products at Northern Manufacturing Company.

On the basis of this information, use the physical units method to allocate the joint costs to products A and B.

	Product A	Product B	Total
Production in gallons	7,500	2,500	10,000
Proportion of gallons of production	$\frac{7,500}{10,000}$ = 75%	$\frac{2,500}{10,000}$ = 25%	
Allocation of joint costs based on the proportion of gallons of production	$30,000 (75%)	$10,000 (25%)	$40,000

B. Sales value method

The sales value method allocates joint costs on the basis of the relative sales value of each joint product at the split-off point. You would compute this value by multiplying the sales price at the split-off point by the units of production. You would then find each product's proportion of the total sales value, and you use this proportion to allocate the joint costs.

EXAMPLE 8-4: From the information in Example 8-3, allocate the joint costs using the sales value method.

You must first compute the sales value at the split-off points for products A and B:

$$\text{Sales value at the split-off point for product A} = \$2.00 \times 7,500 \text{ gallons}$$
$$= \$15,000$$

$$\text{Sales value at the split -off point for product B} = \$4.00 \times 2,500$$
$$= \$10,000$$

These sales values would be used to allocate the joint costs as follows:

	Product A	Product B	Total
Sales value at the split-off point	$15,000	$10,000	$25,000
Proportion of sales value at the split-off point	$\frac{\$15,000}{\$25,000}$ = 60%	$\frac{\$10,000}{\$25,000}$ = 40%	
Allocation of joint costs	$24,000 (60%)	$16,000 (40%)	$40,000

C. Net realizable value method

The net realizable value method allocates joint costs based on the relative net realizable value of the joint products at the split-off point. This method is generally used when the sales value at the split-off point is not known. The net realizable value at the split-off point can be interpreted as an estimate of the sales value at the split-off point. You would compute the net realizable value at the split-off point as follows:

$$\text{A PC}$$

$$\frac{\text{Net realizable value}}{\text{at the split-off point}} = \frac{\text{Sales value}}{\text{at completion}} - \frac{\text{Separable}}{\text{costs}} \qquad (8.1)$$

EXAMPLE 8-5: From the information in Example 8-3, allocate the joint costs using the net realizable value method.

You would first use equation 8.1 to compute the net realizable value at the split-off point for the joint products:

$$\frac{\text{Net realizable value at the}}{\text{split-off point for Product A}} = (\$5.00 \times 7,500) - \$15,000$$

$$= \$37,500 - \$15,000$$

$$= \$22,500$$

$$\frac{\text{Net realizable value at the}}{\text{split-off point for Product B}} = (\$9.00 \times 2,500) - \$15,000$$

$$= \$22,500 - \$15,000$$

$$= \$7,500$$

Next, you would use these values to allocate the joint costs.

	Product A	Product B	Total
Net realizable value at the split-off point	$22,500	$ 7,500	$30,000
Proportion of net realizable value	$\frac{\$22,500}{\$30,000}$ = 75%	$\frac{\$ 7,500}{\$30,000}$ = 25%	
Allocation of joint costs based on net realizable value	$30,000 (75%)	$10,000 (25%)	$40,000

D. Joint products: Sell-or-process-further decision

A major decision involving joint products is whether to sell a joint product at the split-off point or at completion (after further processing). This decision is commonly referred to as the "sell-or-process-further decision." This decision should be based on the comparison of (1) sales value at the split-off point and (2) sales value at completion *minus* separable costs. The allocated joint costs are not relevant (see Chapter 11 for an explanation of relevant cost analysis) and should not affect the decision.

For Product A in Example 8-4, the decision to sell or process further would be based on the following comparison:

Sales value at the split-off point	$15,000
Sales value at completion minus separable costs ($37,500 − $15,000)	$22,500

Northern Manufacturing Company should process Product A further and sell it at completion rather than sell it at the split-off point. Remember that the joint costs are not relevant to the decision and are not considered in the analysis.

8-4. Accounting for Byproducts

A *byproduct* is a product with relatively minor sales value that is produced together with the major product. Byproducts differ from joint products in that byproducts have relatively minor sales value and joint products have relatively significant sales value.

Byproducts are accounted for differently than joint products. In one method of accounting for byproducts, the net realizable value of the byproducts sold is deducted from the cost of the major products sold. In another method, the net realizable value of the byproducts produced is deducted from the cost of the major products produced. The two methods are similar because they both involve deducting the net realizable value of the byproducts (sold or produced) from the cost of the major products (sold or produced).

RAISE YOUR GRADES

Can you explain...?

☑ what cost allocation is
☑ the purpose of cost allocation
☑ the process of cost allocation
☑ the differences between service departments and production departments
☑ the purpose of service department cost allocation
☑ how to choose a cost allocation base for service departments
☑ how to use the direct method of service department cost allocation
☑ how to use the step method of service department cost allocation
☑ how to determine the sequence of service departments when using the step method
☑ what joint products are
☑ the difference between joint costs and separable costs
☑ how to use the physical units method of joint-product cost allocation
☑ how to use the sales value method of joint-product cost allocation
☑ how to use the net realizable value method of joint-product cost allocation
☑ the relevant costs and revenues for the sell-or-process-further decision for joint products
☑ how to account for byproducts

SUMMARY

1. Cost allocation is the process of assigning costs to cost objectives.
2. A cost objective is an object—for instance, a product or department—for which a separate measurement of cost is desired.
3. A cost allocation base is a systematic measure used to allocate costs to cost objectives.
4. The general process of cost allocation involves the identification of cost objectives and the identification of a cost allocation base.
5. Service departments provide services to other departments within a factory, but are not directly involved in the production process.
6. Production departments are directly involved in the production process.
7. The purpose of service department cost allocation is to allocate service department costs to production departments.
8. Allocated service department costs are classified as factory overhead costs.
9. The cost allocation base for service department cost allocation should reflect the services provided to other departments and should be relatively easy to measure.
10. The direct method of service department cost allocation involves the allocation of service department costs directly to production departments.
11. Under the direct method of service department cost allocation, costs are not allocated from one service department to another.
12. The step method of service department cost allocation involves the allocation of service

department costs from one service department to another, and then to the production departments, using a particular sequence of service departments.

13. When using the step method, the sequence, or order, of service departments generally begins with the service department that provides services to the greatest number of other service departments.

14. Joint products are produced together and are not readily identifiable as individual products until after a certain point in the production process.

15. The split-off point is the point in the production process where joint products become separately identifiable.

16. Joint costs are the costs of producing joint products before the split-off point.

17. Separable costs are the costs of producing joint products after the split-off point.

18. The purpose of joint-product cost allocation is to allocate joint costs to the joint products.

19. The physical units method of joint-product cost allocation uses some physical measure to allocate joint costs to joint products.

20. The sales value method of joint-product cost allocation uses the sales value of the joint products at the split-off point to allocate joint costs.

21. The net realizable value of joint-product cost allocation uses the net realizable value of the joint products at the split-off point to allocate joint costs.

22. The net realizable value of joint products is computed as the sales value at completion, minus the separable costs.

23. The net realizable value method is generally used when the sales value at the split-off point is not known.

24. The sell-or-process-further decision is the decision to sell a joint product at the split-off point or to sell it at completion.

25. Joint costs are not relevant to a sell-or-process-further decision.

26. Accounting for byproducts involves deducting the net realizable value of the byproducts sold or produced from the cost of the major products sold or produced.

RAPID REVIEW

1. Cost allocation is the process of assigning costs to cost objectives: (a) true, (b) false. [See Section 8-1.]

2. Cost allocation generally involves (a) identifying cost objectives, (b) identifying a cost allocation base, (c) both of the above, (d) none of the above. [See Section 8-2.]

3. Examples of cost objectives would include (a) production departments, (b) joint products, (c) both of the above, (d) none of the above. [See Sections 8-2, 8-3.]

4. Service departments are (a) directly involved in the production process, (b) not directly involved in the production process. [See Section 8-2.]

5. The purpose of service department cost allocation is to assign service department costs to (a) direct labor hours, (b) production departments, (c) joint products. [See Section 8-2.]

6. Service department costs that are allocated to production departments are classified as (a) direct labor costs, (b) direct materials costs, (c) factory overhead costs. [See Section 8-2.]

7. Which of the following factory departments is likely to be a service department? (a) machining department, (b) assembly department, (c) maintenance department. [See Section 8-2.]

8. A cost allocation base for service department cost allocation should (a) reflect the services provided to other departments, (b) be relatively easy to measure, (c) both of the above. [See Section 8-2.]

9. Which method allocates service department costs directly to the production departments without any intermediate cost allocation between service departments? (a) direct method, (b) step method, (c) reciprocal method. [See Section 8-2.]

10. When using the step method of service department cost allocation, the sequence of service departments should begin with (a) the service department that provides services to the least number of service departments, (b) the service department that provides services to the

greatest number of service departments, (**c**) the service department with the greatest total costs. [See Section 8-2.]

11. Joint costs are incurred (**a**) after the split-off point, (**b**) before the split-off point. [See Section 8-3.]

12. Separable costs are incurred (**a**) after the split-off point, (**b**) before the split-off point. [See Section 8-3.]

13. Joint products are (**a**) produced together, (**b**) not readily identifiable until after the split-off point, (**c**) both of the above. [See Section 8-3.]

14. Which of the following is not a method for joint-product cost allocation? (**a**) physical units method, (**b**) sales value method, (**c**) step method, (**d**) net realizable value method. [See Section 8-3.]

15. The sales value method for allocating joint costs is based on (**a**) the sales value at the split-off point, (**b**) the sales value after completion of the joint products. [See Section 8-3.]

16. Under the net realizable value method for joint-product cost allocation, the net realizable value of each joint product is computed as the sales value at completion *minus* (**a**) joint costs, (**b**) separable costs, (**c**) both of the above. [See Section 8-3.]

17. The net realizable value method is generally used when the sales value of the joint products at the split-off point is not known: (**a**) true, (**b**) false. [See Section 8-3.]

18. The decision to sell a joint product at the split-off point or to process further should be based on (**a**) the sales value of the joint product at the split-off point, (**b**) the separable costs, (**c**) the sales value at completion, (**d**) both (**a**) and (**c**), (**e**) all of the above. [See Section 8-3.]

19. Joint costs are generally not relevant to the decision to sell a joint product at the split-off point: (**a**) true, (**b**) false. [See Section 8-3.]

20. Accounting for byproducts generally involves (**a**) adding the net realizable value of the byproducts to the cost of the major products, (**b**) deducting the net realizable value of the byproducts sold from the cost of the major products sold, (**c**) none of the above. [See Section 8-4.]

Answers
1. (a)   2. (c)   3. (c)   4. (b)   5. (b)   6. (c)   7. (c)   8. (c)   9. (a)   10. (b)   11. (b)
12. (a)   13. (c)   14. (c)   15. (a)   16. (b)   17. (a)   18. (e)   19. (a)   20. (b)

SOLVED PROBLEMS

Problems 8-1 to 8-3 are based on the following data.

The following information is available for Horizon Company:

	Service Department		Production Department	
	A	B	1	2
Department costs	$4,000	$2,000	$9,000	$18,000
Total labor hours	1,000	2,500	4,500	3,000
Square footage	1,000	6,000	8,000	2,000

Assume that both service departments provide services to each other. Costs for service department A are allocated based on square footage, and costs for service department B are allocated based on total labor hours.

PROBLEM 8-1: Using the direct method, allocate the service department costs for Horizon Company.

Solution: You would allocate the service department costs directly to the production departments, as follows:

	Service Department		Production Department		
	A	B	1	2	Total
Department costs to allocate	$4,000	$2,000			
Square footage			8,000	2,000	10,000
Proportion of square footage			$\frac{8,000}{10,000}$ = 80%	$\frac{2,000}{10,000}$ = 20%	
Allocation of service department A costs based on proportion of square footage			$ 3,200 (80%)	$ 800 (20%)	$ 4,000
Total labor hours			4,500	3,000	7,500
Proportion of total labor hours			$\frac{4,500}{7,500}$ = 60%	$\frac{3,000}{7,500}$ = 40%	
Allocation of service department B costs based on the proportion of total labor hours			$ 1,200 (60%)	$ 800 (40%)	$ 2,000

[See Section 8-2.]

PROBLEM 8-2: Prepare a diagram that describes the sequence of departments that Horizon Company would use in the step method of service department cost allocation.

Solution: The sequence of departments begins with the service department that provides services to the greatest number of other service departments. In this problem, both service departments provide services to one other service department. Therefore, the service department that has the greatest total costs (service department A) would be first in the sequence. The diagram of the sequence is presented in Exhibit 8-7. Note that the costs allocated from service department A to service department B in the first step are later reallocated from service department B to the production departments. [See Section 8-2.]

EXHIBIT 8-7

Step Method of Service Department
Cost Allocation

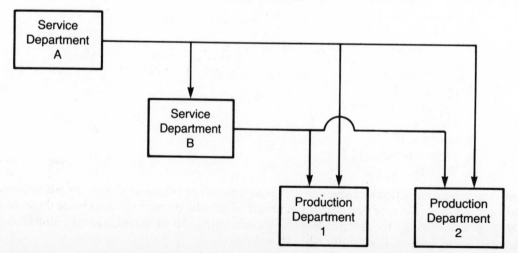

PROBLEM 8-3: Use the step method to allocate service department costs for Horizon Company.

Solution: Using the allocation sequence described in Problem 8-2, you would allocate the service department costs as follows:

	Service Department		Production Department		
	A	B	1	2	Total
Department costs to allocate	$4,000	$2,000			
Square footage		6,000	8,000	2,000	16,000
Proportion of square footage		$\frac{6,000}{16,000}$ = 37.5%	$\frac{8,000}{16,000}$ = 50%	$\frac{2,000}{16,000}$ = 12.5%	
Allocation of service department A costs based on the proportion of square footage		$1,500 (37.5%)	$2,000 (50%)	$500 (12.5%)	$4,000
Service department B costs		$2,000			
Plus: Costs allocated from service department A		1,500			
Total costs to allocate from service department B		$3,500			
Total labor hours			4,500	3,000	7,500
Proportion of total labor hours			$\frac{4,500}{7,500}$ = 60%	$\frac{3,000}{7,500}$ = 40%	
Allocation of service department B costs based on the proportion of total labor hours			$2,100 (60%)	$1,400 (40%)	$3,500

Note that the costs of $1,500 that are allocated from service department A to service department B are part of the total costs allocated from service department B to the production departments. [See Section 8-2.]

Problems 8-4 and 8-5 are based on the following data.

Rochester Company has provided the following information:

	Service Department		Production Department	
	A	B	1	2
Department costs	$20,000	$30,000	$100,000	$120,000
Proportion of service department A services	0%	20%	60%	20%
Proportion of service department B services	0%	0%	50%	50%

Assume that the proportions of the service department's services are based on an appropriate cost allocation base. Service department A provides 20% of its services to service department B and 80% (60% + 20%) to the production departments. In contrast, service department B provides services only to the production departments.

PROBLEM 8-4: Use the direct method to allocate the costs of service department B.

Solution: In this problem, the proportions of the service department's services provided to other departments are given. Using the direct method, you would make the following allocation of the service department B costs:

| | Production Department | | |
	1	2	Total
Proportion of service department B services	50%	50%	
Allocation of service department B costs	$15,000 (50%)	$15,000 (50%)	$30,000

[See Section 8-2.]

PROBLEM 8-5: Use the step method to allocate the costs from service department A.

Solution: To use the step method, you must first determine the sequence of departments for allocation. Service department A would be the first in the sequence, since it provides services to the greatest number of other service departments. Now you can use the step method to allocate service department A costs. Since service department A is first in the sequence, you can simply use the proportions given in the problem to allocate the department costs of $20,000.

| | Service Department | | Production Department | | |
	A	B	1	2	Total
Proportion of service department A services		20%	60%	20%	
Allocation of service department A costs		$4,000 (20%)	$12,000 (60%)	$4,000 (20%)	$20,000

[See Section 8-2.]

Problems 8-6 to 8-9 are based on the following data.

Southeast Company manufactures two joint products, X and Y, in one of their production processes. Joint costs were $60,000. The following information is available:

Product	Units produced	Sales value at split-off	Sales value at completion	Separable costs
X	6,000	$40,000	$65,000	$11,000
Y	4,000	$10,000	$45,000	$ 9,000

PROBLEM 8-6: Allocate the joint costs to products X and Y using the physical units method. Assume that the physical measure used is units of production.

Solution: You would make the following allocation of joint costs using the physical units method:

	Product X	Product Y	Total
Units produced	6,000	4,000	10,000
Proportion of units produced	$\frac{6,000}{10,000}$ = 60%	$\frac{4,000}{10,000}$ = 40%	
Allocation of joint costs based on the proportion of units produced	$36,000 (60%)	$24,000 (40%)	$60,000

[See Section 8-3.]

PROBLEM 8-7: Allocate the joint costs for Southeast Company using the sales value method.

Solution: You would use the sales value method to make the following allocation of the joint costs:

	Product X	Product Y	Total
Sales value at the split-off point	$40,000	$10,000	$50,000
Proportion of sales value at the split-off point	$\dfrac{\$40,000}{\$50,000}$ $= 80\%$	$\dfrac{\$10,000}{\$50,000}$ $= 20\%$	
Allocation of joint costs based on the proportion of sales value	$48,000 (80%)	$12,000 (20%)	$60,000

[See Section 8-3.]

PROBLEM 8-8: Allocate the joint costs for Southeast Company using the net realizable value method.

Solution: You must first use equation 8.1 to compute the net realizable value for the two products:

$$\begin{array}{l}\text{Net realizable value} \\ \text{at the split-off point}\end{array} = \begin{array}{l}\text{Sales value} \\ \text{at completion}\end{array} - \begin{array}{l}\text{Separable} \\ \text{costs}\end{array}$$

$$\begin{array}{l}\text{Net realizable value} \\ \text{of product X}\end{array} = \$65,000 - \$11,000$$
$$= \$54,000$$

$$\begin{array}{l}\text{Net realizable value} \\ \text{of product Y}\end{array} = \$45,000 - \$9,000$$
$$= \$36,000$$

You can now use the net realizable value method to allocate the joint costs.

	Product X	Product Y	Total
Net realizable value at split-off point	$54,000	$36,000	$90,000
Proportion of net realizable value	$\dfrac{\$54,000}{\$90,000}$ $= 60\%$	$\dfrac{\$36,000}{\$90,000}$ $= 40\%$	
Allocation of joint costs based on the proportion of net realizable value	$36,000 (60%)	$24,000 (40%)	$60,000

[See Section 8-3.]

PROBLEM 8-9: Determine if net revenue would be greater for Southeast Company if it sold joint product X at the split-off point or at completion.

Solution: In order to solve this problem, you must compare the sales value of joint product X at the split-off point with its sales value at completion minus the separable cost.

Sales value at split-off point		$40,000
Sales value at completion	$65,000	
− Separable costs	− 11,000	$54,000
Advantage to sell at completion		$14,000

The net revenue is $14,000 greater by selling joint product X at completion. [See Section 8-3.]

Problems 8-10 and 8-11 are based on the following data.

DeKalb Company manufactures products A and B from a joint process. The total joint costs are $60,000. The sales value at the split-off point was $75,000 for 8,000 units of product A and $25,000 for 2,000 units of product B.

PROBLEM 8-10: Assume that DeKalb Company allocates joint costs using the sales value method. What are the joint costs allocated to products A and B?

Solution: You would allocate the joint costs by using the sales value at the split-off point for each product:

	Product A	Product B	Total
Sales value at the split-off point	$75,000	$25,000	$100,000
Proportion of sales value at the split-off point	$\dfrac{\$75,000}{\$100,000}$ $= 75\%$	$\dfrac{\$25,000}{\$100,000}$ $= 25\%$	
Allocation of joint costs based on the proportion of sales value	$45,000 (75%)	$15,000 (25%)	$60,000

[See Section 8-3.]

PROBLEM 8-11: Compute the joint costs that would be allocated to products A and B if DeKalb Company used the physical units method.

Solution: In solving this problem, you would use units of production as the physical measure. You would allocate the joint costs as follows:

	Product A	Product B	Total
Units of production	8,000	2,000	10,000
Proportion of units of production	$\dfrac{8,000}{10,000}$ $= 80\%$	$\dfrac{2,000}{10,000}$ $= 20\%$	
Allocation of joint costs based on the proportion of units of production	$48,000 (80%)	$12,000 (20%)	$60,000

[See Section 8-3.]

9 COST BEHAVIOR DETERMINATION

THIS CHAPTER IS ABOUT

☑ **Types of Cost Behavior**
☑ **Methods of Cost Behavior Determination**
☑ **The Graphical Method**
☑ **The High-Low (Algebraic) Method**
☑ **The Least-Squares Regression Method**

9-1. Types of Cost Behavior

In cost and management accounting, there are basically three types of cost behavior: variable costs, fixed costs, and mixed (semi-variable) costs. This chapter will use linear cost functions to represent these three types of cost behavior.

A. Linear cost functions

The equation for a straight line is:

$$y = a + bx \tag{9.1}$$

y = dependent variable (variable to be predicted)
x = independent variable (observed variable)
a = vertical intercept (the value of y when x = 0)
b = slope (the change in y for each unit change in x)
$$= \frac{\text{change in y}}{\text{change in x}}$$

[handwritten: y = a + θ]

The dependent variable, y, may be expressed as a function of x, the independent variable ($y = f(x)$). The function ($y = f(x)$) describes the relationship between x and y such that for each value of x there is a corresponding value of y.

The equation for a straight line can be used to represent linear cost functions:

$$y = a + bx \tag{9.2}$$

y = total cost *[handwritten: = dependent]*
x = units of production activity *[handwritten: = independent]*
a = fixed cost *[handwritten: — vertical intercept]*
b = variable cost per unit of production activity *[handwritten: = slope]*

The independent variable, x, representing units of production activity, can be measured in terms of one of the following:

1. units of production   3. direct labor dollars
2. direct labor hours   4. machine hours

Figure 9-1 is a graphical representation of equation 9.2. Total cost, y, is on the vertical axis. The vertical axis intercept is a, fixed cost. Units of production activity, x, are on the

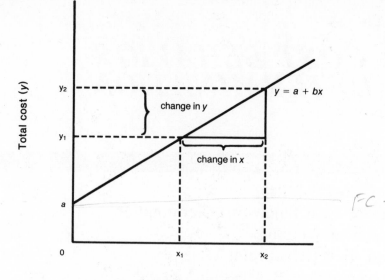

Figure 9-1
Linear Cost Function

horizontal axis. The slope of the line, b, is the change in y divided by the change in x, and represents the variable cost per unit of production activity.

B. Relevant range

Separating costs into variable cost and fixed cost components is based on the assumption of the relevant range. The *relevant range* is the range of production activity levels for which linear cost behavior functions for variable costs, fixed costs, and mixed costs are valid. Within the relevant range, costs can be classified as variable or fixed, and linear functions can be used to describe the relationship between these costs and production activity levels. Outside the relevant range, the classification of costs as fixed or variable is no longer valid.

C. Variable costs

Variable costs, in total, change in direct proportion to changes in production activity, within the relevant range. Equation 9.3 represents the variable cost function:

$$y = bx \tag{9.3}$$

y = total variable cost
x = units of production activity
b = variable cost per unit of production activity

Note that the vertical intercept, a, is zero because the variable cost function does not contain any fixed costs. Figure 9-2 presents a variable cost function.

D. Fixed costs

Fixed costs, in total, remain unchanged when changes in production activity occur, within the relevant range. Equation 9.4 represents the fixed cost function:

$$y = a \tag{9.4}$$

y = total fixed cost
a = fixed cost

Note that the slope of the line, b, is zero because the fixed cost function does not contain any variable cost component. In other words, total fixed cost, y, remains unchanged when changes in production activity, x, occur. Figure 9-3 presents a fixed cost function.

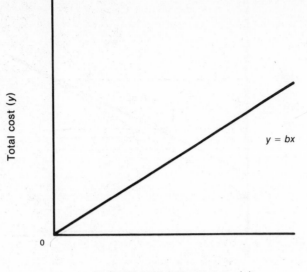

Figure 9-2
Variable Cost Function

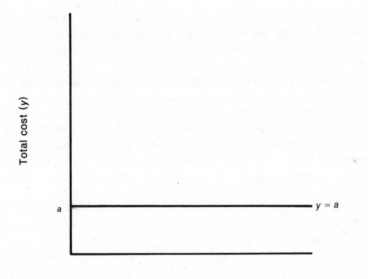

Figure 9-3
Fixed Cost Function

E. Mixed costs

Mixed, or semivariable, costs have both a fixed cost component, *a*, and a variable cost component, *bx*. Equation 9.5 represents the mixed costs function:

$$y = a + bx \qquad \text{(9.5)}$$

y = total mixed cost
a = fixed cost
b = variable cost per unit
x = units of production activity

An example of a mixed cost would be telephone costs. There is a monthly fee, *a*, which is fixed. There is also a charge, *b*, per call or unit, *x*; this amount will vary, depending on the

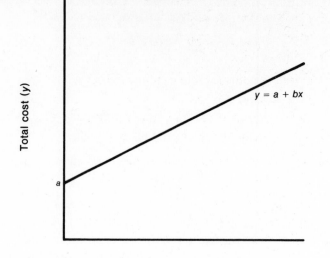

Figure 9-4
Mixed Cost Function

number of calls made. Total cost, *y*, depends on the number of calls made (*x*). That is, *y* is a function of *x* ($y = f(x)$). Figure 9-4 presents a mixed cost function.

EXAMPLE 9-1: The Block Company has summarized the following production cost information based on production of 10,000 units:

Production Cost	Cost Behavior
Direct materials	variable cost—$1.50 per unit
Factory rent	fixed cost—$7,000
Factory maintenance	mixed cost—$5,000 + $.40 per unit

The direct materials cost for 10,000 units of production would be computed using equation 9.3.

$$y = bx$$
$$= (\$1.50)(10{,}000 \text{ units})$$
$$= \$15{,}000$$

The factory rent for 10,000 units of production would be computed using equation 9.4.

$$y = a$$
$$= \$7{,}000$$

The factory maintenance costs for 10,000 units of production would be computed using equation 9.5.

$$y = a + bx$$
$$= \$5{,}000 + \$.40x$$
$$= \$5{,}000 + (\$0.40)(10{,}000 \text{ units})$$
$$= \$9{,}000$$

The direct materials cost (variable cost), in total, changes in direct proportion to changes in production activity. The factory rent (fixed cost) is constant at $7,000. The factory maintenance cost (mixed cost) has both a fixed cost component ($5,000) and a variable cost component ($0.40 per unit).

F. Flexible budgeting.

One of the purposes of separating variable costs and fixed costs is to prepare a flexible budget (see Chapter 5 for a more complete discussion of budgets). A *flexible production budget* is based on actual production activity. The flexible budget for production costs requires budgeted production costs to be separated into fixed costs and variable costs. Use equation 9.6 to compute the flexible budget for production costs:

$$y = a + bx \qquad \text{(9.6)}$$

y = flexible budget production cost

a = fixed cost

b = variable cost per unit of production activity

x = actual units of production activity

Assume that budgeted factory maintenance costs are separated into fixed costs of $5,000 and variable costs of $0.40 per unit. If actual units of production were 12,000, the flexible budget for factory maintenance costs would be $9,800. Use equation 9.6 as follows:

$$y = \$5,000 + (\$0.40)(12,000)$$
$$= \$9,800$$

If actual units of production were 10,000, the flexible budget for factory maintenance costs would be $9,000. Use equation 9.6 as follows:

$$y = \$5,000 + (\$0.40)(10,000)$$
$$= \$9,000$$

9-2. Methods of Cost Behavior Determination

The three methods for cost behavior determination (estimation) presented in the following sections are (1) the graphical (scatter diagram) method, (2) the high-low (algebraic) method, and (3) the least-squares regression method. The purpose of each method is to estimate the values of a and b in the linear cost function ($y = a + bx$), based on observations of costs at different production activity levels. For example, a company may want to determine the fixed cost component and variable cost component of manufacturing overhead.

The methods most often tested on the CPA and CMA examinations are the high-low (algebraic) method and the least-squares regression method.

A. Graphical (scatter diagram) method

The graphical (scatter diagram) method involves plotting observations of cost and production activity. The estimates of a and b in the linear cost function are based on the visual fitting of a line to the plotted observations.

B. High-low (algebraic) method

The high-low method involves using two observations (usually the high observation and the low observation) to compute the slope, b, and the intercept, a, of the line which connects the two points.

C. Least-squares regression method

The least-squares regression method is a statistical model for estimating a and b in the linear cost function and provides statistical information about the estimates of the cost behavior function $y = a + bx$.

9-3. The Graphical Method

The graphical, or scatter diagram, method involves plotting observations of cost and production activity. The estimates of a and b in the cost function are made by visually fitting a line to the plotted observations.

The graphical method involves four steps:

STEP 1. PLOT OBSERVATIONS OF TOTAL COST AND UNITS OF PRODUCTION ACTIVITY.

STEP 2. VISUALLY FIT A LINE TO THE PLOTTED OBSERVATIONS.

STEP 3. MEASURE THE VALUE OF THE VERTICAL INTERCEPT, a.

STEP 4. MEASURE THE VALUE OF THE SLOPE OF THE LINE, b.

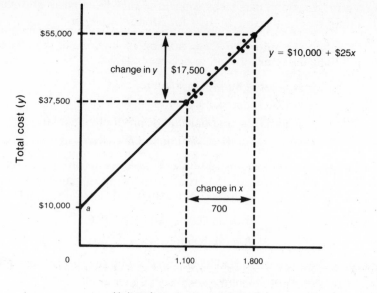

$$b = \frac{\text{change in y}}{\text{change in x}} = \frac{\$17,500}{700} = \$25 \text{ per unit}$$

Figure 9-5
Graphical Method

EXAMPLE 9-2: Central Manufacturing Company would like to estimate the variable and fixed components of its manufacturing overhead cost. The following information is available for each month of the previous year:

	Units of Production	Manufacturing Overhead Costs
January	1,400	$ 44,000
February	1,200	40,000
March	1,600	52,000
April	1,800	55,000
May	1,500	48,500
June	1,300	41,500
July	1,400	46,000
August	1,300	42,000
September	1,200	41,000
October	1,150	38,500
November	1,100	37,500
December	1,150	39,000
Total	16,100	$525,000

You can determine the variable and fixed components of the manufacturing overhead cost by using the graphical method. Figure 9-5 illustrates the graphical method.

STEP 1. PLOT OBSERVATIONS OF TOTAL COST AND UNITS OF PRODUCTION ACTIVITY.

Cost is plotted on the y, or vertical, axis. Units of production activity, which in this example is units of production, is plotted on the x, or horizontal, axis.

STEP 2. VISUALLY FIT A LINE TO THE PLOTTED OBSERVATIONS.
See Figure 9-5.

STEP 3. MEASURE THE VALUE OF THE VERTICAL INTERCEPT, a.

The point at which the line intersects the vertical axis is the amount of fixed cost, a. The fixed cost amount for the fitted line in Figure 9-5 is $10,000.

STEP 4. MEASURE THE VALUE OF THE SLOPE OF THE LINE, b.

The slope of the fitted line, b, in Figure 9-5 can be measured by dividing the change in manufacturing overhead costs by the change in units. Based on the line in Figure 9-5, the change in units of 700 corresponds to a change in manufacturing overhead costs of $17,500.

$$b = \frac{\text{Change in y}}{\text{Change in x}}$$

$$= \frac{\$55,000 - \$37,500}{1,800 - 1,100}$$

$$= \frac{\$17,500}{700}$$

$$= \$25 \text{ per unit}$$

The cost function would be:

$$y = \$10,000 + \$25x$$

It should be noted that the values for a and b are subject to a great deal of error and are dependent on the fit of your line to the plotted observations and the accuracy of your graph.

9-4. The High-Low (Algebraic) Method

The high-low, or algebraic, method uses two observations—usually the high observation and the low observation—to compute the slope of the line, b, and the vertical intercept of the line, a, that connects the two observed points.

The high-low method involves three steps:

STEP 1. IDENTIFY THE TWO OBSERVATIONS THAT YOU WILL USE TO ESTIMATE THE COST BEHAVIOR FUNCTION.

STEP 2. COMPUTE THE SLOPE OF THE LINE, b (VARIABLE COST PER UNIT).

STEP 3. COMPUTE THE VERTICAL INTERCEPT, a (FIXED COST).

A. Identify observations

The high-low method uses only two observations to estimate the cost behavior function ($y = a + bx$). You will usually use the high observation and the low observation. (You might be asked in a problem to use two observations that are not the high and low observations.)

B. Compute the slope of the line

You would compute the slope of the line, b (variable cost per unit), by dividing the change in cost, $y_2 - y_1$, by the change in units of production activity, $x_2 - x_1$. Given the low observation (x_1, y_1) and the high observation (x_2, y_2), the variable cost per unit of production activity is computed using equation 9.7:

$$b = \frac{y_2 - y_1}{x_2 - x_1} \qquad (9.7)$$

C. Compute the vertical intercept

After computing the slope of the line, b, you would compute the vertical intercept, a (fixed cost), using equation 9.8:

$$a = y - bx \qquad (9.8)$$

You can use either the low observation (x_1, y_1) or the high observation (x_2, y_2) to solve for a, the vertical intercept.

EXAMPLE 9-3: Using the information from Example 9-2, determine the cost behavior function of the manufacturing overhead cost of Central Manufacturing Company using the high-low method.

STEP 1. USE THE HIGH AND LOW OBSERVATIONS.

The high observation is April (1,800 units, $55,000) and the low observation is November (1,100 units, $37,500).

STEP 2. COMPUTE THE SLOPE OF THE LINE, b, WHICH IS THE VARIABLE COST PER UNIT.

Use equation 9.7.

$$b = \frac{y_2 - y_1}{x_2 - x_1}$$

$$b = \frac{\$55,000 - \$37,500}{1,800 - 1,100}$$

$$= \$25 \text{ per unit}$$

STEP 3. COMPUTE THE VERTICAL INTERCEPT, a, WHICH IS THE FIXED COST.

Use equation 9.8:

$$a = y - bx$$

Either the low observation or the high observation may be used.

(1) Using the low observation (x_1, y_1):

$$a = \$37,500 - \$25(1,100)$$
$$= \$37,500 - \$27,500$$
$$= \$10,000$$

(2) Using the high observation (x_2, y_2):

$$= \$55,000 - \$25(1,800)$$
$$= \$55,000 - \$45,000$$
$$= \$10,000$$

The solution for the fixed cost amount (a) will always be the same for either the high observation (x_2, y_2) or the low observation (x_1, y_1).

On the basis of the high-low method, you would state the cost behavior function for manufacturing overhead for Central Manufacturing Company as follows:

$$y = \$10,000 + \$25x$$
$$y = \text{total manufacturing overhead cost}$$
$$x = \text{units of production activity}$$

9-5. The Least-Squares Regression Method

The least-squares regression method is a statistical model that provides information about the estimates of a and b in the regression equation for a cost behavior function $y = a + bx$.

The least-squares regression method fits the best regression line to the observations of cost and units of production activity. In particular, the least-squares regression method finds the values of the fixed cost a and the variable cost per unit, b, in the cost behavior function $y = a + bx$ that minimize the sum of the squared deviations between the observations and the regression line. The specific procedures for computing the regression values are beyond the scope of this outline. However, the following regression statistics will be discussed and interpreted:

1. the coefficient of determination
2. the coefficient of correlation
3. the computed t value

1. COEFFICIENT OF DETERMINATION (r^2)

The coefficient of determination describes the proportion of the variation of y (costs) that is explained by the variable x (units of production activity). The value of the coefficient of determination will fall between 0 and 1.00. The coefficient of determination describes how well the units of production activity, x, explain the variation in costs, y. A coefficient of determination that is relatively close to 1.00 is one indicator of a good fit of the regression line to the observations.

2. COEFFICIENT OF CORRELATION (r)

The coefficient of correlation describes both the direction and the strength of the relationship between x and y. The value of the coefficient of correlation will fall between -1.00 and $+1.00$

When x and y move in the same direction, the relationship between x and y is positive, and r is positive. When x and y move in opposite directions, the relationship between x and y is negative, and r is negative.

The strength of the relationship between x and y is indicated by the value of the coefficient of correlation. A value of r that is close to $+1.00$ or -1.00 indicates a strong relationship between x and y. There can be either a strong positive relationship (if r is close to $+1.00$) or a strong negative relationship (if r is close to -1.00).

3. COMPUTED t VALUE

The computed t value is the ratio of the regression coefficient (b) to the standard error of b. In general, for a relatively large sample size, a computed t value of at least 2.0 indicates a relatively good fit of the regression line to the observations.

EXAMPLE 9-4: Beta Manufacturing Company has used the least-squares regression method to estimate the fixed and variable components of manufacturing overhead costs. On the basis of 24 months of data, the following regression results were obtained:

y = manufacturing overhead costs

x = direct labor hours (manufacturing overhead is applied on the basis of direct labor hours)

Regression equation: $y = \$40,000 + \$2.10x$

Coefficient of determination (r^2) = .908

Coefficient of correlation (r) = .953

Computed t value = 5.00

Based on these regression results, we know that the estimated manufacturing fixed overhead is $40,000, and the variable overhead is $2.10 per direct labor hour. The coefficient of determination, .908, means that 90.8% of the variation of y is explained by x. The coefficient of correlation, .953, means that (1) the relationship between x and y is positive (x and y move in the same direction) and (2) the relationship between x and y is relatively strong (r is relatively close to 1.00). The computed t value of 5.00 indicates a relatively good fit of the regression line to the observations. *t > 2.00 = good a significant relationship exist/*

RAISE YOUR GRADES

Can you explain...?

☑ how to use linear cost functions to represent fixed costs, variable costs, and mixed costs

☑ the purpose of the cost-behavior determination methods

☑ how to use the graphical method to estimate cost behavior functions

☑ how to use the high-low method to estimate cost behavior functions

☑ how to interpret a regression equation

☑ how to interpret the coefficient of determination

☑ how to interpret the coefficient of correlation

SUMMARY

1. Linear cost functions can be used to represent variable costs, fixed costs, or mixed costs.
2. In a linear cost function, the vertical intercept a usually represents fixed costs.
3. In a linear cost function, the slope of the line b usually represents the variable cost per unit of production activity.
4. The purpose of each method of cost behavior determination is to estimate the values of the fixed cost a and the variable cost per unit b in the linear cost function $y = a + bx$.
5. The three methods of cost behavior determination are the graphical method, the high-low method, and the least-squares regression method.
6. The graphical method involves plotting observations of costs and production activity and visually fitting a line to the plotted observations.

7. The high-low method involves using observations to compute the slope and the vertical intercept of the line that connects the two points.

8. The least-squares regression method is a statistical model for estimating the values of a and b in the linear cost function $y = a + bx$.

RAPID REVIEW

1. A linear cost behavior function (where y is total cost and x is units of production activity) can be represented by the equation $y = a + bx$: (a) true, (b) false. [See Section 9-1.]

2. A variable cost function is represented by the equation (a) $y = bx$, (b) $y = a$, (c) $y = a + bx$. [See Section 9-1.]

3. A fixed cost function is represented by the equation (a) $y = bx$, (b) $y = a$, (c) $y = a + bx$. [See Section 9-1.]

4. A mixed cost has both a fixed cost component and a variable cost component: (a) true, (b) false. [See Section 9-1.]

5. A mixed cost function is represented by the equation (a) $y = bx$, (b) $y = a$, (c) $y = a + bx$. [See Section 9-1.]

6. The graphical method is based on plotting observations on a graph and visually fitting a line to the plotted observations: (a) true, (b) false. [See Section 9-3.]

7. The high-low method is based on only two observations: (a) true, (b) false. [See Section 9-4.]

8. The coefficient of determination describes the proportion of the variation of x (units of production activity) that is explained by y (costs): (a) true, (b) false. [See Section 9-5.]

9. A coefficient of correlation of $-.987$ indicates that the relationship between x and y is a (a) strong positive relationship, (b) strong negative relationship, (c) weak positive relationship, (d) weak negative relationship. [See Section 9-5.]

10. Using the high-low method, you would compute the slope of the line, b, by dividing the change in costs by the change in units of production activity: (a) true, (b) false. [See Section 9-4.]

Answers
1. (a)   2. (a)   3. (b)   4. (a)   5. (c)   6. (a)   7. (a)   8. (b)   9. (b)   10. (a)

SOLVED PROBLEMS

Problems 9-1 to 9-3 are based on the following data.

Northern Company would like to estimate the fixed cost and variable cost components of maintenance costs in its factory. The following information is available for 19X6:

Month	Maintenance Costs	Units of Production	Machine Hours
January	$25,000	5,000	20,000
February	26,000	7,000	28,000
March	25,500	6,000	24,000
April	37,000	10,000	40,000
May	48,000	15,000	60,000
June	47,000	15,000	60,000
July	52,500	17,000	68,000
August	55,000	20,000	80,000
September	46,000	16,000	64,000
October	52,500	18,000	72,000
November	37,000	10,000	40,000
December	30,000	7,000	28,000

PROBLEM 9-1: Using the high-low method, estimate the fixed maintenance cost and variable maintenance cost per unit of production. Use the high and low cost observations.

Solution: The cost behavior function for maintenance cost is:

$$y = a + bx$$

To solve for this equation, you must first identify the low observation as January and the high observation as August. To compute the variable cost per unit of production, *b*, use equation 9.7:

$$b = \frac{y_2 - y_1}{x_2 - x_1}$$

$$= \frac{\$55,000 - \$25,000}{20,000 - 5,000}$$

$$= \$2.00 \text{ variable cost per unit of production}$$

To compute the fixed cost, *a*, use equation 9.8:

$$a = y - bx$$

Using the low observation:

$$a = \$25,000 - (\$2.00)(5,000)$$

$$= \$15,000$$

Using the high observation:

$$a = \$55,000 - (\$2.00)(20,000)$$

$$= \$15,000$$

The cost behavior function for maintenance costs is:

$$y = \$15,000 + \$2.00x$$

The fixed maintenance cost per month is $15,000, and the variable maintenance cost per unit of production is $2.00. [See Section 9-4.]

PROBLEM 9-2: Using the high-low method, compute the fixed maintenance cost and variable maintenance cost per machine hour. Use the high and low cost observations.

Solution: The cost behavior function for maintenance costs is:

$$y = a + bx$$

To solve for this equation, you would first identify the low observation as January and the high observation as August. To compute the variable cost per machine hour, *b*, use equation 9.7:

$$b = \frac{y_2 - y_1}{x_2 - x_1}$$

$$= \frac{\$55,000 - \$25,000}{80,000 - 20,000}$$

$$= \$0.50 \text{ variable cost per machine hour}$$

To compute the fixed cost, *a*, use equation 9.8:

$$a = y - bx$$

Using the low observation:

$$= \$25,000 - (\$0.50)(20,000)$$

$$= \$15,000$$

Using the high observation:

$$= \$55,000 - (\$0.50)(80,000)$$

$$= \$15,000$$

The cost behavior for maintenance costs is:

$$y = \$15{,}000 + \$0.50x$$

[See Section 9-4.]

PROBLEM 9-3: Using the high-low method, estimate the fixed cost and variable cost per unit for maintenance cost. Use March and October as the two observations for estimating the cost behavior function.

Solution: The cost behavior function for maintenance cost is:

$$y = a + bx$$

To compute the variable cost per unit, b, use equation 9.7:

$$b = \frac{y_2 - y_1}{x_2 - x_1}$$

$$= \frac{\$52{,}500 - \$25{,}500}{18{,}000 - 6{,}000}$$

$$= \$2.25 \text{ variable cost per unit}$$

To compute the fixed cost, a, use equation 9.8:

$$a = y - bx$$

Using the March observation:

$$= \$25{,}500 - (\$2.25)(6{,}000)$$

$$= \$12{,}000$$

Using the October observation:

$$= \$52{,}500 - (\$2.25)(18{,}000)$$

$$= \$12{,}000$$

Note that the fixed cost and variable cost per unit amounts determined in this problem are different than the ones that were found in the solution to Problem 9-1 because each problem used different sets of observations. [See Section 9-4.]

PROBLEM 9-4: The following information is available for different levels of production activity:

Units of Production	Maintenance Costs	Depreciation Expense	Indirect Materials
15,000	$40,000	$11,000	$ 46,500
35,000	80,000	11,000	108,500

On the basis of this information, determine the type of cost behavior (variable cost, fixed cost, or mixed cost) and the cost behavior function for each of the three cost items: (1) maintenance costs, (2) depreciation expense, and (3) indirect materials.

Solution: To solve this problem, you need to determine how each cost item changes in response to changes in production activity. In other words, you need to determine the behavior cost function of each cost item.

(1) MAINTENANCE COSTS

This cost would be classified as a mixed cost because it has both a fixed cost and a variable cost component. The behavior cost function for mixed costs is:

$$y = a + bx$$

To compute the variable cost per unit of production, b, use equation 9.7:

$$b = \frac{y_2 - y_1}{x_2 - x_1}$$

$$= \frac{\$80,000 - \$40,000}{35,000 - 15,000}$$

$$= \$2.00 \text{ variable cost per unit}$$

To compute the fixed cost, a, use equation 9.8:

$$a = y - bx$$

Using the low observation:

$$= \$40,000 - \$2.00(15,000)$$

$$= \$10,000$$

Using the high observation:

$$= \$80,000 - \$2.00(35,000)$$

$$= \$10,000$$

The cost behavior function for maintenance costs is:

$$y = \$10,000 + \$2.00x$$

(2) DEPRECIATION EXPENSE

The depreciation expense would be classified as a fixed cost because this cost remains unchanged with changes in production activity (it is $11,000 whether 15,000 or 30,000 units are produced). The cost behavior function for fixed costs is:

$$y = a$$

$$= \$11,000$$

(3) INDIRECT MATERIALS

The indirect materials cost would be classified as a variable cost because the cost changes in direct proportion to changes in production activity. The cost behavior function for variable costs is:

$$y = bx$$

To solve for b, the variable cost per unit, use equation 9.7:

$$b = \frac{y_2 - y_1}{x_2 - x_1}$$

$$b = \frac{\$108,500 - \$46,500}{35,000 - 15,000}$$

$$= \$3.10 \text{ variable cost per unit}$$

If you use equation 9.8, you find that the fixed cost is zero.

$$a = y - bx$$

Using the high observation:

$$= \$108,500 - \$3.10(35,000)$$

$$= \$0$$

Using the low observation:

$$= \$46,500 - \$3.10(15,000)$$

$$= \$0$$

[See Sections 9-1 and 9-4.]

PROBLEM 9-5: Southern Company has used the least-squares regression method to estimate fixed and variable components of factory overhead costs. The following results were obtained:

$$\text{Regression equation: } y = \$45,000 + \$14x$$
$$y = \text{factory overhead costs}$$
$$x = \text{units of production}$$
$$\text{Coefficient of determination: } .939$$

Discuss the meaning of the regression equation and the coefficient of determination.

Solution: The \$45,000 in the regression equation represents the fixed factory overhead cost. The \$14 represents the variable overhead cost per unit of production. The coefficient of determination of .939 means that 93.9% of the variation in y (factory overhead costs) is explained by x (units of production). [See Section 9-5.]

PROBLEM 9-6: The following information is available for indirect materials for four quarters of 19X3:

Quarter	Units of Production	Indirect Materials
1	48,000	\$206,400
2	56,000	240,800
3	51,000	219,300
4	54,000	232,200
	209,000	\$898,700

Use the high-low method to estimate the cost behavior function for indirect materials.

Solution: The cost behavior function for indirect materials (a variable cost) is:

$$y = bx$$

To solve for this equation, you must first identify the low observation as Quarter 1 and the high observation as Quarter 2. To compute the variable cost per unit of production, b, use equation 9.7:

$$b = \frac{y_2 - y_1}{x_2 - x_1}$$
$$= \frac{\$240,800 - \$206,400}{56,000 - 48,000}$$
$$= \$4.30 \text{ variable cost per unit of production}$$

If you use equation 9.8, you will find that the fixed cost is zero.

$$a = y - bx$$

Using the high observation:

$$= \$240,800 - (\$4.30)(56,000)$$
$$= \$0$$

Using the low observation:

$$= \$206,400 - (\$4.30)(48,000)$$
$$= \$0$$

The indirect materials cost function is:

$$y = \$4.30x$$

[See Section 9-4.]

Problems 9-7 and 9-8 are based on the following data.

The following information is available for Chicago Company:

Machine Hours	Maintenance Costs
3,000	$30,000
7,000	41,000

PROBLEM 9-7: Estimate the cost behavior function for maintenance costs on the basis of these data.

Solution: Maintenance costs are classified as a mixed cost. The cost behavior function is:

$$y = a + bx$$

To solve this equation, we must use equation 9.7 to compute the variable cost per machine hour, b:

$$b = \frac{y_2 - y_1}{x_2 - x_1}$$
$$= \frac{\$41,000 - \$30,000}{7,000 - 3,000}$$
$$= \$2.75 \text{ variable cost per machine hour}$$

To compute the fixed cost, a, use equation 9.8:

$$a = y - bx$$

Using the high observation:

$$= \$41,000 - \$2.75(7,000)$$
$$= \$21,750$$

Using the low observation:

$$= \$30,000 - \$2.75(3,000)$$
$$= \$21,750$$

The cost function for maintenance costs is:

$$y = \$21,750 + \$2.75x$$

[See Section 9-4.]

PROBLEM 9-8: Compute the estimated maintenance costs for 38,000 machine hours.

Solution: You would compute the estimated maintenance costs for 38,000 machine hours using the cost behavior function found in Problem 9-7:

$$y = \$21,750 + \$2.75x$$
$$= \$21,750 + \$2.75(38,000)$$
$$= \$126,250$$

The estimated maintenance costs for 38,000 machine hours are $126,250. [See Section 9-4.]

10 COST-VOLUME-PROFIT RELATIONSHIPS AND THE BREAK-EVEN POINT

THIS CHAPTER IS ABOUT

☑ Cost-Volume-Profit (CVP) Relationships and the Break-Even Point
☑ The Equation Method
☑ The Contribution Margin Method
☑ The Graphical Method
☑ Applications of CVP Analysis and the Break-Even Point
☑ Sales Mix Problems
☑ Assumptions and Limitations of CVP Analysis and Break-Even Analysis
☑ Income Taxes and CVP Analysis

10-1. Cost-Volume-Profit (CVP) Relationships and the Break-Even Point

When presenting break-even or cost-volume-profit relationships, many cost accounting textbooks use the terms *expenses* and *costs* interchangeably and *net income* and *profit* interchangeably. In this outline, the terms *costs* and *profit* will be used.

A. Cost-volume-profit (CVP) relationships

The relationship of cost, volume, and profit is generally presented in the income statement as follows:

$$\text{Revenue} - \text{Total Costs} = \text{Profit (Loss)} \tag{10.1}$$

Total costs can be divided into two components: variable costs and fixed costs. Therefore, we can restate equation 10.1 as follows:

$$\text{Revenue} - \text{Variable Costs} - \text{Fixed Costs} = \text{Profit (Loss)} \tag{10.2}$$

By rearranging the terms in equation 10.2, we can obtain the following general equation for CVP relationships:

$$\text{Revenue} = \text{Variable Costs} + \text{Fixed Costs} + \text{Profit (Loss)} \tag{10.3}$$

Equation 10.3 is the basis for CVP analysis and break-even analysis.

B. Break-even analysis

Break-even analysis is the special case of CVP analysis where profit is assumed to be zero. This is the point where total costs = total revenue and therefore profit equals zero. Equation 10.3 can be used to compute the break-even point for a company in terms of units or sales dollars.

C. CVP analysis

CVP analysis shows the relationship between cost (variable cost and fixed cost), volume (the number of units of production sold), and profit (net income). Equation 10.3 can also be used to compute the number of units that must be sold or the number of sales dollars that must be realized to earn a given amount of profit.

D. Three methods of finding the break-even point

Three methods used to find the break-even point based on the relationship of cost, volume, and profit will be presented in this outline: (1) the equation method, (2) the contribution margin method, and (3) the graphical method.

10-2. The Equation Method

To find the break-even point by the equation method, we will use the following notation:

q = quantity (or volume) of units sold	BEP$ = break-even point in dollars
s = selling price per unit	BEPU = break-even point in units
v = variable costs per unit	S$ = sales in dollars
F = fixed costs per year	
P = profit (loss)	

Equation 10.3 is used as the basis of break-even analysis:

$$\text{Revenue} = \text{Variable Costs} + \text{Fixed Costs} + \text{Profit (Loss)}$$

Using the above notation, we can restate equation 10.3 as follows:

$$(s)(q) = (v)(q) + F + P \tag{10.3 restated}$$

Now we can solve for q by using algebra. First, subtract $[(v)(q)]$ from both sides of the equation:

$$(s)(q) - (v)(q) = F + P$$

Remember that $[(s)(q) - (v)(q)] = [(s - v)(q)]$. Now we can isolate q on the left side of the equation:

$$(s - v)(q) = F + P$$

Finally, divide both sides of the equation by $(s - v)$:

$$q = \frac{F + P}{(s - v)} \tag{10.4}$$

Equation 10.4 represents the number of units that must be sold to achieve a given amount of profit (P).

EXAMPLE 10-1: The HBX Company manufactures and sells a product with the following characteristics:

Selling price:	$10.00 per unit
Variable cost:	$ 8.00 per unit
Fixed cost:	$20,000 per year

HBX desires profit of $15,000. To determine the quantity of units that must be sold to achieve this profit, we can use equation 10.4:

$$
\begin{aligned}
q &= \frac{F + P}{(s - v)} \\
&= \frac{\$20,000 + \$15,000}{(\$10.00 - \$8.00)} \\
&= \frac{\$35,000}{\$2.00} \\
&= 17,500 \text{ units must be sold to earn a profit of } \$15,000
\end{aligned}
$$

To find the number of sales dollars that must be realized to earn a profit of $15,000, multiply the units (q) by the selling price per unit (s):

$$
\begin{aligned}
\genfrac{}{}{0pt}{}{\text{Sales dollars that must be realized}}{\text{to earn a profit of }\$15,000} &= (q)(s) \\
&= 17,500 \times \$10.00 \\
&= \$175,000
\end{aligned}
$$

A. The break-even point in units

At the break-even point, profit (P) equals zero. In equation 10.4, if we assume that $P = 0$, we have the equation for finding the number of units that must be sold in order to break even (total costs = total revenue; profit = 0).

$$BEPU = \frac{F}{(s - v)} \qquad (10.5)$$

EXAMPLE 10-2: Using the information from Example 10-1, assume that HBX wants to know how many units it must sell to break even (profit = 0). We can use equation 10.5 to find the break-even point in units.

$$
\begin{aligned}
BEPU &= \frac{F}{(s - v)} \\
&= \frac{\$20,000}{(\$10.00 - \$8.00)} \\
&= \frac{\$20,000}{\$2.00} \\
&= 10,000 \text{ units to break even}
\end{aligned}
$$

B. The break-even point in dollars

To find the break-even point in sales dollars, BEP\$, (the number of sales dollars that must be realized if $P = 0$), we multiply the break-even point in units by the selling price per unit, BEP\$ = (BEPU)(s).

This can be shown algebraically using equation 10.5:

$$BEPU = \frac{F}{(s - v)} \qquad (10.5)$$

$$(BEPU)(s) = \frac{F}{(s - v)}(s) \qquad (10.6)$$

Since $(s) = 1/(1/s)$, we can restate equation 10.6 as follows:

$$(BEPU)(s) = \frac{F}{(s - v)/s}$$

This equation can also be stated as follows:

$$BEP\$ = \frac{F}{(s - v)/s} \qquad (10.6)$$

Equation 10.6 can also be stated as follows:

$$BEP\$ = (BEPU)(s) \qquad (10.6)$$

EXAMPLE 10-3: Using the information from Example 10-2, we can find the break-even point in sales dollars for HBX. The break-even point in units is 10,000.

$$
\begin{aligned}
BEP\$ &= \frac{F}{(s - v)/s} \\
&= \frac{\$20,000}{(\$10.00 - \$8.00)/\$10.00} \\
&= \frac{\$20,000}{.20} \\
&= \$100,000 \text{ in sales to break even}
\end{aligned}
$$

The break-even point in sales dollars can also be found using the restated equation 10.6:

$$
\begin{aligned}
BEP\$ &= (BEPU)(s) \\
&= (10,000)(\$10.00) \\
&= \$100,000 \text{ in sales to break even}
\end{aligned}
$$

10-3. The Contribution Margin Method

The break-even point can also be determined by using the contribution margin. The contribution margin is equal to the sales revenue minus the variable cost.

A. Contribution margin per unit

The contribution margin per unit (CMU) equals the selling price per unit (s) minus the variable cost per unit (v).

$$CMU = s - v \tag{10.7}$$

The contribution margin per unit can be interpreted as the amount available to cover fixed costs (reduce the loss) below the break-even point and the amount to add to profit above the break-even point for each unit sold.

From the information in Example 10-1, we would find the contribution margin per unit for HBX using equation 10.7:

$$CMU = s - v$$
$$= \$10.00 - \$8.00$$
$$= \$2.00$$

For every unit sold by HBX, $2.00 is available to cover fixed costs before the break-even point and $2.00 is available to add to profit after the break-even point.

B. Contribution margin ratio

The contribution margin ratio (CMR) is the ratio of the contribution margin per unit (CMU) to the selling price per unit (s).

$$CMR = \frac{CMU}{s} \tag{10.8}$$

The contribution margin ratio is usually expressed as a percentage and is interpreted as the percent of each sales dollar that is available to cover fixed costs before the break-even point and the amount to add to profit after the break-even point.

From the information in Example 10-1, we would find the contribution margin ratio for HBX using equation 10.8:

$$CMR = \frac{CMU}{s}$$
$$= \frac{\$2.00}{\$10.00}$$
$$= .20$$
$$= 20\%$$

For each sales dollar earned by HBX, 20% is available to cover fixed costs below the break-even point and 20% is available to add to profit above the break-even point.

C. Contribution margin and the break-even point

BREAK-EVEN POINT IN UNITS

Since the contribution margin per unit (CMU) equals the selling price per unit (s) minus the variable cost per unit (v), it can be substituted in equation 10.5 for finding the break-even point in units:

$$CMU = s - v$$

$$BEPU = \frac{F}{s - v} \tag{10.5}$$

$$BEPU = \frac{F}{CMU} \tag{10.9}$$

This is called the contribution margin method for finding the break-even point in units.

Using the information from Example 10-1, the break-even point in units for HBX is:

$$BEPU = \frac{\$20,000}{\$2.00}$$

$$= 10,000 \text{ units to break even}$$

BREAK-EVEN POINT IN DOLLARS

Since the contribution margin ratio (CMR) is the ratio of the CMU to the selling price per unit (s), it can be substituted in equation 10.6 for finding the break-even point in dollars:

$$CMR = \frac{CMU}{s} = \frac{s - v}{s}$$

$$BEP\$ = \frac{F}{(s - v)/s} \qquad \textbf{(10.6)}$$

$$BEP\$ = \frac{F}{CMR} \qquad \textbf{(10.10)}$$

Using the information from Example 10-1, the break-even point in dollars for the HBX Company would be:

$$BEP\$ = \frac{\$20,000}{20\%}$$

$$= \$100,000 \text{ in sales to break even}$$

10-4. The Graphical Method

The third way to find the break-even point is to use the graphical method. The graphical method is based on the "accountant's break-even chart," a graphical representation of cost-volume-profit relationships and the break-even point.

A. The accountant's break-even chart

A sample accountant's break-even chart is shown in Figure 10-1. This chart graphs the information from Example 10-1.

This chart is based on the assumption that the revenue function and all cost functions are linear within the relevant range. The relevant range is the range of volume within which the firm expects to operate in the short run. The horizontal axis of the chart represents volume (quantity) in units. The vertical axis represents dollars of revenue, costs, and profit (loss).

The Total Sales Revenue (TSR) line represents the sales revenue of the firm at various levels of volume (quantity) of units sold (q). It is determined by multiplying the selling price per unit (s) by the quantity (volume) of units sold (q).

The Fixed Cost (F) line represents the fixed cost per year and is constant for all volume levels within the relevant range.

The Total Cost (TC) line represents the sum of the variable costs [(v)(q)] plus the fixed costs (F). For example, at the volume of 15,000 units, the total costs would equal:

$$\text{Total costs} = \text{Variable costs} + \text{Fixed costs}$$

$$= (\$8.00 \times 15,000) + \$20,000$$

$$= \$140,000$$

The break-even point was defined previously as the point where profit equals zero. By definition, this is also the point where total costs (TC) equal total sales revenue (TSR). On the accountant's break-even chart, this point is where the TC and TSR lines intersect. In Figure 10-1, using the information from Example 10-1, that point's coordinate on the horizontal axis is 10,000 units, which is thus the break-even point in units. The point's coordinate on the vertical axis is $100,000, which is the break-even point in dollars.

The vertical distance between the total costs (TC) line and the total sales revenue (TSR) line represents profit above the break-even point. The vertical distance between the TC line

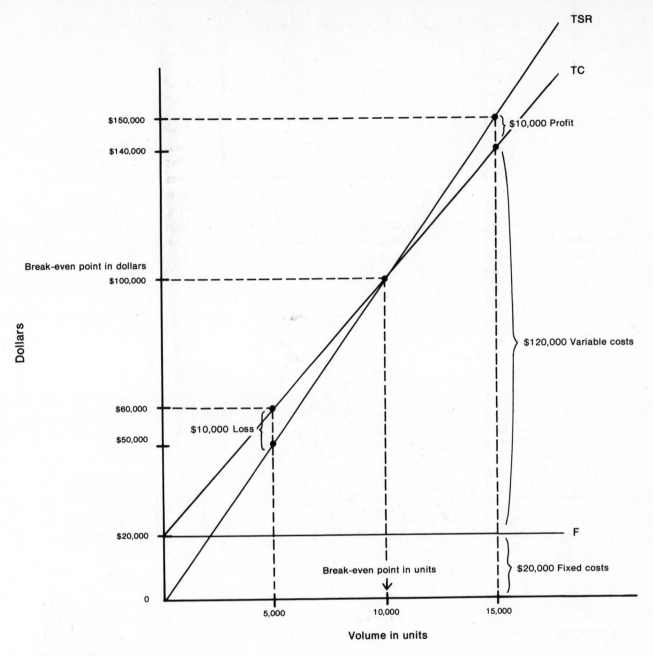

Figure 10-1
The Accountant's Break-even Chart

and the TSR line represents loss below the break-even point. For example, in Figure 10-1, at 5,000 units, the vertical distance from the TC line to the TSR line represents a loss of $10,000. At a volume of 15,000 units, the vertical distance from the TC line to the TSR line reflects a profit of $10,000.

B. The profit-volume (PV) chart

The profit-volume (PV) chart represents the CVP relationships and the break-even point with a single line on a graph. Figure 10-2 is a sample PV chart using the information from Example 10-1 and Figure 10-1.

The horizontal axis represents the volume (quantity) of units sold. The vertical axis represents the dollars of profit (+) or (loss) (−). The PV line intersects the horizontal axis at the break-even point (where profit = 0, and total costs = total sales revenue) of 10,000 units.

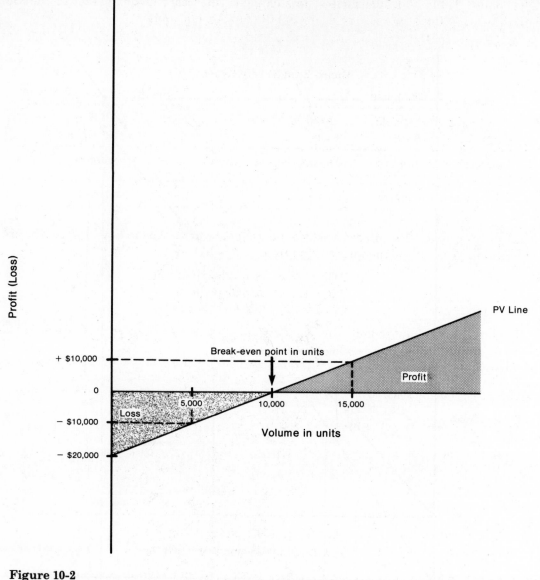

Figure 10-2
Profit-Volume (PV) Chart

Where the PV line is above the horizontal axis, there is a profit corresponding to the vertical distance from the PV line to the horizontal axis. At a volume of 15,000 units, there is a profit of $10,000.

Where the PV line is below the horizontal axis, there is a loss corresponding to the vertical distance from the PV line to the horizontal axis. At a volume of 5,000 units, there is a loss of $10,000.

10-5. Applications of CVP Analysis and the Break-Even Point

CVP analysis and break-even analysis are used to analyze situations where the selling price (s), variable cost per unit (v), fixed cost (F), and profit (P) are all either known or assumed. An application called sensitivity analysis involves determining how changes in one or more variables of a model affect the solution of that model.

A. Break-even sensitivity analysis

Break-even sensitivity analysis is used to determine how changes in the variables (s), (v), and (F) of the break-even formula affect the break-even point. For example, we may want to know whether an increase in the selling price per unit (s) will increase or decrease the break-even point. Table 10-1 summarizes how changes (increases or decreases) in individual variables will affect (increase or decrease) the break-even point.

Table 10-1

Break-Even Sensitivity Analysis

Change in				Change in break-even point
selling price	variable cost	fixed cost		in units or dollars
increase	decrease	decrease	will cause	decrease
decrease	increase	increase	will cause	increase

The following examples will demonstrate how changes in the variables will affect the break-even point. We will use the information from Example 10-1.

Selling price: $10.00 per unit
Variable cost: $ 8.00 per unit
Fixed costs: $20,000 per year

The break-even point in units was 10,000, and the break-even point in dollars was $100,000.

EXAMPLE 10-4: What will happen to the break-even point if we increase the selling price per unit (s) from $10.00 to $12.00? According to Table 10-1, the price increase should cause a decrease in the break-even point. Using equations 10.5 and 10.6, we will solve for the new break-even point in units and dollars:

$$BEPU = \frac{F}{s - v}$$

$$= \frac{\$20,000}{\$12.00 - \$8.00}$$

$$= 5,000 \text{ units to break even}$$

$$BEP\$ = (BEPU)(s)$$

$$= (5,000)(\$12.00)$$

$$= \$60,000 \text{ in sales to break even}$$

The break-even point in units has decreased from 10,000 to 5,000. The break-even point in dollars has decreased from $100,000 to $60,000.

EXAMPLE 10-5: What will happen to the break-even point if we increase the variable cost per unit from $8.00 to $9.00? According to Table 10-1, we could expect the break-even point to increase (more units will have to be sold to break even). Calculate the new break-even points in units and dollars using equations 10.5 and 10.6:

$$BEPU = \frac{F}{s - v}$$

$$= \frac{\$20,000}{\$10.00 - \$9.00}$$

$$= 20,000 \text{ units to break even}$$

$$BEP\$ = (BEPU)(s)$$

$$= (20,000)(\$10.00)$$

$$= \$200,000 \text{ in sales to break even}$$

The increase in variable cost per unit has caused the break-even point in units to increase from 10,000 to 20,000. The break-even point in dollars has increased from $100,000 to $200,000.

EXAMPLE 10-6: What will happen to the break-even point if we increase the fixed costs from $20,000 to

$40,000? According to Table 10-1, we would expect the break-even point to increase. Calculate the new break-even point in units and dollars using equations 10.5 and 10.6.

$$\text{BEPU} = \frac{F}{s - v}$$

$$= \frac{\$40,000}{\$10.00 - \$8.00}$$

$$= 20,000 \text{ units to break even}$$

$$\text{BEP\$} = (\text{BEPU})(s)$$

$$= (20,000)(\$10.00)$$

$$= \$200,000 \text{ in sales to break even}$$

The increase in the fixed costs has caused the break-even point in units to increase from 10,000 to 20,000 and the break-even point in dollars to increase from $100,000 to $200,000.

B. Target profit problems

Target profit problems involve determining how many units must be sold or how many sales dollars must be realized to earn a "target" profit (or loss). The number of units that must be sold to earn a target profit (loss) can be determined by using equation 10.4:

$$q = \frac{F + P}{s - v} \tag{10.4}$$

The sales dollars (S$) that must be realized to earn a target profit can be determined using equation 10.11:

$$S\$ = \frac{F + P}{(s - v)/s} \tag{10.11}$$

This equation can be restated as follows:

$$S\$ = (q)(s) \tag{10.11}$$

EXAMPLE 10-7: The One-Shot Company produces and sells a product with the following cost and price characteristics:

> Selling price: $5.00 per unit
> Variable cost: $4.00 per unit
> Fixed cost: $10,000 per year

The One-Shot Company has set as its target a profit of $30,000 for next year. How many units and sales dollars are needed to achieve that $30,000 profit?

Using equation 10.4, we can determine how many units must be sold to achieve that target profit:

$$q = \frac{F + P}{s - v}$$

$$= \frac{\$10,000 + \$30,000}{\$5.00 - \$4.00}$$

$$= 40,000 \text{ units to achieve } \$30,000 \text{ profit}$$

Using equation 10.11, we can determine how many sales dollars must be realized to achieve that target profit:

$$S\$ = (q)(s)$$

$$= 40,000(\$5.00)$$

$$= \$200,000 \text{ in sales to achieve } \$30,000 \text{ profit}$$

C. Selling price problems

The selling price problem involves finding what the selling price per unit should be to earn a targeted profit, assuming we know how many units will be sold. Equation 10.3 restated can be used to find the selling price:

$$(s)(q) = (v)(q) + F + P$$

(10.3)
restated

EXAMPLE 10-8: The One-Shot Company has predicted the following cost data for next year:

Variable cost: $4.00 per unit
Fixed cost: $100,000 per year

The company has also predicted that it will sell 30,000 units per year. What selling price per unit should the company charge next year to attain a target profit of $50,000?

Using equation 10.3 restated, we can solve for the selling price per unit:

$$(s)(q) = (v)(q) + F + P$$

$$(s)(30,000) = (\$4.00)(30,000) + \$100,000 + \$50,000$$

$$s = \frac{\$270,000}{30,000}$$

$$= \$9.00 \text{ selling price per unit to achieve } \$50,000 \text{ profit}$$

If the predictions of the One-Shot Company are correct regarding cost and number of units to be sold, a selling price of $9.00 per unit would produce the targeted profit of $50,000.

10-6. Sales Mix Problems

When a company sells more than one product, there is a *sales mix problem*. Sales mix is the ratio of the share of each product's sales to total sales for all products. This share is calculated in terms of number of units. For example, suppose the HBX Company makes two products, A and B, and it sells 60 units of A and 40 units of B (100 units total). The company's sales mix is 60% of product A and 40% of product B.

The sales mix will usually affect the break-even point if the different products have different contribution margins (CMU = s − v). For example, if the company starts selling relatively less of the higher contribution margin product and relatively more of the lower contribution margin product, the sales mix shifts from the higher contribution margin product to the lower contribution margin product. This means the break-even point in units will increase.

A. Sales mix break-even problems

To find the break-even point for a multiproduct firm, we must assume a specific sales mix. Based on that assumed sales mix, we will use the average variable cost per unit and the average selling price per unit in the break-even equations 10.5 and 10.6. The following steps are used to compute the break-even units and dollars for a sales mix.

STEP 1. COMPUTE THE COMPANY'S SALES MIX.

Develop a fraction for each product. The numerator is the product's sales in units. The denominator is total number of units sold by the company. Convert this fraction to a percent.

$$\text{Product A}\% = \frac{\text{Product A units sold}}{\text{Total units sold}}$$

(10.12)

$$\text{Product B}\% = \frac{\text{Product B units sold}}{\text{Total units sold}}$$

STEP 2. COMPUTE THE AVERAGE SELLING PRICE PER UNIT (ASU).

Multiply each product's selling price by its percentage that you found in Step 1. Then sum these products.

$$\text{ASU} = (\text{Product A selling price})(\text{Product A}\%) + (\text{Product B selling price})(\text{Product B}\%)$$ (10.13)

STEP 3. COMPUTE THE AVERAGE VARIABLE COST PER UNIT (AVCU).

Multiply each product's variable cost per unit by its percentage that you found in Step 1. Then sum these products.

$$AVCU = \left(\begin{array}{c}\text{Product A variable cost} \\ \text{per unit}\end{array}\right)(\text{Product A\%}) + \left(\begin{array}{c}\text{Product B variable cost} \\ \text{per unit}\end{array}\right)(\text{Product B\%})$$

$$(10.14)$$

STEP 4. COMPUTE THE AVERAGE CONTRIBUTION MARGIN PER UNIT (ACMU).

Find the average contribution margin per unit by subtracting the average variable cost per unit from the average selling price per unit:

$$ACMU = ASU - AVCU \qquad (10.15)$$

The ACMU can also be found by multiplying each product's CMU by the product's percentage that you found in Step 1. Then sum these amounts.

$$ACMU = (\text{Product A CMU})(\text{Product A\%}) + (\text{Product B CMU})(\text{Product B\%}) \quad (10.15a)$$

STEP 5. COMPUTE THE BREAK-EVEN POINT IN UNITS FOR A SALES MIX.

Equation 10.5 is used to compute the break-even point in units for a single product.

$$BEPU = \frac{F}{s - v} \qquad (10.5)$$

For a sales mix, the break-even point in units is found using equation 10.16:

$$SM\ BEPU = \frac{F}{ASU - AVCU} = \frac{F}{ACMU} \qquad (10.16)$$

The SM BEPU must be multiplied by each product's percentage that you found in Step 1 to determine the number of units for each product.

$$\text{Product 1 number of units} = (SM\ BEPU)(\text{Product A\%})$$

$$\text{Product 2 number of units} = (SM\ BEPU)(\text{Product B\%}) \qquad (10.17)$$

(Note that the ACMU can be substituted in the denominator of equation 10.16 for $(ASU - AVCU)$.)

STEP 6. COMPUTE THE BREAK-EVEN POINT IN DOLLARS FOR A SALES MIX.

Equation 10.6 is used to compute the break-even point in dollars for a single product.

$$BEPU = \frac{F}{(s - v)/s} \qquad (10.6)$$

For a sales mix, the break-even point in dollars is found using equation 10.18:

$$SM\ BEP\$ = \frac{F}{(ASU - AVCU)/ASU} \qquad (10.18)$$

Equation 10.18 can be restated as follows:

$$SM\ BEP\$ = (SM\ BEPU)(ASU) \qquad (10.18)$$

EXAMPLE 10-9: The Multiproduct Company produces and sells two products: Product A and Product B. The following are the company's predictions of sales volume, selling price, and variable cost per unit for each product for next year:

	Product A	Product B
Units of sales	10,000	30,000
Selling price per unit	$10.00	$12.00
Variable cost per unit	$ 6.00	$10.00

The total fixed costs for the Multiproduct Company are $50,000. Using the six steps outlined above, we can find the sales mix break-even point in units and dollars.

STEP 1. COMPUTE THE COMPANY'S SALES MIX.

Total units sold = 40,000. Using equation 10.12, we can compute the sales mix.

Product A	Product B
$\% = \dfrac{10,000}{40,000}$	$\% = \dfrac{30,000}{40,000}$
$= 25\%$	$= 75\%$

STEP 2. COMPUTE THE AVERAGE SELLING PRICE PER UNIT (ASU).

Use equation 10.13 to compute ASU.

$$ASU = (\$10.00)(25\%) + (\$12.00)(75\%)$$
$$= \$11.50$$

STEP 3. COMPUTE THE AVERAGE VARIABLE COST PER UNIT (AVCU).

Use equation 10.14 to compute AVCU.

$$AVCU = (\$6.00)(25\%) + (\$10.00)(75\%)$$
$$= \$9.00$$

STEP 4. COMPUTE THE AVERAGE CONTRIBUTION MARGIN PER UNIT (ACMU).

Use equation 10.7 to compute the CMU for each product.

$$\text{Product A CMU} = \$10.00 - \$6.00 \qquad \text{Product B CMU} = \$12.00 - \$10.00$$
$$= \$4.00 \qquad\qquad\qquad\qquad\qquad = \$2.00$$

Use equation 10.15 OR equation 10.15a to compute the ACMU.

$$ACMU = \$11.50 - \$9.00$$
$$= \$2.50$$

OR

$$ACMU = (\$4.00)(25\%) + (\$2.00)(75\%)$$
$$= \$2.50$$

STEP 5. COMPUTE THE BREAK-EVEN POINT IN UNITS FOR A SALES MIX.

Use equation 10.16 to compute the break-even point.

$$SM\ BEPU = \frac{\$50,000}{\$11.50 - \$9.00}$$
$$= \frac{\$50,000}{\$2.50}$$
$$= 20,000 \text{ units}$$

Use equation 10.17 to determine the number of units of each product.

$$\text{Product A number of units} = (20,000)(25\%)$$
$$= 5,000 \text{ units to break even}$$

$$\text{Product B number of units} = (20,000)(75\%)$$
$$= 15,000 \text{ units to break even}$$

STEP 6. COMPUTE THE BREAK-EVEN POINT IN DOLLARS FOR A SALES MIX.

Use equation 10.18 to compute the break-even point in dollars.

$$SM\ BEP\$ = \frac{\$50,000}{(\$11.50 - \$9.00)/\$11.50}$$
$$= \$230,000 \text{ in sales to break even}$$

The restated equation 10.18 can also be used:

$$SM\ BEP\$ = (20,000)(\$11.50)$$
$$= \$230,000 \text{ in sales to break even}$$

You can check this figure of $230,000 by multiplying the number of units found in Step 5 by their selling price:

Product A:
5,000 units × $10.00 $ 50,000
Product B:
15,000 units × $12.00   180,000
Total sales dollars to break even $230,000

B. Sales mix target profit

To find the number of units that a multiproduct company must sell to earn a target profit, we can use equation 10.19:

$$SMq = \frac{F + P}{ASU - AVCU} \tag{10.19}$$

To find the number of sales dollars that a multiproduct company must realize to earn a target profit, use equation 10.20:

$$SMS\$ = \frac{F + P}{(ASU - AVCU)/ASU} \tag{10.20}$$

Equation 10.20 can be restated:

$$SMS\$ = (SMq)(ASU) \tag{10.20}$$

EXAMPLE 10-10: Using the information in Example 10-9 for the Multiproduct Company, we will find the number of units that must be sold and the number of sales dollars that must be realized to earn a target profit of $50,000.

Use equation 10.19 to find the number of units the company must sell to earn a $50,000 profit.

$$SMq = \frac{F + P}{ASU - AVCU}$$

$$= \frac{\$50,000 + \$50,000}{\$11.50 - \$9.00}$$

$$= 40,000 \text{ total units to earn } \$50,000 \text{ profit}$$

Use equation 10.17 to determine the number of units of each product that must be sold. Substitute SMq for SM BEPU in equation 10.17.

Product A number of units = (SMq)(Product A%)
= (40,000)(25%)
= 10,000 units

Product B number of units = (SMq)(Product B%)
= (40,000)(75%)
= 30,000 units

Use equation 10.20 to find the number of sales dollars that must be realized to earn a $50,000 profit

SMS$ = (SMq)(ASU)
= (40,000)($11.50)
= $460,000 in sales to earn $50,000 profit

The Multiproduct Company must sell 40,000 units (10,000 units of Product A and 30,000 units of Product B) to realize $460,000 in total sales dollars and achieve the target profit of $50,000.

10-7. Assumptions and Limitations of CVP Analysis and Break-Even Analysis

CVP analysis and break-even analysis are based on certain assumptions about the relationship of cost, volume, and profit. Both kinds of analysis are reliable only if these assumptions are accepted. In general, these assumptions can reasonably be accepted for the relevant range (the limited range of activity within which a given firm expects to operate in the short run). It is important to know and understand the following assumptions to intelligently apply and interpret CVP analysis and break-even analysis.

A. Costs can be divided into fixed and variable components

This assumption is essential because all costs must be divided into fixed and variable components to perform CVP or break-even analysis.

B. Cost and revenue functions are linear

These functions are linear because total fixed cost, variable cost per unit, and selling price per unit are assumed to be constant at volume levels within the relevant range.

C. Volume determines cost

This assumption is important because the structure of the CVP relationships and break-even analysis allows that the determinant of cost is the volume of activity (in units).

10-8. Income Taxes and CVP Analysis

Income taxes affect CVP analysis because profit is generally taxable. When we used equation 10.4 to determine the number of units that must be sold to earn a target profit, P was assumed to be profit before taxes:

$$q = \frac{F + P}{s - v} \tag{10.4}$$

To account for income taxes, we must calculate the relationship between P, profit before taxes, and PAT, profit after taxes, using equation 10.21:

$$P = \frac{PAT}{(1 - \text{tax rate})} \tag{10.21}$$

When we need to find the number of units to earn a target *after* tax profit, we must substitute equation 10.21 for P in equation 10.4:

$$q = \frac{F + \dfrac{PAT}{(1 - \text{tax rate})}}{s - v} \tag{10.22}$$

When we used equation 10.11 to find the sales dollars that must be realized to earn a target profit, P was profit before taxes:

$$S\$ = \frac{F + P}{(s - v)/s} \tag{10.11}$$

To account for income taxes, we must substitute equation 10.21 for P in equation 10.11:

$$S\$ = \frac{F + \dfrac{PAT}{(1 - \text{tax rate})}}{(s - v)/s} \tag{10.23}$$

Equation 10.23 can also be restated as follows:

$$S\$ = (q)(s) \tag{10.23}$$

EXAMPLE 10-11: Refer to Example 10-7. In that example, the One-Shot Company produces and sells a product with the following cost and price characteristics:

Selling price:	$5.00 per unit
Variable cost:	$4.00 per unit
Fixed cost:	$10,000 per year

In Example 10-7, the One-Shot Company set $30,000 as its target profit. The $30,000 profit was the profit *before* taxes. To achieve the targeted profit before taxes, the company needed to sell 40,000 units and earn $200,000 in sales.

Suppose the One-Shot Company decides to target $30,000 as the profit *after* taxes. Their tax rate is 40%. To determine the number of sales in units to earn an $30,000 after tax profit, we would use equation 10.22:

$$q = \frac{F + \dfrac{PAT}{(1 - \text{tax rate})}}{s - v}$$

$$= \frac{\$10,000 + \dfrac{\$30,000}{1 - .40}}{\$5.00 - \$4.00}$$

$$= \frac{\$10,000 + \$50,000}{\$1.00}$$

$$= 60,000 \text{ units to earn } \$30,000 \text{ profit after taxes}$$

To find the number of sales dollars that must be realized to earn a $30,000 profit after taxes, use equation 10.23:

$$S\$ = (q)(s)$$
$$= (60,000)(\$5.00)$$
$$= \$300,000 \text{ in sales to earn a } \$30,000 \text{ profit after taxes}$$

To earn a profit after taxes of $30,000, the company must sell 60,000 units and earn $300,000 in sales dollars.

EXAMPLE 10-12: Referring to Example 10-7, suppose the One-Shot Company has a before tax profit of $30,000. What will the after tax profit be at a 40% tax rate?

Use equation 10.21 to determine the after tax profit.

$$P = \frac{PAT}{(1 - \text{tax rate})}$$

$$\$30,000 = \frac{PAT}{(1 - .40)}$$

$$(.60)(\$30,000) = PAT$$

$$\$18,000 = PAT$$

A before tax profit of $30,000 equals an after tax profit of $18,000 at the 40% tax rate.

EXAMPLE 10-13: Determine the number of units that must be sold by the One-Shot Company and the number of sales dollars it must realize to earn a profit after taxes of $18,000.

Use equation 10.22 to find the number of units to earn the targeted *after* tax profit of $18,000.

$$q = \frac{F + \dfrac{PAT}{(1 - \text{tax rate})}}{s - v}$$

$$= \frac{\$10,000 + \dfrac{\$18,000}{(1 - .40)}}{\$5.00 - \$4.00}$$

$$= \frac{\$10,000 + \$30,000}{\$1.00}$$

$$= 40,000 \text{ units to earn } \$18,000 \text{ after tax profit}$$

Use equation 10.23 to find the number of sales dollars needed to earn the targeted *after* tax profit of $18,000.

$$S\$ = (q)(s)$$
$$= (40,000)(\$5.00)$$
$$= \$200,000 \text{ in sales to earn } \$18,000 \text{ after tax profit}$$

The One-Shot Company must sell 40,000 units and realize $200,000 in sales to achieve an $18,000 after tax profit. If you compare these figures with the figures you calculated in Example 10-7, you will see that a $30,000 before tax profit equals an $18,000 after tax profit at the 40% tax rate. This was shown in Example 10-12.

RAISE YOUR GRADES

Can you explain...?

☑ the definition of the break-even point
☑ how to find the break-even point in units
☑ how to find the break-even point in dollars
☑ how to find the number of units that must be sold to earn a target profit
☑ how to find the sales price necessary to earn a target profit
☑ the three basic assumptions of CVP analysis and break-even analysis
☑ how changes in price, variable cost per unit, and fixed costs affect the break-even point
☑ how to find the break-even point for a company that produces more than one product
☑ how to compute the contribution margin per unit and the contribution margin ratio
☑ how income taxes affect CVP analysis

SUMMARY

1. Cost-volume-profit (CVP) relationships explain how changes in volume affect cost and profit (loss).
2. Break-even analysis is a special case of CVP analysis where profit is assumed to be zero.
3. The break-even point can be expressed in terms of units of sales or dollars of sales.
4. The equation method of finding the break-even point derives the break-even formulas from the basic CVP equation, 10.3.
5. The contribution margin per unit (CMU) equals the selling price per unit minus the variable cost per unit ($CMU = s - v$).
6. The contribution margin ratio (CMR) equals the contribution margin per unit (CMU) divided by the selling price per unit ($CMR = CMU/s$).
7. To find the break-even point in units using the contribution margin, divide fixed costs by the CMU ($BEPU = F/CMU$).
8. To find the break-even point in dollars using the contribution margin, divide fixed costs by the CMR ($BEP\$ = F/CMR$).
9. The accountant's break-even chart shows total sales revenue, total costs, and profit for all volumes of units sold.
10. The profit volume (PV) chart shows profit or loss for all volume of units sold.
11. An increase in the selling price per unit will result in a decrease in the break-even point; a decrease in the selling price per unit will result in an increase in the break-even point.
12. An increase in the variable cost per unit or in fixed costs will result in an increase in the break-even point; a decrease in the variable cost per unit or in fixed costs will result in a decrease in the break-even point.
13. For firms with more than one product, one must know or assume the specific sales mix to perform CVP analysis or break-even analysis.
14. In the accountant's CVP analysis and break-even analysis, cost functions and revenue functions are assumed to be linear.
15. To perform CVP analysis or break-even analysis, costs must be separable into fixed and variable components.

16. To find the number of units that must be sold to earn a target profit, divide fixed costs plus target profit by the contribution margin per unit ([F + P]/CMU).
17. Target profit before taxes, *P*, equals profit after taxes, *PAT*, divided by one minus the tax rate (P = PAT/(1 − tax rate)).

RAPID REVIEW

1. The break-even point can be expressed in terms of (**a**) units, (**b**) dollars, (**c**) both of the above, (**d**) none of the above. [See Section 10-2.]
2. The break-even point in units can be found by dividing fixed costs by the (**a**) selling price per unit, (**b**) contribution margin per unit, (**c**) contribution margin ratio, (**d**) none of the above. [See Section 10-3.]
3. The break-even point in dollars can be found by dividing fixed costs by the (**a**) selling price per unit, (**b**) contribution margin per unit, (**c**) contribution margin ratio, (**d**) none of the above. [See Section 10-3.]
4. The contribution margin per unit (CMU) equals the selling price per unit minus the (**a**) fixed costs, (**b**) variable cost per unit, (**c**) profit per unit, (**d**) none of the above. [See Section 10-3.]
5. The contribution margin ratio (CMR) equals the CMU divided by the (**a**) variable cost per unit, (**b**) fixed costs, (**c**) selling price per unit, (**d**) none of the above. [See Section 10-3.]
6. The vertical axis of the profit volume (PV) chart represents (**a**) dollars of cost, (**b**) dollars of sales, (**c**) dollars of profit (loss), (**d**) none of the above. [See Section 10-4.]
7. An increase in selling price per unit would (**a**) increase the break-even point, (**b**) decrease the break-even point, (**c**) have no effect on the break-even point. [See Section 10-5.]
8. An increase in the variable cost per unit would (**a**) increase the break-even point, (**b**) decrease the break-even point, (**c**) have no effect on the break-even point. [See Section 10-5.]
9. An increase in fixed costs would (**a**) increase the break-even point, (**b**) decrease the break-even point, (**c**) have no effect on the break-even point. [See Section 10-5.]
10. In the accountant's break-even chart, all cost and revenue functions are assumed to be (**a**) curvilinear, (**b**) nonlinear, (**c**) linear, (**d**) none of the above. [See Section 10-6.]
11. For a multiproduct company, selling relatively more of a low contribution margin product and selling relatively less of a high contribution margin product will cause the break-even point to (**a**) increase, (**b**) decrease, (**c**) remain unchanged. [See Section 10-6.]

Answers
1. (**c**)　2. (**b**)　3. (**c**)　4. (**b**)　5. (**c**)　6. (**c**)　7. (**b**)　8. (**a**)　9. (**a**)　10. (**c**)　11. (**a**)

SOLVED PROBLEMS

Problems 10-1 through 10-4 are based on the following information.

The Chicago Company produces a single product. The company sold 50,000 units last year with the following result:

Sales revenue		$125,000
Less: Variable costs	$75,000	
Fixed costs	30,000	105,000
Profit before taxes		$ 20,000
Less: Income taxes		8,000
Profit after taxes		$ 12,000

PROBLEM 10-1: What was the Chicago Company's break-even point in units last year?

Solution: To solve this problem, we must first compute the selling price per unit (s) and the variable cost per unit (v) as follows:

$$s = \frac{\text{Sales revenue}}{\text{units}}$$

$$= \frac{\$125,000}{50,000}$$

$$= \$2.50 \text{ selling price per unit}$$

$$v = \frac{\text{Variable costs}}{\text{units}}$$

$$= \frac{\$75,000}{50,000}$$

$$= \$1.50 \text{ variable cost per unit}$$

Next, we use equation 10.5 to compute the break-even point in units:

$$\text{BEPU} = \frac{F}{s - v}$$

$$= \frac{\$30,000}{\$2.50 - \$1.50}$$

$$= 30,000 \text{ units to break even}$$

[See Section 10-2.]

PROBLEM 10-2: What was Chicago Company's break-even point in dollars for last year?

Solution: Having computed the variable cost per unit and the selling price per unit in Problem 10-1, we can now use equation 10.6 to compute the break-even point in dollars:

$$\text{BEP\$} = \frac{F}{(s - v)/s}$$

$$= \frac{\$30,000}{(\$2.50 - \$1.50)/\$2.50}$$

$$= \$75,000 \text{ in sales to break even}$$

Equation 10.6 can be restated as follows:

$$\text{BEP\$} = (\text{BEPU})(s) = (30,000)(\$2.50) = \$75,000 \text{ in sales to break even}$$

[See Section 10-2.]

PROBLEM 10-3: How many units would the Chicago Company have had to sell last year to earn $60,000 in profit after taxes (PAT), assuming a tax rate of 40%?

Solution: To find the number of units to earn a target after tax profit of $60,000, use equation 10.22:

$$q = \frac{F + \dfrac{\text{PAT}}{(1 - \text{tax rate})}}{s - v}$$

$$= \frac{\$30,000 + \dfrac{\$60,000}{(1 - .40)}}{(\$2.50 - \$1.50)}$$

$$= 130,000 \text{ in units to earn an after tax profit of \$60,000}$$

[See Section 10-8.]

PROBLEM 10-4: What would the break-even point in units for the Chicago Company be if the selling price per unit were increased by 20%?

Solution: The new selling price per unit would be $3.00 ($2.50 × 120%). To find the new break-even point in units, use equation 10.5:

$$BEPU = \frac{F}{s - v}$$

$$= \frac{\$30,000}{\$3.00 - \$1.50}$$

$$= 20,000 \text{ units to break even}$$

[See Section 10-2.]

PROBLEM 10-5: The One-Shot Company reached the break-even point when it sold 600 units. Its variable costs for those units totaled $600, and its total fixed costs are $300. What amount will the 601st unit sold contribute to the One-Shot Company's profit before taxes?

Solution: To solve this problem, we use equation 10.9, which states that the break-even point in units equals the fixed costs divided by the contribution margin per unit (CMU).

$$BEPU = \frac{F}{CMU}$$

$$600 \text{ units} = \frac{\$300}{CMU}$$

$$(CMU) \, 600 \text{ units} = \$300$$

$$CMU = \frac{\$300}{600 \text{ units}}$$

$$= \$0.50$$

The CMU is $0.50 and represents the amount available to add to profit above the break-even point. Therefore, the 601st units sold will contribute $0.50 to profit before taxes. [See Section 10-3.]

PROBLEM 10-6: If the fixed costs for a product increase and the variable costs also increase, what will happen to the break-even point?

Solution: An increase in fixed costs will generally cause an increase in the break-even point. An increase in variable costs implies that the contribution margin ratio will decrease, which will also cause an increase in the break-even point. Therefore, the increase in fixed costs and in variable costs must result in an increase in the break-even point. [See Section 10-5.]

PROBLEM 10-7: The Multiproduct Company sells three products: A, B, and C. The sales mix is as follows: A, 50%; B, 25%; C, 25%. The contribution margin per unit is $1.00 for A, $2.00 for B, and $3.00 for C. The fixed costs for the company are $17,500. How many units of A would Multiproduct sell at the break-even point?

Solution: Using the six steps outlined in Section 10-6, we can find the number of units of Product A that must be sold to break even.

STEP 1. COMPUTE THE COMPANY'S SALES MIX.

We were told in the problem that the company had the following sales mix:

Product A	Product B	Product C
50%	25%	25%

STEP 2. COMPUTE THE AVERAGE SELLING PRICE PER UNIT (ASU).

We cannot compute the ASU because we do not know the selling prices of the products.

STEP 3. COMPUTE THE AVERAGE VARIABLE COST PER UNIT (AVCU).

We cannot compute the AVCU because we do not know the variable cost per unit.

STEP 4. COMPUTE THE AVERAGE CONTRIBUTION MARGIN PER UNIT (ACMU).

The contribution margin for products A, B, and C are as follows:

Product A	Product B	Product C
$1.00	$2.00	$3.00

Multiply each product's CMU by the product's percentage that you found in Step 1.

$$ACMU = (\$1.00)(50\%) + (\$2.00)(25\%) + (\$3.00)(25\%)$$
$$= \$1.75$$

STEP 5. COMPUTE THE BREAK-EVEN POINT IN UNITS FOR A SALES MIX.

Use equation 10.16 to find the break-even point in units for a sales mix:

$$SM\ BEPU = \frac{F}{ASU - AVCU}$$

The ACMU can be substituted in the denominator of equation 10.16 for ASU − AVCU.

$$SM\ BEPU = \frac{F}{ACMU}$$

$$= \frac{\$17,500}{\$1.75}$$

$$= 10,000\ \text{total units to break even}$$

Use equation 10.17 to find the number of units of Product A that must be sold to break even:

$$\text{Product A number of units} = (SM\ BEPU)(\text{Product A}\%)$$
$$= (10,000)(50\%)$$
$$= 5,000\ \text{units of Product A sold}$$
$$\text{at the break-even point}$$

[See Section 10-6.]

PROBLEM 10-8: The Hot-Shot Company would like to market a new product at a selling price of $2.00 per unit. The fixed costs to manufacture this product are $60,000, and the contribution margin ratio is 20%. How many units must be sold to earn a target profit of $40,000?

Solution: To solve this problem, we must find the contribution margin using equation 10.8:

$$CMR = \frac{CMU}{s}$$

$$20\% = \frac{CMU}{\$2.00}$$

$$(\$2.00)20\% = CMU$$

$$\$0.40 = CMU$$

Use equation 10.4 to find the number of units that must be sold to earn a profit of $40,000:

$$q = \frac{F + P}{s - v}$$

Remember that s − v equals the CMU. Therefore, the CMU can be substituted in the denominator of equation 10.4:

$$q = \frac{F + P}{CMU}$$

$$= \frac{\$60,000 + \$40,000}{\$0.40}$$

$$= 250,000 \text{ units to earn a } \$40,000 \text{ profit}$$

[See Sections 10-2 and 10-3.]

Problems 10-9 and 10-10 are based on the following information.

The Dual Company produces and sells two products, Alpha and Beta. Alpha accounts for 60% of unit sales and Beta accounts for 40%. The contribution margin per unit is $2.00 for Alpha and $4.00 for Beta. Fixed costs are $280,000.

PROBLEM 10-9: What is the break-even point in units for the Dual Company?

Solution: Use the six steps outlined in Section 10-6 to find the break-even point in units.

STEP 1. COMPUTE THE COMPANY'S SALES MIX.

Alpha	Beta
60%	40%

STEP 2. COMPUTE THE AVERAGE SELLING PRICE PER UNIT (ASU).

We cannot compute the ASU because we do not know the selling price of Alpha or Beta.

STEP 3. COMPUTE THE AVERAGE VARIABLE COST PER UNIT (AVCU).

We cannot compute the AVCU because we do not know the variable cost per unit of Alpha or Beta.

STEP 4. COMPUTE THE AVERAGE CONTRIBUTION MARGIN PER UNIT (ACMU).

The contribution margins for Alpha and Beta are as follows:

Alpha	Beta
$2.00	$4.00

Multiply each product's CMU by the product's percentage that you found in Step 1.

$$ACMU = (\$2.00)(60\%) + (\$4.00)(40\%)$$
$$= \$2.80$$

STEP 5. COMPUTE THE BREAK-EVEN POINT IN UNITS FOR A SALES MIX.

Use equation 10.16 to find the break-even point in units for a sales mix:

$$SM \ BEPU = \frac{F}{ASU - AVCU}$$

The ACMU can be substituted in the denominator of equation 10.16 for ASU − AVCU.

$$SM \ BEPU = \frac{F}{ACMU}$$

$$= \frac{\$280,000}{\$2.80}$$

$$= 100,000 \text{ units to break even}$$

[See Sections 10-3 and 10-6.]

PROBLEM 10-10: Suppose that the fixed costs of the Dual Company increased by 10%. How many units would have to be sold to earn a target profit of $28,000?

Solution: Calculate the new fixed cost amount as follows:

$$F = (\$280,000)(110\%)$$
$$= \$308,000$$

Calculate the number of units to earn the target profit of $28,000 using equation 10.19:

$$SMq = \frac{F + P}{ACMU}$$
$$= \frac{\$308,000 + \$28,000}{\$2.80}$$
$$= 120,000 \text{ units to earn a } \$28,000 \text{ profit}$$

[See Sections 10-5 and 10-6.]

11 RELEVANT COST ANALYSIS

THIS CHAPTER IS ABOUT

- ☑ The Role of Relevant Cost Analysis
- ☑ Identifying Relevant Costs and Revenues
- ☑ Short-Run Pricing Decisions
- ☑ Make-or-Buy Decisions
- ☑ Sell-or-Process-Further Decisions

11-1. The Role of Relevant Cost Analysis

Relevant cost analysis involves the identification and comparison of the relevant costs and revenues for each alternative being considered. The costs and revenues that affect a decision are relevant. The costs and revenues that do not affect a decision are irrelevant. Relevant cost analysis is used primarily in making short-run decisions.

11-2. Identifying Relevant Costs and Revenues

Relevant costs or revenues are expected future costs or revenues that differ among the alternatives being considered. It is important to remember that for a cost or revenue to be *relevant*, it must satisfy both of the following conditions.

It must be:

1. an expected future cost or revenue and
2. a cost or revenue that differs among the alternatives being considered

Any cost or revenue that fails to satisfy either one or both of these two conditions is irrelevant.

Relevant costs and revenues of the alternatives being considered are compared so that the alternative that best suits the company's needs can be chosen.

EXAMPLE 11-1: Micro Company has 1,000 computer disk drives that have become obsolete. The inventory cost of the disk drives is $100,000. Micro is considering two alternatives: (1) sell the disk drives for a scrap value of $3,000; (2) remachine the disk drives at a cost of $20,000 and then sell them for $25,000. Which alternative should Micro choose to produce the largest net revenue?

To make this decision, Micro must first identify the relevant costs and revenues of the alternatives under consideration.

The following table lists the costs and revenues in this example and tests each to see if it satisfies *both* of the relevant cost conditions.

	Relevant Conditions					
	Expected future cost or revenue		Differs among alternatives		Relevant	
	yes	no	yes	no	yes	no
Inventory costs ($100,000)		X		X		X
Remachining costs ($20,000)	X		X		X	
Scrap revenue ($3,000)	X		X		X	
Sales revenue ($25,000)	X		X		X	

Note that the inventory cost of $100,000 is not a relevant cost. It is not an expected future cost, and it does not differ between the two alternatives.

Now Micro can compare the scrap and remachining alternatives:

	Alternatives	
	Scrap	Remachine
Relevant revenue	$3,000	$25,000
Relevant costs	− −0−	− 20,000
Net relevant revenue	$3,000	$ 5,000

Micro should choose the remachining alternative because it will produce the largest net relevant revenue.

The following costs will be analyzed: variable costs, opportunity costs, fixed costs, and sunk (past) costs.

A. Variable costs

To be relevant to a short-run decision, a variable cost must meet the two relevant cost conditions.

It must:

1. be an expected future cost and
2. differ among alternatives

A variable cost is relevant if it differs, in total, among the alternatives under consideration and it is an expected future cost.

A variable cost is irrelevant if it does not differ among the alternatives under consideration or it is not an expected future cost.

B. Opportunity costs

An opportunity cost is the amount of income foregone or the amount of cost savings foregone if one alternative were chosen instead of another. In other words, it is the economic benefit (income or cost savings) that was foregone by choosing one alternative over another. There is no actual payment for an opportunity cost nor is it usually recorded in any accounting records. However, an opportunity cost is relevant to short-run decisions because it meets the two relevant cost conditions:

1. it is an expected future cost and
2. it differs among alternatives.

A widely used example for demonstrating an opportunity cost is factory capacity. There is either an alternative use for the factory capacity or there is no alternative use. An opportunity cost exists if there is an alternative use for the factory capacity that can generate income or cost savings.

EXAMPLE 11-2: Part of the Techno Company factory capacity is used to produce 1,000 keyboard components for its final product. Variable production costs are $100 per unit. An outside supplier has offered to sell the same keyboard component to Techno for $120 per unit. Techno has also been approached by a firm that wants to rent for $40,000 the part of the factory that is used to produce the keyboard components. Which alternative should Techno choose to incur the lowest cost?

To analyze this situation, you must identify the costs associated with each alternative—produce or purchase, determine which costs are relevant, and then compare total costs for each alternative to find the lowest total cost.

The costs associated with the produce alternative are variable costs of $100,000 (1,000 units × $100) and opportunity costs of $40,000. The opportunity cost arises for Techno because there is an alternative use for a part of the factory capacity (rent it to another firm for $40,000). Note that the $40,000 rental income must be foregone if Techno Company produces the keyboard components. That is the definition of an opportunity cost—the amount of economic benefit that is foregone by choosing one alternative over another.

The cost associated with the purchase alternative is the purchase cost of the keyboard components for $120,000 (1,000 units × $120).

We must now test these costs to see if they satisfy the relevant conditions.

| | Relevant Conditions | | |
	Expected future cost or revenue	Differs among alternatives	Relevant
	yes no	yes no	yes no
Variable costs ($100,000)	X	X	X
Opportunity costs ($40,000)	X	X	X
Purchase cost ($120,000)	X	X	X

The relevant cost analysis would be as follows:

| | Alternatives | |
	Produce	Purchase
Variable costs	$100,000	—
Opportunity costs	40,000	—
Purchase cost	—	$120,000
	$140,000	$120,000

Since the cost of purchasing the keyboard components from the outside supplier would be $20,000 lower, Techno should choose the purchase alternative.

EXAMPLE 11-3: Use the information from Example 11-2, but suppose that there is no firm that wants to rent the part of the factory used to produce the keyboard components. Which alternative should Techno choose to incur the lowest cost?

To analyze this situation, you must identify the cost associated with each alternative, determine which costs are relevant, and then compare total costs for each alternative to find the lowest total cost.

The only cost that changes between Examples 11-2 and 11-3 is the opportunity cost. There is no opportunity cost for Techno in this example because there is no alternative use for the factory capacity. No other company wants to rent the factory capacity.

The relevant cost analysis would be as follows:

| | Alternatives | |
	Produce	Purchase
Variable cost	$100,000	—
Purchase cost	—	$120,000
Total costs	$100,000	$120,000

In this example, Techno should produce the keyboard components in house because it will cost $20,000 less.

C. Fixed costs

A fixed cost by definition is constant. Therefore, a fixed cost will usually be irrelevant because it will not satisfy the second relevant cost condition.

The exception to the general rule that a fixed cost is irrelevant is if the fixed cost is an *avoidable fixed cost*. An avoidable fixed cost is a fixed cost that can be eliminated under one of the alternatives being considered.

An avoidable fixed cost will be relevant because it satisfies both of the relevant cost conditions: it is a future expected cost and it differs among alternatives.

D. Sunk (past) costs

Sunk costs are always irrelevant. A sunk cost is a cost that has already been incurred. Therefore, a sunk cost is always irrelevant because it does not satisfy the first relevant cost condition. In Example 11-1, Micro Company had inventory costs of $100,000. This cost was irrelevant because it was a past cost and thus did not meet the first relevant cost condition.

EXAMPLE 11-4: Use the information from Example 11-2. Assume that another firm wants to rent from Techno the factory building that is used to produce the keyboard components.

Techno employs a factory security guard for $5,000. The firm that wants to rent the factory wishes to use its own guards. Therefore, the $5,000 cost for the security guard would be avoided if the other firm rents the factory capacity.

How does the relevant cost analysis differ from that of Example 11-2?

The cost of Techno's security guard is considered a fixed cost. Now, however, that $5,000 that Techno pays its security guard is an avoidable fixed cost because it can be eliminated under the purchase alternative, but not under the produce alternative. It is a relevant cost because it meets both of the relevant cost conditions.

In this situation, the relevant cost analysis would be as follows:

	Alternatives	
	Produce	Purchase
Variable costs	$100,000	—
Opportunity costs	40,000	—
Avoidable fixed cost	5,000	—
Purchase cost	—	$120,000
Total costs	$145,000	$120,000

The purchase alternative is even more attractive now than it was in Example 11-2. Techno should purchase the keyboard components from the outside supplier.

11-3. Short-Run Pricing Decisions

A short-run pricing decision involves setting a sales price for a special order—an order that does not displace regular sales of the company.

In the long run, total revenue must exceed total costs for a company to earn a profit. However, in the short run, according to the contribution approach to pricing, a selling price is acceptable if it exceeds the variable cost.

According to the contribution approach to pricing, a short-run sales price is acceptable if that sale will increase the contribution margin of the firm. Remember from Chapter 10 that the contribution margin per unit equals the selling price per unit minus the variable cost per unit ($CMU = s - v$). Below the break-even point, the CMU can be interpreted as the amount available to cover fixed costs. Above the break-even point, the CMU can be interpreted as the amount available to add to profit.

If the short-run sales price exceeds the variable cost per unit, then the short-run special order will generate a positive contribution margin. In the short run, if the break-even point has been reached, an increase in the CMU will increase profit. If the break-even point has not been reached, an increase in the CMU will increase the amount available to cover fixed costs. Therefore, a company should accept a short-run special order if the CMU is positive and the order will not displace regular sales of the company.

The variable production costs are relevant to a short-run pricing decision if they satisfy both of the relevant cost conditions. The selling price is also relevant if it is an expected future revenue and differs among the alternatives. The fixed costs are irrelevant if they do not differ among the alternatives.

EXAMPLE 11-5: The Boston Company, a manufacturer of athletic shoes, has enough idle factory capacity available to accept a short-run special order for 10,000 pairs of shoes at a sales price of $50 per pair. The normal sales price is $75 per pair. Variable production costs are $40 per pair, and the fixed production costs are $20 per pair. The company is operating above the break-even point, and this short-run special order will not displace any of the company's regular sales. What would be the effect on Boston Company's net income if the company accepts the short-run special order?

To analyze this situation, you must identify the costs and revenues associated with the acceptance or rejection of the short-run special order, determine which costs and revenues are relevant, and then subtract relevant costs from relevant revenues to determine if the contribution margin is positive.

We must now test these costs and revenues to see if they satisfy the relevant conditions.

	Relevant Conditions					
	Expected future cost or revenue		Differs among alternatives		Relevant	
	yes	no	yes	no	yes	no
Variable costs ($40 per pair)	X		X		X	
Sales price ($50 per pair)	X		X		X	
Fixed costs ($20 per pair)	X			X		X

Note that the fixed costs are not relevant because they do not differ between the alternatives.

Now we can subtract relevant costs from relevant revenues to determine if the contribution margin is positive. Remember that the contribution margin per unit is found by subtracting variable costs from the sales price (CMU = s − v).

Sales price	$50
Variable cost	40
Contribution margin	$10
×	10,000 pairs of shoes
Increase in profit	$100,000

Accepting the short-run special order would generate $100,000 of contribution margin. Because Boston Company is operating above the break-even point and fixed costs are assumed to be constant, the $100,000 will increase the profit. Therefore, because the short-run special order will not displace any of the company's regular sales and the contribution margin is positive, Boston Company should accept the short-run special order.

11-4. Make-or-Buy Decisions

The make-or-buy decision involves the comparison of two alternatives: making an item in-house or buying that item from an outside supplier. The relevant cost of buying the item is the purchase price per unit. The relevant costs of making the item in-house can include (1) variable production costs, (2) avoidable fixed costs, and (3) opportunity costs. It is important to remember that fixed costs are not avoidable unless they are specifically stated to be avoidable.

EXAMPLE 11-6: The Boston Company can make the 100,000 soles for the athletic shoes that it produces or it can buy the soles from an outside supplier. The in-house production cost per unit for 100,000 soles is as follows:

Direct materials	$ 5.00
Direct labor	2.00
Variable overhead	3.00
Fixed cost	7.00
Total production costs	$17.00

The BCD Company has offered to sell 100,000 soles to Boston Company for $13 each. If Boston Company buys the soles from BCD, then $1.00 of fixed cost per unit would be avoided. Which alternative will create the lowest cost for Boston Company?

To analyze this situation, you must identify the costs associated with each alternative, determine which costs are relevant, and then compare total costs for each alternative to find the lowest cost.

The $1.00 of avoidable fixed cost is a relevant cost to the make alternative.

Now we must test the costs to see if they satisfy the relevant conditions.

	Relevant Conditions					
	Expected future cost or revenue		Differs among alternatives		Relevant	
	yes	no	yes	no	yes	no
Make:						
Direct material	X		X		X	
Direct labor	X		X		X	
Variable overhead	X		X		X	
Avoidable fixed cost	X		X		X	
Unavoidable fixed cost	X			X		X
Buy:						
Purchase price	X		X		X	

The relevant cost analysis would be as follows:

	Alternatives	
	Make	Buy
Direct materials	$ 5.00	—
Direct labor	2.00	—
Variable costs	3.00	—
Avoidable fixed costs	1.00	—
Purchase price	—	$13.00
Total relevant cost per unit	$11.00	$13.00

The alternative with the lowest cost is the make-in-house alternative. The total savings from choosing this alternative would be:

$$(\$13.00 - \$11.00) \times 100{,}000 \text{ units} = \$200{,}000$$

Notice that all the variable costs (direct materials, direct labor, and variable overhead) are relevant, but only the avoidable portion of the fixed cost is relevant.

11-5. Sell-or-Process-Further Decisions

The sell-or-process-further decision involves the comparison of two alternatives: selling a product without additional processing costs or selling the product after incurring additional processing costs. The important factor to remember in this type of decision is that sunk (past) costs are always irrelevant.

EXAMPLE 11-7: The XYZ Company has 1,000 gallons of product Z–1, which it can sell now for $10.00 per gallon or process further at an additional processing cost of $2.00 per gallon and sell as product Z–2 for $14.00 per gallon. The inventory cost of Z–1 is $7.00 per gallon. Which alternative will generate the most revenue for XYZ?

To analyze this situation, you must identify the costs and revenues associated with the sell now or process further alternatives, determine which costs and revenues are relevant, and then subtract relevant costs from relevant revenues to determine the net relevant revenue.

We must now test these costs and revenues to see if they satisfy the relevant conditions.

	Relevant Conditions					
	Expected future cost or revenue		Differs among alternatives		Relevant	
	yes	no	yes	no	yes	no
Inventory costs		X		X		X
Sell-now revenue	X		X		X	
Processing cost	X		X		X	
Process-further revenue	X		X		X	

Note that the $7.00 inventory cost of Z–1 is a sunk cost and is therefore irrelevant.

The relevant cost analysis would be as follows:

	Alternatives	
	Sell now	Process further
Relevant revenue	$10.00	$14.00
Relevant cost	—	2.00
Net relevant revenue	$10.00	$12.00

The process further alternative will generate the most revenue for XYZ. The total net relevant revenue from choosing this alternative would be:

$$\$12.00 \text{ per gallon} \times 1,000 \text{ gallons} = \$12,000$$

RAISE YOUR GRADES

Can you explain...?

☑ the definition of relevant costs
☑ when variable costs are relevant
☑ when opportunity costs are relevant
☑ when sunk costs are relevant
☑ when fixed costs are relevant
☑ the relevant costs for short-run pricing decisions
☑ the relevant costs for make-or-buy decisions
☑ the relevant costs for sell-or-process-further decisions

SUMMARY

1. Relevant cost analysis is used in making short-run decisions.
2. Relevant costs or revenues affect short-run decisions.
3. Relevant costs or revenues are expected future costs or revenues that differ among alternatives.
4. Any costs or revenues that are not expected future costs or revenues or that do not differ among alternatives are irrelevant.
5. Variable costs are usually relevant.
6. Opportunity costs are relevant.
7. Opportunity costs are the amount of income that could be earned or the amount of cost savings that must be foregone if one alternative were chosen instead of another.
8. If there is an alternative use for the factory capacity that can generate income or cost savings, then there is an opportunity cost associated with using that capacity.
9. If there is no alternative use for the factory capacity, there is no opportunity cost.
10. Sunk (past) costs are always irrelevant.
11. Fixed costs are usually irrelevant unless they are avoidable under one alternative.
12. Short-run pricing decisions involve setting short-run prices for special orders that do not displace part of a company's regular sales.
13. Short-run sales prices are usually acceptable if they exceed variable costs (that is, if the contribution margin is positive).
14. Make-or-buy decisions involve comparing the costs of making an item in-house versus buying the item from an outside supplier.
15. Sell-or-process-further decisions involve comparing the costs of selling a product with or without additional processing.

RAPID REVIEW

1. Costs or revenues that do not affect a short-run decision are (**a**) relevant, (**b**) irrelevant. [See Section 11-1.]

2. A relevant cost must be (**a**) a past cost, (**b**) a cost that differs between alternatives, (**c**) an expected future cost, (**d**) both (**b**) and (**c**). [See Section 11-2.]

3. Variable costs are usually (**a**) relevant, (**b**) irrelevant. [See Section 11-2.]

4. Opportunity costs are usually (**a**) relevant, (**b**) irrelevant. [See Section 11-2.]

5. An opportunity cost of using factory capacity will usually exist if there is an alternative use for that capacity: (**a**) true, (**b**) false. [See Section 11-2.]

6. Sunk (past) costs are always (**a**) relevant, (**b**) irrelevant. [See Section 11-2.]

7. Fixed costs that are not avoidable are (**a**) relevant, (**b**) irrelevant. [See Section 11-2.]

8. Fixed costs that are avoidable under one alternative in the short run are (**a**) relevant, (**b**) irrelevant. [See Section 11-2.]

9. In a short-run pricing decision, a short-run sales price is usually acceptable if it exceeds (**a**) variable costs, (**b**) fixed costs, (**c**) direct materials (**d**) opportunity costs. [See Section 11-3.]

10. In the make-or-buy decision, the relevant costs of making the item in-house may include (**a**) variable production costs, (**b**) opportunity costs, (**c**) avoidable fixed costs, (**d**) all of the above. [See Section 11-4.]

11. In the sell-or-process-further decision, it is important to remember that the following cost is irrelevant: (**a**) variable cost, (**b**) sunk cost, (**c**) additional processing cost. [See Section 11-5.]

Answers
1. (**b**)　　2. (**d**)　　3. (**a**)　　4. (**a**)　　5. (**a**)　　6. (**b**)　　7. (**b**)　　8. (**a**)　　9. (**a**)　　10. (**d**)
11. (**b**)

SOLVED PROBLEMS

PROBLEM 11-1: Northern Company incurs the following costs per unit in producing 500,000 units of product N–1:

Variable manufacturing cost	$5.00
Sales commission	1.00
Fixed manufacturing cost	2.00
Fixed nonmanufacturing cost	1.00
Total cost per unit	$9.00

The normal selling price for N–1 is $10.00 per unit. Southern Company has placed a special order with Northern to buy 10,000 units for $7.00 per unit. The production and sale to Southern would not displace any regular sales of N–1, and no sales commissions would be paid on Southern's order. Northern is operating above the break-even point. By how much would the profit of Northern increase or decrease if Southern's order is accepted?

Solution: To analyze this situation, you must identify the costs and revenues associated with the acceptance or rejection of the short-run special order, determine which costs and revenues are relevant, and then subtract relevant costs from relevant revenues to determine if the contribution margin is positive or negative.

The fixed manufacturing and nonmanufacturing costs are irrelevant to this short-run pricing decision because the fixed costs will not differ between the alternatives. No sales commission will be paid on Southern's order so that cost is also irrelevant.

Only the variable manufacturing costs are relevant. The relevant revenue is $7.00 per unit. You can now subtract relevant costs from relevant revenues to determine the contribution margin.

Sales price	$7.00
Variable cost	5.00
Contribution margin	$2.00
	× 10,000 units
Increase in profit	$20,000

Northern should accept Southern's special order for 10,000 units at $7.00 each. [See Section 11-3.]

PROBLEM 11-2: Chicago Company manufactures part no. 118 for use in the production of its final product. The costs per unit for 10,000 units of part no. 118 are as follows:

Direct materials	$ 4
Direct labor	24
Variable overhead	10
Fixed overhead applied	8
Total cost per unit	$46

New York Company has offered to sell Chicago Company 10,000 units of part no. 118 for $43 per unit. If Chicago Company accepts the offer, some of the facilities presently used to manufacture part no. 118 could be used to manufacture part no. 119. This would save $40,000 of relevant costs in the manufacture of part no. 119, and $3 per unit of fixed overhead applied to part no. 118 would be eliminated. By what amount would net relevant costs be increased or decreased if Chicago Company decides to buy part no. 118 from New York Company?

Solution: To solve this make-or-buy problem, you must identify the relevant costs per unit of making part no. 118 in-house.

Variable manufacturing costs:		
Direct materials	$ 4	
Direct labor	24	
Variable overhead	10	$38
Avoidable fixed overhead		3
Opportunity cost $\left(\dfrac{\$40,000}{10,000\ units}\right)$		4
Total relevant cost per unit		$45

Notice that the $40,000 ($4 per unit) potential savings in relevant costs for part no. 119 represents an opportunity cost of using the factory capacity for the production of part no. 118. Also notice that the avoidable fixed overhead cost of $3 per unit is relevant but the remaining unavoidable fixed overhead cost is not.

The relevant cost of producing part no. 118 in-house is $45 per unit as compared to the relevant cost of $43 per unit of buying part no. 118 from New York Company. The amount of the decrease in net relevant costs by buying from New York Company would be as follows:

Relevant cost to make in-house (per unit)	$45
Relevant cost to buy (per unit)	43
	$ 2
	× 10,000 units
Decrease in net relevant costs	$20,000

[See Section 11-4.]

PROBLEM 11-3: Star Company has 4,000 obsolete light fixtures in inventory with a manufacturing cost of $60,000. The company can rework the fixtures for $20,000 and then sell them for $36,000. Alternatively, it can sell them as scrap for $12,000. Which alternative should Star Company choose?

Solution: The following is a list of the relevant costs and revenues for each alternative of this sell-or-process-further decision.

	Rework	ll as scrap
Relevant revenue	$36,000	$12,000
Relevant costs	20,000	—
Net relevant revenue	$16,000	$12,000

Notice that the inventory cost of $60,000 is a sunk cost and is therefore irrelevant.

In this problem, Star Company should rework the fixtures, since the net relevant revenue of $16,000 from choosing this alternative exceeds the $12,000 from selling the fixtures as scrap. [See Section 11-2.]

PROBLEM 11-4: Computer Company manufactures 10,000 units of part C-1 annually for use in the production of minicomputers. The following costs are incurred at 10,000 units of production:

Direct materials	$ 20,000
Direct labor	50,000
Variable overhead	40,000
Fixed overhead	80,000
Total cost	$190,000

Disk Drive Company has offered to sell 10,000 units of C–1 to Computer Company for $14 per unit. If Computer Company accepts this offer, some of the facilities presently used to manufacture C–1 could be rented to a third party at an annual rental of $16,000. Should Computer Company accept Disk Drive Company's offer?

Solution: To solve this make-or-buy problem, you must first identify the relevant costs of making C–1 in-house.

Direct materials	$ 20,000
Direct labor	50,000
Variable overhead	40,000
Opportunity cost	16,000
Relevant costs of making C–1	$126,000

In comparison, the relevant costs of buying C–1 from Disk Drive Company are $140,000 ($14 × 10,000 units).

Computer Company would prefer to make C–1 in-house, since it would cost $14,000 less ($140,000 − $126,000) to make the part in-house than to buy it from Disk Drive Company. [See Section 11-4.]

PROBLEM 11-5: Southeast Company has an annual plant capacity of 2,000 units of product X, and the plant is currently operating at 50% of capacity (i.e., 1,000 units). Southeast is operating above the break-even point. Annual costs at a production level of 1,000 units are as follows:

Variable manufacturing cost	$10 per unit
Fixed manufacturing cost	$5 per unit
Variable selling cost	$1 per unit
Fixed selling and administrative costs	$5,000 per year

The normal selling price per unit for product X is $25. Central Company has offered to buy 100 units of product X for $20 per unit. The sale of the 100 units to Central Company would not displace any normal sales of product X. Southeast Company would incur variable selling costs of $1 per unit for the sale of the 100 units. There is no alternative use for the idle capacity at Southeast Company in the short run. Should Southeast Company accept Central Company's offer?

Solution: To solve this short-run pricing problem, you must compare the relevant costs and revenue of the special order:

Relevant revenue (per unit)		$ 20
Relevant costs (per unit):		
Variable manufacturing cost	$10	
Variable selling cost	1	11
Contribution margin (per unit)		$ 9
		× 100 units
Increase in profit		$900

Notice that the fixed manufacturing cost and fixed selling and administrative costs are irrelevant to this decision.

Southeast Company should accept the order of 100 units, since this order would increase the net income of the company by $900. [See Section 11-3.]

PROBLEM 11-6: Chemical Research Company has produced 1,000 gallons of product Z–1, which costs $5 per gallon to manufacture and sells for $8 per gallon. Alternatively, the company can refine Z–1 into a new product, Z–2, by incurring an additional processing cost of $4 per gallon. Z–2 sells for $15 per gallon. Should Chemical Research Company refine Z–1 further to produce Z–2?

Solution: In order to solve this sell-or-process-further problem, you must compare the relevant cost and revenue per unit for each alternative:

	Sell Z–1	Sell Z–2
Relevant revenue	$8	$15
Relevant cost	–	4
Net relevant revenue	$8	$9

Producing product Z–2 would increase Chemical Research Company's profit margin by $1 per unit ($9 − $8) and would therefore increase its profit by $1,000 ($1 × 1,000 units). The company should therefore refine Z–1 into Z–2. [See Section 11-5.]

PROBLEM 11-7: Micro Company manufactures part no. 15 for use in producing its final product, the Executive IV computer. The annual costs of producing 20,000 units of part no. 15 are as follows:

Direct materials	$ 120,000
Direct labor	600,000
Variable overhead	240,000
Fixed overhead	320,000
Total cost	$1,280,000

Alpha Company has offered to sell 20,000 units of part no. 15 to Micro Company for $60 per unit. If Micro accepts Alpha's offer, Micro will eliminate $180,000 of fixed overhead. In addition, Micro will be able to rent for $85,000 per year the factory capacity presently used in the production of part no. 15. Should Micro accept Alpha's offer?

Solution: In order to solve this make-or-buy problem, you must identify the relevant costs of making 20,000 units of part no. 15 in-house:

Direct materials	$ 120,000
Direct labor	600,000
Variable overhead	240,000
Opportunity cost (rent)	85,000
Avoidable fixed overhead	180,000
Total relevant costs	$1,225,000

In contrast, the relevant costs to buy part no. 15 from Alpha Company would be $1,200,000 ($60 × 20,000 units).

Micro Company should buy the parts from Alpha Company, since this alternative will save Micro $25,000 ($1,225,000 − $1,200,000). [See Section 11-4.]

PROBLEM 11-8: A truck with a cost of $20,000 is totally destroyed during its first day of use. Unfortunately, the truck was uninsured. The truck can be sold as scrap for $3,000 cash and replaced with a new truck costing $20,500, or it can be rebuilt for $16,000. Which alternative should be selected?

Solution: When solving this repair-or-replace decision, it is important to remember that the cost of the truck is a sunk cost and is therefore irrelevant. Only the expected future costs and revenues that differ between alternatives are relevant.

	Replace	Rebuild
Relevant revenue:		
Scrap value of old truck	$ 3,000	—
Relevant costs:		
Cost of new truck	20,500	—
Cost of rebuilding old truck	—	$16,000
Net relevant cost of each alternative	$17,500	$16,000

It would be preferable to rebuild the truck at a cost of $16,000 instead of replacing the truck at a net cost of $17,500. [See Section 11-2.]

PROBLEM 11-9: Digit Company currently buys 5,000 units of a subcomponent part for $20 per unit. The management of Digit feels that some of the company's idle capacity can be utilized to produce the part in-house. Following are the estimated costs of manufacturing the subcomponent.

	Per unit	Total
Direct materials	$ 5	$ 25,000
Direct labor	10	50,000
Variable overhead	2	10,000
Fixed overhead	5	25,000
Total costs	$22	$110,000

Assuming that there is no opportunity cost of using its idle capacity, and no additional fixed overhead costs will be incurred if the part is made in-house, should Digit Company make or buy the subcomponent part?

Solution: In order to solve this make-or-buy problem, you must remember that fixed costs are irrelevant unless they are avoidable. In this problem, the fixed costs are not avoidable and are therefore not relevant to the decision.

The relevant costs of making 5,000 units of the subcomponent part in-house are as follows:

	Per unit	Total
Direct materials	$ 5	$25,000
Direct labor	10	50,000
Variable overhead	2	10,000
Relevant costs to make	$17	$85,000

In contrast, the costs of buying 5,000 units of the part from an outside supplier are as follows:

	Per unit	Total
Relevant costs to buy	$20	$100,000

Digit Company could save $15,000 ($100,000 − $85,000) by making the subcomponent part in-house instead of buying it from an outside supplier. [See Section 11-4.]

PROBLEM 11-10: Mini Company annually produces 10,000 disk drives, which it sells to computer manufacturers for $200 each. The cost per unit of manufacturing each disk drive is as follows:

Direct materials	$ 75
Direct labor	25
Variable overhead	25
Fixed overhead	50
Total	$175

Mini Company has enough idle capacity, in the short run, to produce an additional 1,000 units of disk drives. A computer repair service, CRS Company (which is not a regular customer of Mini), has offered to buy 1,000 disk drives for $150 each. Should Mini Company accept this offer?

Solution: In this short-run pricing decision, you must remember that the fixed overhead costs are not relevant. By identifying the relevant costs and revenue, you can determine if accepting CRS Company's offer will increase or decrease Mini Company's profit.

Relevant revenue (per unit)		$ 150
Relevant costs (per unit):		
Direct materials	$75	
Direct labor	25	
Variable overhead	25	125
Contribution margin (per unit)		$ 25
		× 1,000 units
Increase in profit		$25,000

Based on this analysis, Mini Company should accept the offer to sell 1,000 units at $150 each because this would increase the company's profit by $25,000. [See Section 11-3.]

PROBLEM 11-11: Assume the same facts as presented in Problem 11-10, except that Mini Company could rent its idle capacity to Computer Company in the short run for $40,000. Should Mini Company sell the 1,000 units to CRS Company for $150 each?

Solution: The potential rental income of $40,000 represents an opportunity cost to the alternative of producing the 1,000 units for CRS Company. Therefore, the relevant costs and revenue are as follows:

Relevant revenue per unit		$ 150
Relevant costs per unit:		
Direct materials	$75	
Direct labor	25	
Variable overhead	25	
Opportunity cost $\left(\dfrac{\$40,000}{1,000 \text{ units}}\right)$	40	165
Loss per unit		($ 15)
		× 1,000 units
Decrease in profit		($15,000)

Based on the facts in this problem, Mini Company should not sell the 1,000 units to CRS Company for $150 per unit, since this alternative would result in a $15,000 decrease in profit. [See Section 11-3.]

12 DIRECT COSTING AND ABSORPTION COSTING

THIS CHAPTER IS ABOUT

☑ **Production Costs**
☑ **Differences Between Absorption Costing and Direct Costing**
☑ **Inventory Costing**
☑ **Income Measurement**
☑ **Income Statements**

12-1. Production Costs

Production costs can be divided into four components: (1) direct materials, (2) direct labor, (3) variable factory overhead, and (4) fixed factory overhead. Variable production costs include direct materials, direct labor, and variable factory overhead. Fixed production costs are the fixed factory overhead costs.

These four components of production costs can be classified as either product costs or period costs. *Product costs* are production costs that are inventoried (assigned to units of production). In other words, product costs are production costs that are included in product inventories (i.e., Work-in-Process Inventory and Finished Goods Inventory). Product costs are not expensed until the related units of production are sold. In contrast, *period costs* are expensed in the period incurred and are not included in product inventories.

This chapter describes two methods of accounting for production costs: absorption costing (also called full costing); and direct costing (also called variable or marginal costing). Variable production costs are accounted for in the same way under both absorption costing and direct costing. The variable production costs are classified as product costs and are assigned to units of production under both methods.

12-2. Differences Between Absorption Costing and Direct Costing

The primary difference between absorption costing and direct costing is each method's treatment of fixed factory overhead costs.

Absorption costing includes fixed factory overhead costs in product inventories. This approach is consistent with the concept of assigning all production costs to product inventories. Therefore, under absorption costing, both variable production costs and fixed factory overhead costs are absorbed or assigned to product inventories.

Direct costing considers the fixed factory overhead cost as the cost of providing production capacity for a certain period. Under direct costing, the fixed factory overhead cost is a period cost and is expensed in the period incurred and is not included in product inventories.

Another difference between absorption costing and direct costing is that absorption costing is required by generally accepted accounting principles (GAAP) for external financial reporting and by the Internal Revenue Service (IRS) for tax reporting. In contrast, direct costing is more useful for internal reporting, management decision making, and cost-volume-profit analysis because direct costing separates production costs into fixed and variable cost categories.

The following three sections will discuss the three major differences between absorption costing and direct costing:

1. inventory costing
2. income measurement
3. income statements

12-3. Inventory Costing

Absorption costing is the traditional method of inventory costing where all production costs—both variable and fixed—are assigned to inventory. Under both job-order costing (Chapter 3) and process costing (Chapter 4) the absorption costing method is generally used, and fixed overhead costs are applied to units of production.

Direct costing includes only variable production costs in inventory; the fixed production costs are expensed as period costs in the period incurred. Exhibit 12-1 illustrates the flow of production costs for both absorption costing and direct costing for inventory costing purposes.

EXHIBIT 12-1

Use of Absorption Costing vs. Direct Cost

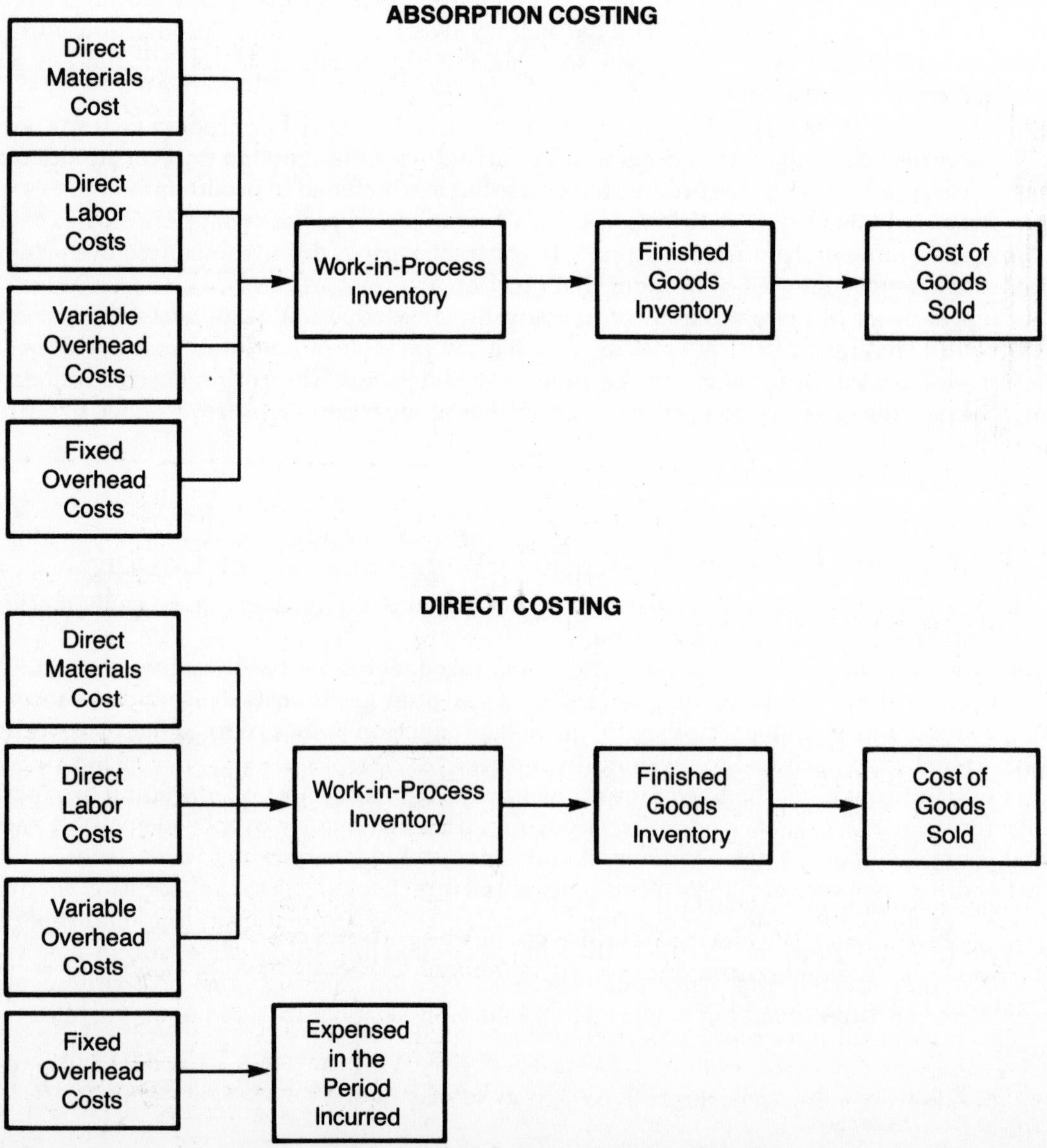

ABSORPTION COSTING

DIRECT COSTING

EXAMPLE 12-1: ABC Company, which began operations on January 1, 19X1, produces a product that sells for $10 per unit. During 19X1, 100,000 units were produced and 80,000 units were sold. Production costs and other costs were as follows:

Direct materials	$2.00/unit
Direct labor	$1.00/unit
Variable factory overhead	$0.50/unit
Fixed factory overhead	$150,000

Variable selling and administrative expenses	$ 50,000
Fixed selling and administrative expenses	80,000
Total selling and administrative expenses	$130,000

Assume that ending Work-in-Process Inventory is zero.

On the basis of this information, determine the production cost per unit for inventory costing based on (1) absorption costing and (2) direct costing.

Using absorption costing for inventory costing purposes, you would include all unit production costs (including fixed factory overhead costs per unit) in the unit cost.

ABSORPTION COSTING

Direct materials	$2.00/unit
Direct labor	1.00/unit
Variable factory overhead	0.50/unit
Fixed factory overhead cost per unit ($150,000/100,000 units)	1.50/unit
Production cost per unit, Absorption costing	$5.00/unit

The production cost per unit based on the direct costing method does not include the fixed overhead cost per unit. When using direct costing, only variable costs are included in inventory.

DIRECT COSTING

Direct materials	$2.00/unit
Direct labor	1.00/unit
Variable factory overhead	0.50/unit
Production cost per unit, Direct costing	$3.50/unit

12-4. Income Measurement

The measurement of net income (revenues minus expenses) under absorption costing and direct costing may differ for a particular period. The difference results from the amount of fixed factory overhead cost that is expensed in a particular period. Under absorption costing, the fixed overhead cost that is assigned to the units sold during the period is expensed. Under direct costing, the total fixed overhead cost incurred during that period is expensed.

In general, the income measurements under the two methods will differ when production and sales (in units) differ. For example, if more units are produced than are sold, net income under absorption costing will generally be greater than net income under direct costing. This is because absorption costing will only expense the fixed overhead costs assigned to the units sold, while direct costing will expense the total fixed overhead costs for the period.

The following is a summary of the differences in income measurement under various conditions:

1. If production = sales → absorption costing income = direct costing income
2. If production > sales → absorption costing income > direct costing income
3. If production < sales → absorption costing income < direct costing income

This summary is based on the assumption that production costs per unit are constant.

EXAMPLE 12-2: For the information given in Example 12-1, compute the net income using (1) absorption costing and (2) direct costing.

To find net income using absorption costing, you must first find the cost of goods sold. The cost of goods sold equals the number of units sold times the production cost per unit. The production cost per unit for absorption costing was found in Example 12-1 to be $5.00/unit. The selling and administrative expenses must also be subtracted from revenue to find net income.

ABSORPTION COSTING NET INCOME

Sales revenue (80,000 units × $10/unit)	$800,000
Cost of goods sold (80,000 units × $5.00/unit)	− 400,000
Selling and administrative expenses	− 130,000
Net income	$270,000

To find net income using direct costing, you must find the variable cost of goods sold. This is found by multiplying the number of units sold by the production cost per unit. Remember that when using direct costing, only the variable production costs are assigned to the units of production. The fixed factory overhead cost is expensed in the period incurred.

DIRECT COSTING NET INCOME

Sales revenue (80,000 units × $10/unit)	$800,000
Variable cost of goods sold	
(80,000 units × $3.50/unit)	− 280,000
Fixed factory overhead	− 150,000
Selling and administrative expenses	− 130,000
Net income	$240,000

In this example, production is greater than sales (100,000 units were produced and 80,000 units were sold). Therefore, absorption costing net income is greater than direct costing net income. The difference of $30,000 ($270,000 − $240,000) represents the fixed factory overhead costs of $1.50/unit that are assigned to the 20,000 units in the ending Finished Goods Inventory.

Units of production	100,000
Units of sales	− 80,000
Ending Finished Goods Inventory	20,000
Fixed factory overhead cost per unit	× $ 1.50
Fixed factory overhead costs assigned to ending Finished Goods Inventory (Absorption costing)	$30,000

Another way to explain the difference between the net income amounts is to compare the amount of fixed overhead cost expensed under each method.

Fixed overhead expensed (Direct costing)	$150,000
Fixed overhead expensed (Absorption costing)	
(80,000 units × $1.50/unit)	120,000
Difference	$ 30,000

This example demonstrates that the difference between the net income amounts under absorption costing and direct costing is the difference between treating fixed factory overhead cost as a product cost or as a period cost.

12-5. Income Statements

The income statements of absorption costing and direct costing differ with respect to the classification of expenses and the subtotals within the statements.

A. Absorption costing income statement

The absorption costing income statement is the traditional income statement, in which expenses are classified as either production expenses (cost of goods sold) or selling and administrative expenses. Fixed factory overhead costs assigned to the units sold are included in the cost of goods sold amount. Under absorption costing, the difference between sales revenue and the cost of goods sold is called the gross margin (or gross profit).

The basic format of an absorption costing income statement is as follows:

Sales revenue	$XXX
Cost of goods sold	– XXX
Gross margin	$XXX
Selling and administrative expenses	– XXX
Net income	$XXX

B. Direct costing income statements

The direct costing income statement is based on the classification of expenses by cost behavior (expenses are variable or fixed). The difference between sales revenue and variable expenses is called the *contribution margin*. The variable expenses include the variable cost of goods sold as well as other variable expenses such as variable selling and administrative expenses. Fixed expenses (fixed factory overhead costs and fixed selling and administrative expenses) are subtracted from the contribution margin to determine the net income.

A direct costing income statement has the following basic format:

Sales revenue	$XXX
Variable expenses:	
Variable cost of goods sold	– XXX
Variable selling and administrative expenses	– XXX
Contribution margin	$XXX
Fixed factory overhead expenses	– XXX
Fixed selling and administrative expenses	– XXX
Net income	$XXX

EXAMPLE 12-3: For the information given in Example 12-1, prepare the income statements using (1) absorption costing and (2) direct costing.

The income statement using absorption costing would be prepared as follows:

ABC Company
Income Statement
For the Year Ended, December 31, 19X1
Absorption Costing

Sales revenue (80,000 units × $10/unit)	$800,000
Cost of goods sold (80,000 units × $5.00/unit)	– 400,000
Gross margin	$400,000
Selling and administrative expenses	– 130,000
Net income	$270,000

The income statement using direct costing would be prepared as follows:

ABC Company
Income Statement
For the Year Ended, December 31, 19X1
Direct Costing

Sales revenue (80,000 × $10/unit)	$800,000
Variable cost of goods sold (80,000 units × $3.50/unit)	– 280,000
Variable selling and administrative expenses	– 50,000
Contribution margin	$470,000
Fixed factory overhead cost	– 150,000
Fixed selling and administrative expenses	– 80,000
Net income	$240,000

Remember that under direct costing, total fixed factory overhead costs are expensed in the period in which they are incurred.

RAISE YOUR GRADES

Can you explain...?

☑ the four components of production costs
☑ what product costs are
☑ what period costs are
☑ what costs are included in product inventories when using absorption costing
☑ what costs are included in product inventories when using direct costing
☑ how to account for fixed factory overhead costs when using absorption costing
☑ how to account for fixed factory overhead costs when using direct costing
☑ the types of reporting that absorption costing and direct costing are used for
☑ the differences in net income under absorption costing and direct costing
☑ the income statement format for absorption costing
☑ the income statement format for direct costing

SUMMARY

1. Production costs can be divided into four components: direct materials, direct labor, variable factory overhead, and fixed factory overhead.
2. Product costs are production costs that are assigned to units of production (inventoried).
3. Period costs are production costs that are expensed in the period incurred and are not included in inventory.
4. When using absorption costing, all production costs—variable and fixed—are classified as product costs.
5. When using direct costing, variable production costs are classified as product costs, and fixed production costs are classified as period costs.
6. Absorption costing is required by generally accepted accounting principles (GAAP) and by the Internal Revenue Service (IRS) for tax reporting.
7. Direct costing is useful for internal reporting, for management decision making, and for cost-volume-profit analysis because it separates costs into fixed and variable components.
8. Absorption costing and direct costing differ with respect to inventory costing, income measurement, and income statements.
9. Absorption costing is the traditional method of inventory costing where all production costs are included in product inventories.
10. Direct costing includes only variable production costs in product inventories and expenses the fixed production costs (fixed factory overhead) in the period incurred.
11. If production is greater than sales in a given period, then absorption costing net income will be greater than direct costing net income.
12. If production is less than sales in a given period, then absorption costing net income will generally be less than direct costing net income.
13. If production equals sales in a given period, then absorption costing net income will generally equal direct costing net income.
14. The absorption costing income statement is the traditional income statement and includes the subtotal of gross margin.
15. Under absorption costing, gross margin represents sales revenue minus cost of goods sold.
16. The direct costing income statement classifies expenses as variable or fixed and includes the subtotal of contribution margin.
17. Under direct costing, the contribution margin represents sales revenue minus variable expenses (variable cost of goods sold and variable selling and administrative expenses).

RAPID REVIEW

1. Product costs are production costs that are (a) expensed in the period incurred, (b) included in product inventories, (c) expensed before the related units of production are sold. [See Section 12-1.]

2. Which of the following production costs are classified as product costs when using absorption costing? (a) direct materials, (b) direct labor, (c) variable factory overhead, (d) fixed factory overhead, (e) all of the above. [See Section 12-2.]

3. Which of the following production costs are classified as period costs when using direct costing? (a) direct materials, (b) direct labor, (c) variable factory overhead, (d) fixed factory overhead, (e) none of the above. [See Section 12-2.]

4. For absorption costing, all production costs (including fixed factory overhead costs) are included in product inventories: (a) true, (b) false. [See Section 12-3.]

5. For direct costing, all production costs (including fixed factory overhead costs) are included in product inventories: (a) true, (b) false. [See Section 12-3.]

6. Product inventories include (a) Work-in-Process Inventory, (b) Finished Goods Inventory, (c) both of the above, (d) none of the above. [See Section 12-1.]

7. Absorption costing is required by generally accepted accounting principles (GAAP) for external financial reporting and by the Internal Revenue Service (IRS) for tax reporting: (a) true, (b) false. [See Section 12-2.]

8. Direct costing is useful for internal reporting, for management decision making, and for cost-volume-profit analysis: (a) true, (b) false. [See Section 12-2.]

9. If production is greater than sales (in units), then absorption costing net income will generally be (a) less than direct costing net income, (b) greater than direct costing net income, (c) equal to direct costing net income. [See Section 12-4.]

10. The difference in net income using absorption costing and direct costing reflects the difference between the amount expensed in that period for (a) variable factory overhead, (b) fixed factory overhead, (c) direct labor, (d) direct materials. [See Section 12-4.]

11. The absorption costing income statement includes (a) gross margin, (b) contribution margin, (c) none of the above. [See Section 12-5.]

12. The direct costing income statement includes (a) gross margin, (b) contribution margin, (c) none of the above. [See Section 12-5.]

Answers
1. (b) 2. (e) 3. (d) 4. (a) 5. (b) 6. (c) 7. (a) 8. (a) 9. (b) 10. (b)
11. (a) 12. (b)

SOLVED PROBLEMS

Problems 12-1 and 12-2 are based on the following information.

Geneva Company has incurred the following costs during the month of June:

Direct materials used	$300,000
Direct labor	300,000
Variable factory overhead	80,000
Fixed factory overhead	120,000

PROBLEM 12-1: Using absorption costing, identify and total the production costs that should be included in the product inventories Work-in-Process Inventory and Finished Goods Inventory.

Solution: Absorption costing includes all production costs (including fixed factory overhead costs) in product inventories:

Direct materials used	$300,000
Direct labor	300,000
Variable factory overhead	80,000
Fixed factory overhead	120,000
Total production costs,	
Absorption costing	$800,000

This $800,000 is included in inventory, and it will flow through the Work-in-Process Inventory, Finished Goods Inventory, and Cost of Goods Sold accounts, as described in Exhibit 12-1. [See Section 12-3.]

PROBLEM 12-2: Using direct costing, identify and total the production costs that should be included in product inventories.

Solution: Direct costing includes only the variable production costs in product inventories:

Direct materials used	$300,000
Direct labor	300,000
Variable factory overhead	80,000
Variable production costs,	
Direct costing	$680,000

[See Section 12-3.]

Problems 12-3 through 12-6 are based on the following information.

Cara Company has provided the following information for the year ended, December 31, 19X8:

Sales revenue	$1,400,000
Units produced	70,000
Units sold	60,000
Production costs:	
Variable	$ 630,000
Fixed	315,000
Total	$ 945,000
Selling and administrative expenses:	
Variable	$ 98,000
Fixed	140,000
Total	$ 238,000

Beginning Finished Goods Inventory was zero, and the ending Finished Goods Inventory was 10,000 units. In addition, there was no Work-in-Process Inventory at the beginning or end of 19X8.

PROBLEM 12-3: Determine the cost of the ending Finished Goods Inventory using the absorption costing method.

Solution: The absorption costing method includes total production costs (including fixed factory overhead) in inventory. You would compute the absorption costing production cost per unit by dividing total production costs by the number of units of production:

$$\text{Absorption costing production cost per unit} = \frac{\$945,000}{70,000 \text{ units}}$$

$$= \$13.50/\text{unit}$$

The cost of the ending Finished Goods Inventory under absorption costing is computed by multiplying the number of units in this ending inventory by the production cost per unit:

$$\text{Ending Finished Goods Inventory,} = 10,000 \text{ units} \times \$13.50/\text{unit}$$
$$\text{Absorption costing}$$
$$= \$135,000$$

[See Section 12-3.]

PROBLEM 12-4: Determine the cost of the ending Finished Goods Inventory using direct costing.

Solution: Only variable production costs are included in inventory under direct costing. You would compute the direct costing production cost per unit by dividing variable production costs by the number of units of production:

$$\text{Direct costing production} = \frac{\$630,000}{70,000 \text{ units}}$$
$$\text{cost per unit}$$
$$= \$9.00/\text{unit}$$

The cost of the ending Finished Goods Inventory under direct costing is computed by multiplying the number of units in this ending inventory by the production cost per unit:

$$\text{Ending Finished Goods Inventory,} = 10,000 \text{ units} \times \$9.00/\text{unit}$$
$$\text{Direct costing}$$
$$= \$90,000$$

[See Section 12-3.]

PROBLEM 12-5: Compute the net income for Cara Company using absorption costing.

Solution: When computing net income under absorption costing, you must first determine the cost of goods sold. To do this, multiply the number of units sold by the absorption costing production cost per unit, which was found in Problem 12-3 to be $13.50. The net income is found as follows:

Sales revenue	$1,400,000
Cost of goods sold	
(60,000 units × $13.50)	− 810,000
Selling and administrative	
expenses	− 238,000
Net income, absorption costing	$ 352,000

Remember that under absorption costing, the unit cost includes both fixed and variable production costs. [See Section 12-4.]

PROBLEM 12-6: Compute the net income for Cara Company using direct costing.

Solution: To find net income, you must compute the variable cost of goods sold using the direct costing production cost per unit, which was found in Problem 12-4 to be $9.00/unit. The net income under direct costing for Cara Company would be as follows:

Sales revenue	$1,400,000
Variable cost of goods sold	
(60,000 units × $9.00/unit)	− 540,000
Fixed production costs	− 315,000
Selling and administrative	
expenses	− 238,000
Net income, direct costing	$ 307,000

Remember that under direct costing, the unit cost includes only variable production costs. The entire amount of fixed production costs ($315,000) is expensed. [See Section 12-4.]

Problems 12-7 and 12-8 are based on the following information.

During the month of July 19X1, CM Company produced 10,000 units with the following costs:

Direct materials	$40,000
Direct labor	22,000
Variable factory overhead	13,000
Fixed factory overhead	10,000
Total production costs	$85,000

PROBLEM 12-7: Using direct costing, compute the production cost per unit for CM Company.

Solution: Using direct costing, you would compute the production cost per unit using only variable production costs:

Direct materials	$40,000
Direct labor	22,000
Variable factory overhead	13,000
Variable production costs	$75,000

The production cost per unit is computed by dividing the variable production costs by the number of units of production:

$$\text{Direct costing production cost per unit} = \frac{\$75,000}{10,000 \text{ units}}$$
$$= \$7.50/\text{unit}$$

[See Section 12-3.]

PROBLEM 12-8: Using absorption costing, compute the production cost per unit for CM Company.

Solution: Using absorption costing, the production cost per unit includes all production costs, including fixed factory overhead. Thus, the production cost per unit is computed by dividing total production costs by the number of units of production:

$$\text{Absorption costing production cost per unit} = \frac{\$85,000}{10,000 \text{ units}}$$
$$= \$8.50/\text{unit}$$

Note that the $1.00 difference between the absorption costing unit cost and the direct costing unit cost is the amount of fixed factory overhead applied to each unit ($10,000/10,000 units = $1.00 per unit). [See Section 12-3.]

PROBLEM 12-9: Micro Company incurred the following production costs in 19X4:

Direct materials used	$400,000
Direct labor	$400,000
Variable factory overhead	$ 35,000
Fixed factory overhead	$160,000

Identify the production costs that should be included in product inventories when using absorption costing.

Solution: Under absorption costing, all production costs are inventoried.

Direct materials used	$400,000
Direct labor	400,000
Variable factory overhead	35,000
Fixed factory overhead	160,000
Total production costs	$995,000

[See Section 12-3.]

Problems 12-10 to 12-13 are based on the following data.

The following information relates to the operations of San Francisco Company for 19X7:

Sales price per unit	$20
Units produced	10,000
Units sold	8,000
Direct materials used	$40,000
Direct labor incurred	$20,000
Fixed factory overhead	$25,000
Variable factory overhead	$12,000
Fixed selling and administrative expenses	$25,000
Variable selling and administrative expenses	$ 4,500

The beginning Finished Goods Inventory was zero, and the ending Finished Goods Inventory was 2,000 units. Work-in-Process Inventory was zero at the beginning and end of 19X7.

PROBLEM 12-10: What was the ending Finished Goods Inventory cost using absorption costing?

Solution: You must first determine the production cost per unit. Under absorption costing, this unit cost is based on both variable and fixed production costs:

Direct materials used	$40,000
Direct labor incurred	20,000
Fixed factory overhead	25,000
Variable factory overhead	12,000
Total production costs	$97,000

The absorption costing production cost per unit would be:

$$\text{Absorption costing production cost per unit} = \frac{\$97,000}{10,000 \text{ units}}$$
$$= \$9.70/\text{unit}$$

Based on this unit cost, you can determine the cost of the 2,000 units in the ending Finished Goods Inventory:

$$\text{Ending Finished Goods Inventory, Absorption costing} = 2,000 \text{ units} \times \$9.70/\text{unit}$$
$$= \$19,400$$

[See Section 12-3.]

PROBLEM 12-11: What was the ending Finished Goods Inventory cost using direct costing?

Solution: You must first determine the production cost per unit. Under direct costing, this unit cost is based on only the variable production costs:

Direct materials used	$40,000
Direct labor incurred	20,000
Variable factory overhead	12,000
Total production costs	$72,000

The direct costing production cost per unit would be:

$$\text{Direct costing production cost per unit} = \frac{\$72,000}{10,000 \text{ units}}$$
$$= \$7.20/\text{unit}$$

Based on this unit cost, you can determine the cost of the 2,000 units in the ending Finished Goods Inventory;

$$\frac{\text{Ending Finished Goods Inventory}}{\text{Direct costing}} = 2{,}000 \text{ units} \times \$7.20/\text{unit}$$

$$= \$14{,}400$$

[See Section 12-3.]

PROBLEM 12-12: Prepare an income statement based on absorption costing for San Francisco Company.

Solution: To prepare the absorption costing income statement, you would compute the cost of goods sold using the absorption costing production cost per unit of $9.70 that was found in Problem 12-10. The income statement would be as follows:

San Francisco Company
Income Statement
For the Year Ended December 31, 19X7
Absorption Costing

Sales revenue	
(8,000 units × $20/unit)	$160,000
Cost of goods sold	
(8,000 units × $9.70/unit)	− 77,600
Gross margin	$ 82,400
Selling and administrative expenses	− 29,500
Net income	$ 52,900

[See Section 12-5.]

PROBLEM 12-13: Prepare an income statement based on direct costing for San Francisco Company.

Solution: To prepare the direct costing income statement, you would compute the variable cost of goods sold using the direct costing production cost per unit of $7.20 that was found in Problem 12-11. The income statement would be as follows:

San Francisco Company
Income Statement
For the Year Ended December 31, 19X7
Direct Costing

Sales revenue	
(8,000 units × $20/unit)	$160,000
Variable cost of goods sold	
(8,000 units × $7.20/unit)	− 57,600
Variable selling and administrative expenses	− 4,500
Contribution margin	$ 97,900
Fixed factory overhead costs	− 25,000
Fixed selling and administrative expenses	− 25,000
Net income	$ 47,900

[See Section 12-5.]

PROBLEM 12-14: Chicago Manufacturing Company manufactures 1,000 units of Product A with a variable production cost of $6.00 per unit and a fixed production cost of $2.00 per unit. The beginning Finished Goods Inventory was zero, and the ending Finished Goods Inventory was 100 units. There was no Work-in-Process inventory at the beginning or end of the period. Using this information, compute the cost of the ending Finished Goods Inventory using (1) absorption costing and (2) direct costing.

Solution: To compute the cost of the ending Finished Goods Inventory using absorption costing, multiply the number of units in the ending inventory by the total production cost per unit. This unit cost is equal to the variable production cost per unit of $6.00 plus the fixed production cost per unit of $2.00 = $8.00 per unit.

$$\text{Ending Finished Goods Inventory, Absorption costing} = 100 \text{ units} \times \$8.00/\text{unit}$$
$$= \$800$$

To compute the cost of the ending Finished Goods Inventory using direct costing, you would use a production cost per unit of only $6.00, since only variable production costs are included in inventory under direct costing.

$$\text{Ending Finished Goods Inventory, Direct costing} = 100 \text{ units} \times \$6.00/\text{unit}$$
$$= \$600$$

[See Section 12-3.]

13 CAPITAL BUDGETING

THIS CHAPTER IS ABOUT

☑ **The Capital Budgeting Process**
☑ **Discounting Cash Flows**
☑ **Net Present Value Method**
☑ **Internal Rate-of-Return Method**
☑ **Payback Method**
☑ **Accounting Rate-of-Return Method**
☑ **Impact of Income Taxes on Capital Budgeting Decisions**

13-1. The Capital Budgeting Process

Capital budgeting is the process of evaluating and selecting major capital investment projects. These are long-term projects that involve cash inflows and cash outflows. Examples of capital investment projects are the purchase of new equipment and the purchase of plant facilities.

The evaluation of capital investment projects generally involves the use of capital budgeting methods that provide some measure of the profitability of a project. Beginning with Section 13-3, this chapter will describe four capital budgeting methods: (1) the net present value method, (2) the internal rate-of-return method, (3) the payback method, and (4) the accounting rate-of-return method.

The net present value method and the internal rate-of-return method are discounted cash flow methods. Discounted cash flow methods take into account the time value of money. Cash flows that will occur at various future dates cannot be compared as if they were of equal value. These cash flows must be discounted to their present values in order to make a valid comparison.

13-2. Discounting Cash Flows

In order to apply a discounted cash flow method when making a capital budgeting decision, you must first understand the concept of discounting cash flows.

The value of a cash flow today is called its present value. For example, the present value of one dollar today is $1, while the present value of $1 that will be received at some time in the future is less than $1.

Discounting is a process used to convert the cash flows for each year to their present value by multiplying each year's cash flow by the appropriate factor from a present value factor table.

Two present value factor tables are included in this chapter. Table 13-1 contains the present value factors for a single cash flow to be received n years from now. To use this table, find the number of years (n) from now when the cash flow occurs. Go across that row to the column that shows the interest rate (i) in your problem. That present value factor will be multiplied by the single future cash flow to find its present value.

You will use the present value factors in Table 13-1 to discount a single future cash flow when you solve net present value problems and internal rate-of-return problems.

Table 13-1
Present Value of $1.00

Years n	5%	6%	8%	10%	12%	14%	16%	18%	20%	22%	24%	25%
1	0.952	0.943	0.926	0.909	0.893	0.877	0.862	0.847	0.833	0.820	0.806	0.800
2	0.907	0.890	0.857	0.826	0.797	0.769	0.743	0.718	0.694	0.672	0.650	0.640
3	0.864	0.840	0.794	0.751	0.712	0.675	0.641	0.609	0.579	0.551	0.524	0.512
4	0.823	0.792	0.735	0.683	0.636	0.592	0.552	0.516	0.482	0.451	0.423	0.410
5	0.784	0.747	0.681	0.621	0.567	0.519	0.476	0.437	0.402	0.370	0.341	0.328
6	0.746	0.705	0.630	0.564	0.507	0.456	0.410	0.370	0.335	0.303	0.275	0.262
7	0.711	0.665	0.583	0.513	0.452	0.400	0.354	0.314	0.279	0.249	0.222	0.210
8	0.677	0.627	0.540	0.467	0.404	0.351	0.305	0.266	0.233	0.204	0.179	0.168
9	0.645	0.592	0.500	0.424	0.361	0.308	0.263	0.225	0.194	0.167	0.144	0.134
10	0.614	0.558	0.463	0.386	0.322	0.270	0.227	0.191	0.162	0.137	0.116	0.107
11	0.585	0.527	0.429	0.350	0.287	0.237	0.195	0.162	0.135	0.112	0.094	0.086
12	0.557	0.497	0.397	0.319	0.257	0.208	0.168	0.137	0.112	0.092	0.076	0.069
13	0.530	0.469	0.368	0.290	0.229	0.182	0.145	0.116	0.093	0.075	0.061	0.055
14	0.505	0.442	0.340	0.263	0.205	0.160	0.125	0.099	0.078	0.062	0.049	0.044
15	0.481	0.417	0.315	0.239	0.183	0.140	0.108	0.084	0.065	0.051	0.040	0.035
16	0.458	0.394	0.292	0.218	0.163	0.123	0.093	0.071	0.054	0.042	0.032	0.028
17	0.436	0.371	0.270	0.198	0.146	0.108	0.080	0.060	0.045	0.034	0.026	0.023
18	0.416	0.350	0.250	0.180	0.130	0.095	0.069	0.051	0.038	0.028	0.021	0.018
19	0.396	0.331	0.232	0.164	0.116	0.083	0.060	0.043	0.031	0.023	0.017	0.014
20	0.377	0.312	0.215	0.149	0.104	0.073	0.051	0.037	0.026	0.019	0.014	0.012

Table 13-2 contains the present value factors for a series of equal cash flows received (or paid) annually for any given number of years—an annuity. To use this table, find the number of years for which the annuity will be received or paid. Go across that row to the column that shows the interest rate (*i*) in your problem. That present value factor will be multiplied by the annual cash flow to find the present value of the annuity.

Table 13-2
Present Value of an Ordinary Annuity of $1.00

Years n	5%	6%	8%	10%	12%	14%	16%	18%	20%	22%	24%	25%
1	0.952	0.943	0.926	0.909	0.893	0.877	0.862	0.847	0.833	0.820	0.806	0.800
2	1.859	1.833	1.783	1.736	1.690	1.647	1.605	1.566	1.528	1.492	1.457	1.440
3	2.723	2.673	2.577	2.487	2.402	2.322	2.246	2.174	2.106	2.042	1.981	1.952
4	3.546	3.465	3.312	3.169	3.037	2.914	2.798	2.690	2.589	2.494	2.404	2.362
5	4.330	4.212	3.993	3.791	3.605	3.433	3.274	3.127	2.991	2.864	2.745	2.689
6	5.076	4.917	4.623	4.355	4.111	3.889	3.685	3.498	3.326	3.167	3.020	2.951
7	5.786	5.582	5.206	4.868	4.564	4.288	4.039	3.812	3.605	3.416	3.242	3.161
8	6.463	6.210	5.747	5.335	4.968	4.639	4.344	4.078	3.837	3.619	3.421	3.329
9	7.108	6.802	6.247	5.759	5.328	4.946	4.607	4.303	4.031	3.786	3.566	3.463
10	7.722	7.360	6.710	6.145	5.650	5.216	4.833	4.494	4.192	3.923	3.682	3.571
11	8.306	7.887	7.139	6.495	5.937	5.453	5.029	4.656	4.327	4.035	3.776	3.656
12	8.863	8.384	7.536	6.814	6.194	5.660	5.197	4.793	4.439	4.127	3.851	3.725
13	9.394	8.853	7.904	7.103	6.424	5.842	5.342	4.910	4.533	4.203	3.912	3.780
14	9.899	9.295	8.244	7.367	6.628	6.002	5.468	5.008	4.611	4.265	3.962	3.824
15	10.380	9.712	8.559	7.606	6.811	6.142	5.575	5.092	4.675	4.315	4.001	3.859
16	10.838	10.106	8.851	7.824	6.974	6.265	5.669	5.162	4.730	4.357	4.033	3.887
17	11.274	10.477	9.122	8.022	7.120	6.373	5.749	5.222	4.775	4.391	4.059	3.910
18	11.690	10.828	9.372	8.201	7.250	6.467	5.818	5.273	4.812	4.419	4.080	3.928
19	12.085	11.158	9.604	8.365	7.366	6.550	5.877	5.316	4.844	4.442	4.097	3.942
20	12.462	11.470	9.818	8.514	7.469	6.623	5.929	5.353	4.870	4.460	4.110	3.954

The present value factors in Table 13-2 will be used to compute the net present value and the internal rate of return when the cash inflows of a project are in the form of an annuity.

Both Tables 13-1 and 13-2 are based on the assumption that cash flows are received or paid at the end of the period.

If you understand discounting, go to Section 13-3, Net Present Value Method.

If you need more help to understand discounting, finish this section. We will give a short review of compounding and illustrate the relationship between compounding and discounting.

A. Compound (future) value of a single cash flow

Compounding is the process of determining what the amount that you have today will be worth in the future. In other words, you are finding the future value of a present value amount. Compounding is, therefore, the opposite of discounting.

You would compute the compound value of a single cash flow by using equation 13.1:

$$F_n = P(1 + i)^n \qquad \text{(13.1)}$$

F_n = the compound (future) value of a single cash flow for n periods at i% interest

P = the present value of a single cash flow

i = the interest rate per period

n = the number of periods

EXAMPLE 13-1: You deposited $100 at 5% interest compounded annually for 1 year. (Ignore income taxes.) You would compute the compound value (future value) at the end of 1 year using equation 13.1:

$$
\begin{aligned}
F_n &= P(1 + i)^n \\
&= \$100(1 + .05)^1 \\
&= \$100(1.05) \\
&= \$105
\end{aligned}
$$

Suppose you left your $100 deposited at 5% interest for 2 years instead of 1 year. You would also compute this compound value using equation 13.1, only now $n = 2$:

$$
\begin{aligned}
F_n &= P(1 + i)^n \\
&= \$100(1 + .05)^2 \\
&= \$100(1.1025) \\
&= \$110.25
\end{aligned}
$$

A cash flow diagram can be used to illustrate these compound cash flow values:

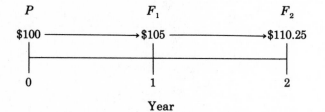

In equation 13.1, the factor $(1 + i)^n$ is called the *compound (future) value factor*. The compound value factor for $n = 2$ and $i = 5$% would be:

$$
\begin{aligned}
CVF &= (1 + i)^n \\
&= (1 + .05)^2 \\
&= 1.1025
\end{aligned}
$$

B. Present value of a single future cash flow

If you will receive an amount of money in the future (a single future cash flow), you can compute its present value using equation 13.2. Finding the present value of a single future cash flow is called discounting.

$$P = F_n \frac{1}{(1 + i)^n} \qquad \text{(13.2)}$$

EXAMPLE 13-2: You have a decision to make. You just won the lottery and it will pay you (a) $100 today, (b) $105 one year from today, or (c) $110.25 two years from today. Which alternative should you choose?

To solve this problem, you must find the present value of each amount. Assume a 5% interest rate.

(*a*) The present value of $100 received today is $100.

(*b*) To find the present value of $105 to be received one year from today, we must use equation 13.2:

$$P = F_n \frac{1}{(1 + i)^n}$$

$$= \$105 \frac{1}{(1 + .05)^1}$$

$$= \$105(.952)$$

$$= \$100$$

The present value of $105 to be received one year from today discounted at 5% is $100.

(*c*) To find the present value of $110.25 to be received two years from today, we must use equation 13.2:

$$P = F_n \frac{1}{(1 + i)^n}$$

$$= \$110.25 \frac{1}{(1 + .05)^2}$$

$$= \$110.25(.907)$$

$$= \$100$$

The present value of $110.25 to be received two years from today discounted at 5% is $100.

Alternatives (a), (b), and (c) all have the same present value ($100).

The following cash flow diagram illustrates the discounting of the cash flows that you have just computed. Note that the arrows pointing to the left indicate that the cash flows are being discounted.

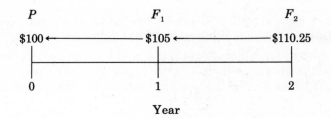

C. Present value factors

In equation 13.2, the factor $\frac{1}{(1 + i)^n}$ is called the *present value factor*. The present value factor for $n = 2$ and $i = 5\%$ would be:

$$PVF = \frac{1}{(1 + i)^n}$$

$$= \frac{1}{(1 + .05)^2}$$

$$= .907029478$$

The present value factors are presented in Table 13-1. To use this table, find the number of years (n). Go across this row to the column that shows the interest rate (i) in your problem. For our example, $n = 2$ and $i = 5\%$. You can see that the present value factor in the second row (2 years) and first column (5%) is .907, the same answer (rounded) as in our example.

You will use the present value factors to discount a single future cash flow whenever you solve net present value problems and internal rate-of-return problems.

EXAMPLE 13-3: What is the present value of $3,250 to be received in 7 years at a 10% interest rate? To find the present value, use Table 13-1. Go down the year column to 7 years and go across this row to the 10%

column. The present value factor is .513. Multiply the present value factor by the future amount to find its present value.

$$P = (F_n)(PVF)$$
$$= (\$3{,}250)(.513)$$
$$= \$1{,}667.25$$

The present value of $3,250 discounted at 10% for 7 years is $1,667.25.

D. Annuities

An annuity is a series of cash flows that (1) are equal in amount and (2) occur at equal intervals. An example of an annuity is the receipt of $1,000 at the end of each year for 3 years. The cash flow diagram of this annuity would be as follows:

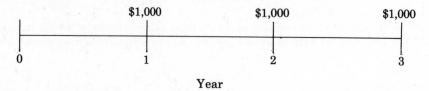

Year

There are two types of annuities: (1) an ordinary annuity (annuity in arrears) and (2) an annuity due. An *ordinary annuity* is an annuity whose cash flows occur at the end of the period. In contrast, an *annuity due* is an annuity whose cash flows occur at the beginning of the period.

E. Present value factor of an annuity

The present value factor of an annuity is the sum of the present value factors of a single future cash flow for the number of years (*n*) of the annuity. To find the present value of an annuity (PA), multiply the annual cash flow (AC) by the present value factor of an annuity (PVFA):

$$PA = (AC)(PVFA) \qquad \textbf{(13.3)}$$

Table 13-2 presents the present value factors of an ordinary annuity. To use this table, find the number of years (*n*) for which the annuity will be received. Go across this row to the column that shows the interest rate (*i*). That number will be your present value factor of that ordinary annuity (PVFA). To find the present value of the ordinary annuity, you would use equation 13.3.

EXAMPLE 13-4: You will receive $1,000 at the end of each year for 3 years. Assume an interest rate of 10%. From Table 13-2, you would find the present value factor of an annuity to be 2.487. This is found by finding the number of years (3) and going across this row to the 10% column. Using equation 13.3, you would compute the present value of this annuity as follows:

$$PA = (AC)(PVFA)$$
$$= (\$1{,}000)(2.487)$$
$$= \$2{,}487$$

The present value of $1,000 to be received at the end of each year for 3 years discounted at 10% is $2,487.

13-3. Net Present Value Method

You can use the net present value method to determine whether a capital investment project should be accepted or rejected. The net present value (NPV) is equal to the present value of cash inflows [cash inflows discounted at the minimum acceptable rate of return (MARR)] minus the present value of cash outflows.

A. Minimum acceptable rate of return

The minimum acceptable rate of return (*MARR*) is sometimes referred to as the hurdle rate or minimum required rate of return. The *MARR* represents the minimum rate of return that management is willing to accept. For example, a *MARR* of 10% means that investment projects must have a rate of return of at least 10% in order to be approved by management.

B. Computing the net present value

You would compute the net present value of a project as follows:

> Present value of cash inflows
> − Present value of cash outflows
> = Net present value

EXAMPLE 13-5: A capital investment project has the following expected cash flows:

> Initial investment (cash outflow): $2,246
> Annual cash inflow (at the end of
> each year for 3 years): $1,000

Assume that the MARR is 10%. From Table 13-2, the present value factor of an annuity for 3 years at 10% interest is 2.487. You would compute the net present value of this project as follows:

Present value of cash inflows ($1,000 × 2.487)	$2,487
− Present value of cash outflows	− 2,246
= Net present value	$ 241

C. Net present value decision rules

Once you have calculated the net present value, you can use this figure to determine whether a capital investment project is acceptable.

Reject projects with a negative NPV.

An independent project (one whose acceptance or rejection would not be affected by the acceptance or rejection of another project) would be accepted if the net present value is greater than or equal to zero.

For mutually exclusive projects (the acceptance of one project precludes the acceptance of the other), the project with the higher net present value should be accepted, assuming that the NPV is greater than or equal to zero.

In summary, the decision rules for evaluating capital investment projects using the net present value method are:

1. Reject projects with a negative NPV
2. Independent projects
   Accept the project if NPV $\geq$ 0
3. Mutually exclusive projects
   Accept the project with the higher NPV, assuming that NPV $\geq$ 0

Thus, the project described in Example 13-5, which has a net present value of $241, would be acceptable since that net present value is greater than zero.

13-4. Internal Rate-of-Return Method

The internal rate of return (time-adjusted rate of return) is the interest rate that equates the present value of cash inflows with the present value of cash outflows.

A. Computing the internal rate of return

You would compute the internal rate of return (IRR) by finding the interest rate that will result in the present value of cash inflows being equal to the present value of cash outflows. There are two ways to compute the IRR, depending on the project's pattern of cash inflows.

1. PRESENT VALUE FACTOR METHOD

You can use this method for projects where the annual cash inflows are constant and occur at equal intervals (i.e., the cash inflows are an annuity), and the initial investment is the only investment cash outflow. Using this method, you would first compute the present value factor of an annuity (PVFA) for the project using equation 13.4:

$$\text{PVFA} = \frac{\text{Initial investment}}{\text{Annual cash inflow}} \tag{13.4}$$

After computing the PVFA, you would go to Table 13-2 and find the row for the number of years over which the annuity is to be received. You would go across this row until you found the PVFA that you just computed. The interest rate at the top of this column is the internal rate of return.

2. TRIAL-AND-ERROR METHOD

You would use this method for projects where the annual cash inflows are not constant. Under this method, you would use the present value factors in Table 13-1 to compute the present values of cash inflows and cash outflows. The objective is to find the interest rate that will make the present value of cash inflows equal to the present value of cash outflows.

EXAMPLE 13-6: Assume that two projects, A and B, have the following cash flows:

Project A:
Initial investment = $2,246
Annual cash inflows (at the end of
each year for 3 years) = $1,000

Project B:
Initial investment = $4,110
Cash inflow at the end of year 1 = $1,000
Cash inflow at the end of year 2 = $2,000
Cash inflow at the end of year 3 = $3,000

You would compute the IRR for Project A using the present value factor method, since the annual cash inflows are in the form of an annuity. You would first compute the present value factor of an annuity using equation 13.4:

$$\text{PVFA} = \frac{\text{Initial investment}}{\text{Annual cash inflow}}$$

$$= \frac{\$2,246}{\$1,000}$$

$$= 2.246$$

Now, looking in Table 13-2 for $n = 3$ years, you would find that the factor 2.246 corresponds to an interest rate of 16%. Therefore, the internal rate of return for Project A is 16%.

The IRR for Project B would be computed using the *trial-and-error method*, since the annual cash inflows are not constant. The objective is to find the interest rate that will equate the present value of cash inflows with the present value of cash outflows. You would start with an arbitrary interest rate, say 16%. Go to Table 13-1 and find the 16% interest column. In year 1, the PVF = .862; year 2 = .743; year 3 = .641. Compute the present value of each cash inflow by multiplying the appropriate PVF by the cash inflow:

Present value of cash inflows (at 16%):
$1,000 × .862 = $ 862
$2,000 × .743 = $1,486
$3,000 × .641 = $1,923
                 $4,271

Present value of
cash outflows   = $4,110

Since the present value of cash inflows is greater than the initial investment of $4,110, you will need to use a higher interest rate to obtain a lower present value of cash inflows. Your next attempt would be at 18% interest:

Present value of cash inflows (at 18%):
$1,000 × .847 = $ 847
$2,000 × .718 = $1,436
$3,000 × .609 = $1,827
                 $4,110

Present value of
cash outflows   = $4,110

The *IRR* for Project *B* is 18%, since the present value of cash inflows equals the present value of cash outflows at that interest rate. If the *IRR* is between two interest rates, you would need to consult a more detailed present value factor table, or you would estimate the value of the *IRR*, using the two interest rates as a guide (linear interpolation).

B. *IRR* decision rules

The decision rules for evaluating projects using the *IRR* method are as follows:

1. Independent projects:
   Accept the project if $IRR \geq MARR$
   Reject the project if $IRR < MARR$
2. Mutually exclusive projects:
   Accept the project with the higher *IRR*, assuming that $IRR \geq MARR$

For example, if the *IRR* of an independent project is 16% and the *MARR* is 10%, the project would be accepted.

C. Net present value profile

The NPV profile is useful for showing the relationship between the NPV and the IRR. The NPV profile is a graph of the net present value at various interest rates.

The NPV profile for the project described in Example 13-5 is presented in Figure 13-1. The net present value at the interest rate of 10% is $241. The net present value at an interest rate of 0% would be $754 (cash inflows of $3,000 minus cash outflows of $2,246). The point where the NPV profile intersects the horizontal axis (NPV = 0) represents the internal rate of return (IRR). Remember that the IRR is the interest rate that equates the present value of cash inflows with the present value of cash outflows. In Table 13-2, the present value factor for 3 years at 16% interest is 2.246. Using the information in Example 13-5 and the present value factor of 2.246, you can see that cash inflows ($1,000 × 2.246 = $2,246) would equal cash outflows ($2,246) at 16%.

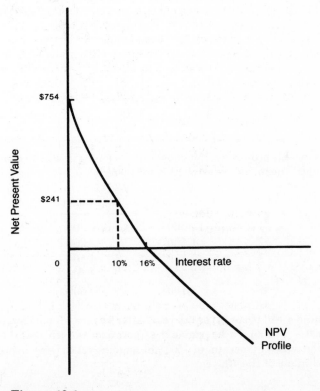

Figure 13-1
Net Present Value Profile

13-5. Payback Method

The *payback* (payout, payoff) of a project measures the amount of time necessary to recover the initial investment in a project. In other words, the payback determines how long it will take for accumulated cash inflows to equal the initial investment (cash outflow).

A. Computing the payback

You can compute the payback of a project for which the cash inflows are constant by using the following equation:

$$\text{Payback} = \frac{\text{Initial investment}}{\text{Annual cash inflow}} \qquad (13.5)$$

If the cash inflows are not constant, then you would determine the payback by computing the number of years it will take for accumulated cash inflows to equal the initial investment.

EXAMPLE 13-7: Assume that the cash flows for a project are as follows:

$$\text{Initial investment} = \$3,000$$
$$\text{Annual cash inflows (at the end}$$
$$\text{of each year for 5 years)} = \$1,000$$

The payback for this project would be computed using equation 13.5:

$$\text{Payback} = \frac{\text{Initial investment}}{\text{Annual cash inflow}}$$
$$= \frac{\$3,000}{\$1,000}$$
$$= 3 \text{ years}$$

EXAMPLE 13-8: Assume that the cash flows for a project are as follows:

$$\text{Initial investment} = \$5,000$$
Cash Inflows

Year	Cash Inflow
1	$ 500
2	1,500
3	2,500
4	3,000
5	3,100

Because the cash inflows for this project are not constant, the payback will be computed by accumulating each year's cash inflow until the initial investment is recovered.

Year	Cash Inflow	Accumulated
1	$ 500	$ 500
2	1,500	2,000
3	2,500	4,500
4	3,000	7,500
5	3,100	10,600

The payback for this project will occur in the 4th year. After 3 years, all but $500 of the initial investment has been recovered ($5,000 − $4,500). To determine the fraction of the 4th year that it will take to recover the $500, develop a fraction with a numerator of $500 (the amount yet to be recovered in the 4th year) and a denominator of the cash inflow of the 4th year:

$$3 \text{ years} + \frac{500}{3,000} = 3.167 \text{ years to recover initial investment}$$

B. Payback decision rules

The decision rules for the payback method are as follows:

1. Independent projects:
   Accept the project if payback $\leq$ maximum acceptable payback set by management
2. Mutually exclusive projects:
   Accept the project with the lower payback, assuming that the payback $\leq$ maximum acceptable payback set by management

C. Payback reciprocal

You can use the payback reciprocal to approximate the internal rate of return if (*1*) the life of the project is at least twice the payback period and (*2*) the cash inflows per year are constant. You would compute the payback reciprocal as follows:

$$\text{Payback reciprocal} = \frac{1}{\text{Payback}} \qquad \textbf{(13.6)}$$

For example, if the payback of a project is 5 years, the payback reciprocal of 1/5 (i.e., 20%) would be an approximation of the project's *IRR*.

13-6. Accounting Rate-of-Return Method

The accounting rate of return (accrual accounting rate of return) is the ratio of the annual operating income of the project to either total or average investment. Each problem will specify whether to use total investment or average investment.

A. Computing the accounting rate of return

You would compute the accounting rate of return (AROR) as follows:

$$\text{AROR} = \frac{\text{Average annual operating income}}{\text{Total investment (or average investment)}} \qquad \textbf{(13.7)}$$

EXAMPLE 13-9: The average annual operating income of a project is $5,000, and the initial investment is $50,000. The AROR based on total investment would be computed using equation 13.7:

$$\text{AROR} = \frac{\text{Average annual operating income}}{\text{Total investment}}$$

$$= \frac{\$5,000}{\$50,000}$$

$$= 10\%$$

The AROR based on average investment would be:

$$\text{AROR} = \frac{\text{Average annual operating income}}{\text{Average investment}}$$

$$= \frac{\$5,000}{(\$50,000/2)}$$

$$= 20\%$$

Notice that the average investment is computed by dividing the total investment by 2.

B. AROR decision rules

The decision rules for using the AROR to evaluate projects are as follows:

1. Independent projects:
   Accept a project if AROR $\geq$ minimum acceptable AROR set by management
2. Mutually exclusive projects:
   Accept the project with the higher AROR, assuming that the AROR $\geq$ minimum acceptable AROR set by management

13-7. Impact of Income Taxes on Capital Budgeting Decisions

The net present value method, internal rate-of-return method, and the payback method as presented in the previous sections have ignored the effect of income taxes on capital budgeting decisions. To take income taxes into account when using the above methods, you must use after-tax cash flows in your calculations. Also, when computing the NPV and when evaluating the IRR computations, you would use the after-tax minimum acceptable rate of return (MARR). In this section, you will learn how to compute (1) the after-tax annual cash flows and (2) the after-tax AROR. The after-tax MARR will usually be given to you in problems.

A. Total after-tax annual cash flows

Total after-tax annual cash flows usually include after-tax cash flows + the depreciation tax effect.

1. AFTER-TAX CASH FLOWS

You would compute after-tax cash flows using equation 13.8:

$$\frac{\text{After-tax}}{\text{cash flows}} = \frac{\text{Before-tax}}{\text{cash flows}} \times \left(1 - \frac{\text{marginal}}{\text{tax rate}}\right) \tag{13.8}$$

$$\text{ATCF} = (\text{BTCF})(1 - t)$$

You can use equation 13.8 to compute after-tax cash flows for both cash inflows and cash outflows.

2. DEPRECIATION TAX EFFECT

Taxable income is reduced by the amount of depreciation expense taken (for tax purposes) in that year. The depreciation tax effect represents the amount of tax dollars saved due to decreasing taxable income by the amount of the tax depreciation expense. You would compute the depreciation tax effect (DTE) by multiplying the depreciation expense by the marginal tax rate:

$$\text{Depreciation tax effect} = (\text{Depreciation expense})(\text{marginal tax rate})$$

$$\text{DTE} = (\text{DE})(t) \tag{13.9}$$

Remember that depreciation expense is not a cash flow, but that the reduction in tax payments due to the deductibility of depreciation expense (i.e., the depreciation tax effect) *is* a cash flow.

B. After-tax accounting rate of return

You would compute the after-tax accounting rate of return (AT AROR) using equation 13.10:

$$\text{AT AROR} = \frac{\text{After-tax annual operating income}}{\text{Total investment (or Average investment)}} \tag{13.10}$$

$$\text{AT AROR} = \frac{\text{AT AOI}}{\text{TI (or AI)}}$$

The after-tax annual operating income (AT AOI) would be calculated using equation 13.11:

$$\text{AT AOI} = (\text{Annual operating income})(1 - \text{marginal tax rate})$$

$$\text{AT AOI} = (\text{AOI})(1 - t) \tag{13.11}$$

EXAMPLE 13-10: The following information is given for a capital investment project:

> Initial investment: $5,000
> Annual net operating cash inflows
>   (at the end of each year for 5 years): $2,000
> Marginal tax rate: 40%
> Maximum acceptable payback: 3.5 years
> After-tax MARR: 8%
> Minimum acceptable accounting rate of return: 11%
> Annual depreciation (Straight line, 5 year,
>   no salvage value: $5,000/5 yrs.) $1,000

Find the total after-tax annual cash flows and use them in each of the four capital budgeting methods to evaluate the investment project.

TOTAL AFTER-TAX ANNUAL CASH FLOWS

Total after-tax annual cash flows equal after-tax cash flows + the depreciation tax effect.

After-tax cash flows

Use equation 13.8 to compute the ATCF:

$$\begin{aligned} \text{ATCF} &= (\text{BTCF})(1 - t) \\ &= (\$2{,}000)(1 - .40) \\ &= \$1{,}200 \end{aligned}$$

Depreciation tax effect

Use equation 13.9 to compute the DTE:

$$\begin{aligned} \text{DTE} &= (\text{DE})(t) \\ &= (\$1{,}000)(.40) \\ &= \$400 \end{aligned}$$

$$\begin{aligned} \text{Total after-tax annual cash flows} &= \text{ATCF} + \text{DTE} \\ &= \$1{,}200 + \$400 \\ &= \$1{,}600 \end{aligned}$$

AFTER-TAX NET PRESENT VALUE METHOD

The after-tax net present value method (AT NPV) is equal to the after-tax cash flows discounted at the after-tax minimum acceptable rate of return minus the present value of cash outflows (initial investment). The after-tax MARR is 8%. From Table 13-2, the present value factor for 5 years at an 8% return is 3.993.

Present value of total after-tax cash inflows ($1,600 × 3.993)	$6,389
Present value of cash outflows	5,000
After-tax net present value	$1,389

Because the project has a positive AT NPV, it should be accepted.

AFTER-TAX INTERNAL-RATE-OF-RETURN METHOD

For this particular investment project, you can use the present value method to determine the after-tax IRR because the cash inflow is an annuity and the initial investment is the only investment cash outflow. Use equation 13.4 to compute the present value factor of an annuity (PVFA).

$$\begin{aligned} \text{PVFA} &= \frac{\text{Initial investment}}{\text{Annual after-tax cash flow}} \\ &= \frac{\$5{,}000}{\$1{,}600} \\ &= 3.125 \end{aligned}$$

Looking in Table 13-2 under $n = 5$ years, you would find that the present value factor of 3.127 is closest to the computed factor of 3.125. The corresponding interest rate is 18%. Therefore, the after-tax IRR is approximately 18%. The after-tax MARR is 8%. Therefore, you would accept this project because the after-tax IRR is greater than the after-tax MARR.

AFTER-TAX PAYBACK METHOD

To determine how long it will take for the accumulated after-tax cash flows to equal the initial investment, use equation 13.5, substituting after-tax annual cash flows for annual cash flows:

$$\begin{aligned} \text{Payback (After tax)} &= \frac{\text{Initial investment}}{\text{After-tax annual cash flow}} \\ &= \frac{\$5{,}000}{\$1{,}600} \\ &= 3.125 \text{ years} \end{aligned}$$

This payback is less than the maximum acceptable payback set by management (3.5 years), so this project should be accepted.

AFTER-TAX ACCOUNTING RATE OF RETURN METHOD

To compute the after-tax AROR, you must first compute the annual operating income, which equals annual net operating cash inflows of $2,000 minus the depreciation expense of $1,000, which equals $1,000. Remember that the after-tax annual operating income is found by multiplying the annual operating income by (1 − marginal tax rate).

$$\text{AT AROR} = \frac{(\text{AOI})(1 - t)}{\text{Total investment}}$$

$$= \frac{(\$1,000)(1 - .40)}{\$5,000}$$

$$= 12\%$$

The AT AROR is 12%, and the minimum acceptable AROR set by management is 11%. Therefore, this project should be accepted.

RAISE YOUR GRADES

Can you explain...?

☑ what capital budgeting is
☑ how to compute the present value of a single future cash flow
☑ how to compute the present value of an annuity
☑ what the net present value of a project is
☑ how to compute the net present value
☑ what the internal rate of return is
☑ how to compute the internal rate of return
☑ what the payback is
☑ how to compute the payback of a project
☑ what the accounting rate of return is
☑ how to compute the accounting rate of return
☑ how to compute after-tax cash flows
☑ how to compute the after-tax accounting rate of return
☑ how to evaluate a capital budgeting project using each of the four capital budgeting methods

SUMMARY

1. Capital budgeting is the process of evaluating and selecting capital investment projects.
2. The net present value method and internal rate of return method are discounted cash flow methods.
3. Discounting a cash flow involves computing the present value of the cash flow.
4. The present value of a single future cash flow equals the cash flow multiplied by the appropriate present value factor.
5. An annuity is a series of cash flows that are equal in amount and occur at equal time intervals.
6. The present value of an annuity equals the annual cash flow multiplied by the appropriate present value factor of an annuity.
7. The net present value (NPV) is equal to the cash inflows discounted at the minimum acceptable rate of return (MARR) minus the present value of cash outflows (initial investment).
8. A project will generally be accepted if the net present value is greater than or equal to zero.
9. The internal rate of return (IRR) is the interest rate that equates the present value of cash inflows with the present value of cash outflows.
10. A project will generally be accepted if the internal rate of return is greater than or equal to the minimum acceptable rate of return.

11. The payback is the amount of time necessary to recover the initial investment in a project.
12. The payback reciprocal provides an approximation of the internal rate of return if the life of the project is at least twice the payback period and the annual cash inflows are constant.
13. The accounting rate of return is the ratio of the annual operating income to total (or average) investment.
14. After-tax cash flows equal before-tax cash flows multiplied by (1 − marginal tax rate).
15. The depreciation tax effect equals the depreciation expense multiplied by the marginal tax rate.

RAPID REVIEW

1. Capital budgeting methods provide some measure of the profitability of capital budgeting projects: (a) true, (b) false. [See Section 13-1.]
2. The net present value method and accounting rate-of-return method are both discounted cash flow methods: (a) true, (b) false. [See Section 13-1.]
3. The minimum acceptable rate of return (MARR) is necessary in order to compute (a) internal rate of return, (b) net present value, (c) payback, (d) accounting rate of return. [See Section 13-3.]
4. The payback of a project equals the initial investment in a project divided by the (a) discount rate, (b) annual cash inflow, (c) minimum acceptable rate of return. [See Section 13-5.]
5. The accounting rate of return on a project equals the annual operating income divided by (a) total (or average) investment, (b) annual cash flows, (c) minimum acceptable rate of return. [See Section 13-6.]
6. The internal rate of return is the interest rate that equates the present value of cash inflows with the present value of cash outflows: (a) true, (b) false. [See Section 13-4.]
7. An annuity is a series of cash flows that (a) are equal in amount, (b) occur at equal time intervals, (c) both (a) and (b). [See Section 13-2.]
8. The net present value is equal to the cash inflows discounted at the minimum acceptable rate of return minus (a) the accounting rate of return, (b) internal rate of return, (c) minimum acceptable rate of return, (d) the present value of cash outflows. [See Section 13-3.]
9. When using the present value factor method to compute the internal rate of return, you divide the initial investment by (a) accumulated cash flows, (b) minimum acceptable rate of return, (c) annual cash inflow. [See Section 13-4.]
10. You can use the payback reciprocal to approximate the (a) net present value, (b) internal rate of return, (c) accounting rate of return. [See Section 13-5.]
11. If the net present value of a project is greater than or equal to zero, the project should generally be accepted: (a) true, (b) false. [See Section 13-3.]

Answers
1. (a)   2. (b)   3. (b)   4. (b)   5. (a)   6. (a)   7. (c)   8. (d)   9. (c)   10. (b)
11. (a)

SOLVED PROBLEMS

Problems 13-1 to 13-3 are based on the following data.

Northern Company is considering a project that requires an initial investment of $72,100 and that is expected to result in annual cash inflows from operations of $20,000 for 5 years.

PROBLEM 13-1: Compute the internal rate of return for the project.

Solution: In order to compute the *IRR* for this project, you would use the present value factor method, since the annual cash inflows are constant.

$$\text{Present value factor} = \frac{\$72,100}{\$20,000}$$

$$= 3.605$$

Looking in Table 13-2, you would find that the present value of an annuity for 5 years with a factor of 3.605 corresponds to an interest rate of 12%. Therefore, the *IRR* of this project is 12%. [See Section 13-4.]

PROBLEM 13-2: Compute the net present value for the project, assuming a minimum acceptable rate of return of 10%.

Solution: To compute the net present value of the project, you must first find the present value of annuity factor. From Table 13-2, the factor for $n = 5$ years and $i = 10\%$ is 3.791. Thus,

Present value of cash inflows	
($20,000)(3.791)	$75,820
— Present value of cash outflows	— 72,100
= Net present value	$ 3,720

[See Section 13-3.]

PROBLEM 13-3: Compute the payback for the project.

Solution: You would compute the payback for the project by using equation 13.5:

$$\text{Payback} = \frac{\$72,100}{\$20,000}$$

$$= 3.605 \text{ years}$$

[See Section 13-5.]

Problems 13-4 and 13-5 are based on the following data.

DePaul Company is considering a project with an initial investment of $100,000 and with annual cash inflows from operations of $35,000 for 10 years. The initial investment (purchase of new equipment) will be depreciated for tax purposes and accounting purposes over the 10 years using the straight-line method and zero salvage value.

PROBLEM 13-4: Compute the accounting rate of return of the project based on total investment.

Solution: In order to compute the accounting rate of return, you must first compute the annual operating income by subtracting the annual depreciation from the annual cash inflow. Note that you find the depreciation expense to be $10,000 by dividing the initial investment of $100,000 by the 10-year life of the equipment.

Annual operating income = Annual operating cash inflow — Depreciation

$$= \$35,000 - \$10,000$$

$$= \$25,000$$

The accounting rate of return by using equation 13.7 would be:

$$AROR = \frac{\$25,000}{\$100,000}$$

$$= 25\%$$

[See Section 13-6.]

PROBLEM 13-5: Compute the payback and payback reciprocal of the project.

Solution: You would compute the payback of the project by using equation 13.5:

$$\text{Payback} = \frac{\$100,000}{\$35,000}$$
$$= \underline{\underline{2.86 \text{ years}}}$$

You would compute the payback reciprocal using equation 13.6:

$$\text{Payback reciprocal} = \frac{1}{2.86 \text{ years}}$$
$$= \underline{\underline{35.0\%}}$$

[See Section 13-5.]

Problems 13-6 and 13-7 are based on the following data.

SSS Company plans to purchase a machine with a cost of $125,000, which will be depreciated on a straight-line basis over the 5-year life of the machine, with no salvage value. The cash inflows from operations will be $50,000 per year. Assume that the marginal tax rate for SSS Company is 40%.

PROBLEM 13-6: Compute the payback after taxes for the investment in the machine.

Solution: In order to compute the payback after taxes, you must first compute the annual cash inflows after taxes.

Operating cash inflow after taxes	
($50,000)(1 − .40)	$30,000
+ Depreciation tax effect	
($125,000/5)(.40)	10,000
= Total cash inflow after taxes	$40,000

Now you can compute the payback after taxes.

$$\text{Payback (after taxes)} = \frac{\$125,000}{\$40,000}$$
$$= \underline{\underline{3.125 \text{ years}}}$$

[See Section 13-7.]

PROBLEM 13-7: Using a minimum acceptable rate of return of 10%, compute the net present value after taxes of the investment in the project.

Solution: To compute the net present value after taxes, you must first look in Table 13-2 for $n = 5$ years and $i = 10\%$ to find the present value factor of 3.791. From Problem 13-6, you know that the after-tax cash inflow is $40,000.

Present value of after-tax cash	
inflow ($40,000)(3.791)	$151,640
− Present value of cash outflow	− 125,000
= Net present value after taxes	$ 26,640

[See Sections 13-3 and 13-7.]

Problems 13-8 to 13-10 are based on the following data.

Cara Company is planning to invest in a project with an initial investment of $411,100 and annual after-tax cash inflows of $100,000 for 6 years.

PROBLEM 13-8: Compute the internal rate of return after taxes.

Solution: In order to compute the after-tax internal rate of return, you would use the present value factor method, since the annual cash inflows are constant.

$$\text{Present value factor} = \frac{\$411,100}{\$100,000}$$

$$= 4.111$$

From Table 13-2, the interest rate corresponding to the factor 4.111 for $n = 6$ years is 12%, so this is the internal rate of return. Note that it was assumed that the annual cash inflows after taxes of $100,000 included the depreciation tax effect. [See Section 13-7.]

PROBLEM 13-9: Compute the net present value after taxes using a 10% minimum acceptable rate of return.

Solution: From Table 13-2 for $n = 6$ years and $i = 10\%$, you find the present value factor of 4.355. You would compute the net present value after taxes as follows:

Present value of after-tax cash inflows ($100,000)(4.355)	$435,500
— Present value of cash outflow	— 411,100
= Net present value after taxes	$ 24,400

[See Section 13-7.]

PROBLEM 13-10: Compute the payback after taxes.

Solution: You would compute the payback after taxes as follows:

$$\text{Payback (after taxes)} = \frac{\$411,100}{\$100,000}$$

$$= 4.111 \text{ years}$$

[See Section 13-7.]

PROBLEM 13-11: Michael Company is considering buying a new machine that would require an initial investment of $6,479 and that would yield the following cash inflows:

Year 1	$1,000
Year 2	$2,000
Year 3	$3,000
Year 4	$4,000

Compute the internal rate of return for this investment project.

Solution: Since the annual cash inflows for this project are not constant, you must compute the internal rate of return using the trial-and-error method. The objective is to find the interest rate that makes the present value of cash inflows equal to the present value of cash outflows. If you guess the *IRR* is 16%, then you must look in Table 13-1 to find the present values for $n = 1,2,3,$ and 4 years and $i = 16\%$. The present values of cash inflows and outflows at 16% interest would be as follows:

Present value of cash inflows (at 16%):	
($1,000)(.862)	$ 862
($2,000)(.743)	1,486
($3,000)(.641)	1,923
($4,000)(.552)	2,208
Present value of cash outflows	$6,479

Since an interest rate of 16% equates the present value of cash inflows and outflows, the internal rate of return is 16%. If the present values had not turned out to be equal, you would have had to try a different interest rate. [See Section 13-4.]

FINAL EXAMINATION

Chapters 1–13

DIRECTIONS: This examination consists of two parts worth a total of **100 points**. Part I contains multiple-choice questions that cover basic concepts from chapters 1–13. Part II contains multiple-choice problems which involve numerical calculations. You should be able to complete the examination in approximately 120 minutes. The answers to the examination questions and problems are included at the end of the examination.

Part I: Multiple-Choice Questions (20 points)

1. Production costs that do not change during significant changes in production activity within the relevant range are
   (a) variable costs   (b) fixed costs   (c) mixed costs   (d) none of the above

2. Direct labor costs and direct materials costs are referred to as
   (a) conversion costs   (b) prime costs   (c) mixed costs   (d) none of the above

3. Direct labor costs and factory overhead costs are referred to as
   (a) conversion costs   (b) prime costs   (c) mixed costs   (d) none of the above

4. Factory overhead costs are classified as
   (a) direct production costs   (c) prime costs
   (b) indirect production costs   (d) none of the above

5. When direct materials are issued to production, the journal entry to record this transaction would include a credit to the Materials Control account and a debit to
   (a) Finished Goods Inventory   (c) Work-in-Process Inventory
   (b) Accounts Payable   (d) none of the above

6. If the year-end balance in the Factory Overhead Control account is less than the balance in the Factory Overhead Applied account, factory overhead is
   (a) overapplied   (b) underapplied   (c) neither underapplied or overapplied

7. For process costing using the weighted-average method, cost per equivalent unit is based on
   (a) current production costs   (b) total production costs   (c) none of the above

8. For process costing using the FIFO method, cost per equivalent unit is based on
   (a) current production costs   (b) total production costs   (c) none of the above

9. A budgeted income statement would be a component of the
   (a) operating budget   (b) financial budget   (c) none of the above

10. The direct materials quantity variance is unfavorable if the actual quantity of direct materials used in production is
    (a) less than the standard quantity allowed for production
    (b) greater than the standard quantity allowed for production
    (c) equal to the standard quantity allowed for production

11. The direct labor rate variance is unfavorable if the standard rate per direct labor hour is
    (b) greater than the actual rate per direct labor hour
    (c) equal to the actual rate per direct labor hour

12. The variable overhead spending variance is unfavorable if the standard overhead rate times the actual direct labor hours is:
(a) less than the actual variable overhead costs incurred
(b) greater than the actual variable overhead costs incurred
(c) equal to the actual variable overhead costs incurred

13. The fixed-overhead production-volume variance is favorable when the applied fixed overhead is
(a) greater than budgeted fixed overhead   (c) less than actual fixed overhead
(b) less than budgeted fixed overhead   (d) none of the above

14. In the production of two joint products, joint costs are production costs incurred
(a) before the split-off point   (b) after the split-off point

15. The break-even point in units can be computed by dividing fixed costs by
(a) selling price per unit   (d) contribution margin ratio
(b) variable cost per unit   (e) none of the above
(c) contribution margin per unit

16. The break-even point in dollars can be computed by dividing fixed costs by
(a) selling price per unit   (d) contribution margin ratio
(b) variable cost per unit   (e) none of the above
(c) contribution margin per unit

17. In a make or buy decision, which of the following costs would *not* be a relevant cost of producing a component in-house?
(a) variable production costs to produce the component
(b) fixed production costs that can be avoided if the component is not produced in-house
(c) fixed production costs that will be incurred whether the component is produced in-house or not
(d) none of the above

18. Under direct costing, which of the following production costs would *not* be included in work-in-process and finished goods inventories?
(a) direct materials   (d) fixed overhead
(b) direct labor   (e) none of the above
(c) variable overhead

19. The net present value of a capital budgeting project is equal to the present value of cash inflows minus the present value of cash outflows discounted at
(a) the accounting rate of return   (c) the minimum acceptable rate of return
(b) the internal rate of return   (d) none of the above

20. The difference between net income using absorption costing versus direct costing reflects the difference between the amount of expense for
(a) variable overhead   (c) direct labor
(b) fixed overhead   (d) direct materials

Part II: Multiple-Choice Problems (80 points)

Problems 1 through 5 are based on the following information for the XYZ Company for the month of September

	Beginning balance	Ending balance
Direct Materials Inventory	$15,000	$20,000
Work-in-Process Inventory	$65,000	$75,000
Finished Goods Inventory	$90,000	$85,000

Costs incurred during the period:

Direct materials purchased	$ 90,000
Direct labor costs	$129,000
Factory overhead costs	$100,000

1. The direct materials issued to production during the period were
   (a) $90,000　　(b) $80,000　　(c) $85,000　　(d) $100,000　　(e) none of the above

2. The cost of goods manufactured for the period were
   (a) $304,000　　(b) $309,000　　(c) $314,000　　(d) $229,000　　(e) none of the above

3. The cost of goods sold were.
   (a) $304,000　　(b) $309,000　　(c) $314,000　　(d) $229,000　　(e) none of the above

4. The prime costs transferred to work-in-process inventory during the period were
   (a) $129,000　　(b) $210,000　　(c) $214,000　　(d) $229,000　　(e) none of the above

5. The conversion costs incurred during the period were
   (a) $129,000　　(b) $210,000　　(c) $214,000　　(d) $229,000　　(e) none of the above

Problems 6 through 9 are based on the following production cost information for the Southern Company:

Direct labor costs incurred	
(10,000 direct labor hours)	$162,000
Factory overhead costs incurred	$150,000
Budgeted factory overhead costs	
(at 8,000 budgeted direct labor hours)	$128,000

Assume that factory overhead costs are applied to production based on actual direct labor hours.

6. The predetermined overhead rate per direct labor hour would be
   (a) $15.00　　(b) $16.00　　(c) $16.20　　(d) $17.00　　(e) none of the above

7. The factory overhead costs applied would be:
   (a) $150,000　　(b) $165,000　　(c) $160,000　　(d) $172,000　　(e) none of the above

8. The journal entry to record the factory overhead costs applied to production (assume applied overhead of $180,000) would be:

   (a) Factory Overhead Applied　　　　　　　$180,000
   　　　Factory Overhead Control　　　　　　　　　　　$180,000
   (b) Factory Overhead Applied　　　　　　　$180,000
   　　　Work-in-Process Inventory　　　　　　　　　　$180,000
   (c) Work-in-Process Inventory　　　　　　　$180,000
   　　　Factory Overhead Control　　　　　　　　　　　$180,000
   (d) Work-in-Process Inventory　　　　　　　$180,000
   　　　Factory Overhead Applied　　　　　　　　　　　$180,000
   (e) none of the above

9. The factory overhead costs applied to production would be
   (a) $10,000 underapplied　　　　　　　(d) $20,000 overapplied
   (b) $10,000 overapplied　　　　　　　　(e) none of the above
   (c) $20,000 underapplied

The following information is available for the DePaul Company for the month of June.

Direct materials purchased on account	$100,000
Direct materials issued to production	$150,000
Direct labor costs	$ 82,000

10. The journal entry to record the purchase of direct materials would be

(a) Materials Control	$100,000	
Work-in-Process Control		$100,000
(b) Materials Control	$100,000	
Accounts Payable		$100,000
(c) Work-in-Process Control	$100,000	
Materials Control		$100,000
(d) Materials Control	$100,000	
Factory Overhead Control		$100,000
(e) none of the above		

11. The journal entry to record the direct labor costs incurred would be

(a) Accrued Payroll	$82,000	
Work-in-Process		$82,000
(b) Work-in-Process	$82,000	
Accrued Payroll		$82,000
(c) Work-in-Process	$82,000	
Finished Goods		$82,000
(d) Finished Goods	$82,000	
Accrued Payroll		$82,000
(e) none of the above		

Problems 12 through 17 are based on the following information for the Clemson Company.

	PHYSICAL UNITS	EQUIVALENT UNITS direct materials	EQUIVALENT UNITS conversion costs
Beginning WIP inventory	10,000	10,000 (100%)	4,000 (40%)
Units started	40,000		
Current production		40,000	42,000
Ending WIP inventory	8,000	8,000 (100%)	4,000 (50%)
Units completed	42,000	42,000	42,000

		direct materials	conversion costs
Production costs:			
Beginning WIP inventory		$ 20,000	$ 12,400
Current production costs		100,000	226,800
Total production costs		$120,000	$239,200

Assume that direct materials are applied to units of production at the beginning of the production process and that conversion costs are applied to units of production uniformly throughout the production process.

12. Using the weighted-average method, the cost per equivalent unit for direct materials would be:
   (a) $2.50   (b) $2.40   (c) $3.00   (d) $2.00   (e) none of the above

13. Using the weighted-average method, the cost per equivalent unit for conversion costs would be
   (a) $5.20   (b) $5.30   (c) $5.00   (d) $5.10   (e) none of the above

14. Using the FIFO method, the cost per equivalent unit for direct materials would be
   (a) $2.00   (b) $2.40   (c) $2.50   (d) $2.60   (e) none of the above

15. Using the FIFO method, the cost per equivalent unit for conversion costs would be
   (a) $5.40   (b) $5.20   (c) $5.30   (d) $5.10   (e) none of the above

16. Assume that the cost per equivalent unit using the weighted average method was $2.00 for direct materials and $4.00 for conversion costs. The amount of production costs allocated to ending work-in-process inventory would be
   (a) $16,000   (b) $32,000   (c) $48,000   (d) $24,000   (e) none of the above

17. Assume that the cost per equivalent unit using the FIFO method was $2.40 for direct materials and $4.40 for conversion costs. The amount of production costs allocated to units completed would be
   (a) $322,400   (b) $200,800   (c) $284,800   (d) $184,800   (e) none of the above

Problems 18 through 19 are based on the following information.

	Budgeted beginning balance	Budgeted ending balance
Finished Goods Inventory (units)	10,000	8,000
Direct Materials Inventory (pounds)	40,000	60,000
Budgeted sales in units	200,000	
Selling price per unit	$10.00	
Budgeted total production costs per unit	$ 6.00	
Budgeted direct materials per unit of production	1 pound per unit	

18. The budgeted production in units would be.
   (a) 200,000 units
   (b) 198,000 units
   (c) 190,000 units
   (d) 208,000 units
   (e) none of the above

19. The budgeted direct materials purchased would be
   (a) 198,000 pounds
   (b) 190,000 pounds
   (c) 218,000 pounds
   (d) 208,000 pounds
   (e) none of the above

Problems 20 through 23 are based on the following information.

Standard price per pound of direct materials	$10.00
Standard quantity of direct materials needed per unit of production	10 lbs
Actual price per pound of direct materials	$10.50
Actual quantity of direct materials used in production	41,000 pounds
Quantity of direct materials purchased	50,000 pounds
Actual production in units	4,000 units
Standard rate per direct labor hour	$12.00
Actual rate per direct labor hour	$10.00
Standard direct labor hours per unit	2 hours per unit
Actual direct labor hours used	9,000 hours

20. The direct materials price variance (recorded when direct materials are purchased) would be
   (a) $15,000 favorable
   (b) $25,000 unfavorable
   (c) $20,500 favorable
   (d) $20,500 unfavorable
   (e) none of the above

21. The direct materials quantity variance would be:
   (a) $12,000 favorable
   (b) $10,000 unfavorable
   (c) $20,000 favorable
   (d) $22,000 unfavorable
   (e) none of the above

22. The direct labor rate variance would be
- (a) $18,000 favorable
- (b) $16,000 unfavorable
- (c) $10,000 favorable
- (d) $12,000 unfavorable
- (e) none of the above

23. The direct labor efficiency variance would be
- (a) $15,000 favorable
- (b) $12,000 unfavorable
- (c) $11,000 favorable
- (d) $10,000 unfavorable
- (e) none of the above

Problems 24 through 27 are based on the following information.

Budgeted fixed overhead (at 10,000 budgeted direct labor hours)	$120,000
Standard fixed overhead rate per direct labor hour	$12.00/hr.
Standard variable overhead rate per direct labor hour	$16.00/hr.
Actual fixed overhead	$100,000
Actual variable overhead	$140,000
Actual direct labor hours	9,200
Standard direct labor hours allowed for production	9,000

Assume that overhead costs are applied to production based on direct labor hours.

24. The variable-overhead spending variance would be
- (a) $3,200 favorable
- (b) $3,200 unfavorable
- (c) $7,200 favorable
- (d) $7,200 unfavorable
- (e) none of the above

25. The variable-overhead efficiency variance would be
- (a) $3,200 favorable
- (b) $3,200 unfavorable
- (c) $7,200 favorable
- (d) $7,200 unfavorable
- (e) none of the above

26. The fixed-overhead budget variance would be
- (a) $20,000 favorable
- (b) $22,000 unfavorable
- (c) $12,000 favorable
- (d) $15,000 unfavorable
- (e) none of the above

27. The fixed-overhead production-volume variance would be
- (a) $20,000 favorable
- (b) $10,000 unfavorable
- (c) $6,000 favorable
- (d) $12,000 unfavorable
- (e) none of the above

The Northern Company has two service departments and two production departments in its plant. The following information is available.

	Service Departments		Production Departments	
	A	B	1	2
Department costs	$8,000	$ 4,000	$18,000	$36,000
Total labor hours	2,000	5,000	9,000	3,000
Square footage	2,000	12,000	16,000	4,000

Service department A's costs are allocated based on square footage and service department B's costs are allocated based on total labor hours. Assume that each service department provides services to each other.

28. Using the direct method, what amount of service department A's costs would be allocated to production department 2?
- (a) $6,400
- (b) $1,600
- (c) $3,200
- (d) $4,000
- (e) none of the above

29. Using the step method, what amount of service department A's costs would be allocated to service department B?
    (a) $3,000   (b) $3,750   (c) $4,000   (d) $4,200   (e) none of the above

30. The Southeast Company produced 12,000 pounds (final sales value of $130,000) of product X and 8,000 pounds (final sales value of $90,000) of product Y. Products X and Y are jointly produced. Joint costs were $120,000. Separable costs were $22,000 for product X and $18,000 for product Y. Using the relative sales value method, what amount of joint costs would be allocated to product X?
    (a) $30,000   (b) $60,000   (c) $72,000   (d) $120,000   (e) none of the above

The XYZ Company wants to estimate the fixed and variable components of maintenance costs based on the following information:

Quarter	Machine hours	Maintenance costs
1	10,000	$29,000
2	8,000	$25,000
3	6,800	$21,000
4	7,500	$22,500

31. Based on this information, using the high-low (algebraic) method, what is the variable cost per machine hour?
    (a) $2.00   (b) $2.50   (c) $2.25   (d) $3.00   (e) none of the above

32. Using the high-low method, what is the fixed maintenance cost per month?
    (a) $4,000   (b) $3,000   (c) $5,000   (d) $4,500   (e) none of the above

33. The Chicago Company has fixed costs of $100,000 and sells one product with a selling price per unit of $25.00. Variable costs are $15.00 per unit. Based on this information, what is the break-even point in units for the Chicago Company?
    (a) 10,000 units
    (b) 15,000 units
    (c) 20,000 units
    (d) 8,000 units
    (e) none of the above

34. Based on the information in Problem 33, how many units must be sold in order to earn a profit (before taxes) of $30,000?
    (a) 10,000 units
    (b) 12,000 units
    (c) 13,000 units
    (d) 15,000 units
    (e) none of the above

35. The Micro Company produces disk drives for microcomputer manufacturers. Micro Company's production costs per unit are:

	Cost per unit
Direct materials	$25.00
Direct labor	10.00
Variable overhead	12.00
Fixed overhead	15.00
Total production costs	$62.00

Assume that Micro Company has the opportunity to sell 1,000 disk drives for $60.00 per unit as a special order to a company outside of its normal marketing region. The Micro Company has enough idle capacity to produce the 1,000 units for the special order and the special order would not displace any sales at the normal selling price. How much would operating income increase or decrease if the special order is accepted?

(a) $2,000 decrease
(b) $5,000 increase
(c) $13,000 increase

(d) $10,000 decrease
(e) none of the above

36. The Beta Company manufactures computer Part No. 16 for use in producing its final product, The Beta II Microcomputer. The cost of producing 10,000 units of Part No. 16 are:

Direct materials	$200,000
Direct labor	150,000
Variable overhead	100,000
Fixed overhead	200,000
Total production costs	$650,000

The Alpha Company has offered to sell 10,000 units of Part No. 16 for $60.00 per unit. If Beta Company accepts Alpha's offer, $100,000 of fixed overhead would be eliminated. What is the relevant cost of producing 10,000 units of Part No. 16 in-house?
(a) $650,000   (b) $550,000   (c) $500,000   (d) $450,000   (e) none of the above

The following information is provided for the Reno Company for 19X1:

Sales price per unit	$10.00
Units produced	10,000
Units sold	8,000
Direct materials used	$30,000
Direct labor costs	$10,000
Variable overhead costs	$12,000
Fixed overhead costs	$15,000
Fixed selling and administrative expenses	$15,000
Variable selling and administrative expenses	$4,500

Beginning and ending work-in-process inventories had zero balances. Beginning finished goods inventory had a zero balance and ending finished goods inventory was 2,000 units.

37. What is the net income before taxes for the Reno Company using absorption costing?
(a) $6,900   (b) $3,900   (c) $6,000   (d) $3,000   (e) none of the above

38. What is the net income before taxes for the Reno Company using direct costing?
(a) $6,900   (b) $3,900   (c) $6,000   (d) $3,000   (d) none of the above

The Jackson Company is reviewing a capital budgeting project which requires an initial investment of $36,050 and is expected to result in cash flows from operations of $10,000 for five years. The minimum acceptable rate of return at Jackson Company is 10%. The present value factor of an annuity of $1.00 at 10% for 5 years is 3.791.

39. What is net present value of the project?
(a) $1,800   (b) $1,860   (c) $2,160   (d) $3,791   (e) none of the above

40. What is the payback period of the project?
(a) 3.791 years
(b) 3.000 years
(c) 3.605 years

(d) 3.780 years
(e) none of the above

Answers

DIRECTIONS: Score your examination as follows: In Part 1, score 1 point for each of the 20 items that you answered correctly. In Part 2, score 2 points for each of the 40 items that you answered correctly. **Total possible points: 100.**

Part I: Multiple-Choice Questions

1. (b)	2. (b)	3. (a)	4. (b)	5. (c)
6. (a)	7. (b)	8. (a)	9. (a)	10. (b)
11. (a)	12. (a)	13. (a)	14. (a)	15. (c)
16. (d)	17. (c)	18. (d)	19. (c)	20. (b)

Part II: Multiple-Choice Problems

1. (c)	2. (a)	3. (b)	4. (c)	5. (d)
6. (b)	7. (c)	8. (d)	9. (b)	10. (b)
11. (b)	12. (b)	13. (a)	14. (c)	15. (a)
16. (b)	17. (a)	18. (b)	19. (c)	20. (b)
21. (b)	22. (a)	23. (b)	24. (c)	25. (b)
26. (a)	27. (d)	28. (b)	29. (a)	30. (c)
31. (b)	32. (a)	33. (a)	34. (c)	35. (c)
36. (b)	37. (a)	38. (b)	39. (b)	40. (c)

GLOSSARY

absorption costing Absorption (full) costing is the traditional method of accounting for production costs where all production costs are included in product inventories.

accounting rate of return The accounting rate of return is the ratio of the operating income of a project divided by either the total investment or average investment of the project.

applied factory overhead Factory overhead allocated to products based upon a predetermined overhead rate.

average (units) costs Computed by dividing total costs by a measure of output.

break-even point The break-even point represents the number of units or the number of sales dollars where total revenue equals total costs.

budget A plan which is expressed in quantitative terms and reflects the objectives of management. A budget reflects the planned operating and financial activities of an organization.

byproducts Products with relatively minor sales value that are produced together with the major products.

capital budgeting Capital budgeting is the process of evaluating and selecting major capital investment projects.

certificate in management accounting (CMA) A program established to recognize professional competence and to establish educational standards in management accounting.

coefficient of correlation Describes the direction of the relationship between x and y and the strength of the relationship between x and y.

coefficient of determination Describes the proportion of the variation of y (costs) which is explained by the variable x (units of production).

contribution margin Contribution margin represents the difference between sales revenue and variable expenses.

contribution margin per unit The contribution margin per unit equals selling price per unit minus variable costs per unit.

contribution margin ratio The contribution margin ratio is the ratio of contribution margin per unit to sales price per unit. The contribution margin ratio is interpreted as the percent of each sales dollar that is available to cover fixed costs before the break-even point and to add to profit after the break-even point.

controller The controller is usually the chief accountant within an organization.

conversion costs Conversion costs consist of direct labor costs plus factory overhead costs.

cost accounting Cost accounting is primarily concerned with the recording and reporting of the cost of manufacturing products and performing services.

cost accumulation Involves the collection of cost data within the accounting system.

cost allocation The process of assigning costs to cost objectives within a firm.

cost objective An activity for which a separate measurement of cost is desired.

cost variances Cost variances are computed as the difference between actual costs and standard costs.

costs Resources foregone to achieve a specific cost objective expressed in terms of monetary units.

direct allocation method The direct method of service department cost allocation involves allocation of each service department's costs directly to production departments.

direct costing Direct (variable) costing assigns only variable production costs to units of production.

direct labor costs Costs of labor which are traceable to the finished units of output.

direct material costs Costs of materials that are traceable to the finished units of output.

discounted cash flow methods Discounted cash flow methods involve the analysis of the discounted cash flows of a project. The net present value method and the internal rate of return method are discounted cash flow methods.

equivalent units Equivalent units measure the relative amount of production completed.

factory overhead costs Product costs that are not classified as direct materials or direct labor costs (also referred to as indirect manufacturing costs).

financial accounting The purpose of financial accounting is to provide accounting information to external users such as stockholders, creditors, and governmental agencies.

fixed costs Fixed costs are costs, which in total, remain unchanged, when changes in production activity occur within the relevant range.

fixed overhead costs Fixed overhead costs are overhead costs which do not change with changes in production activity.

flexible budget A flexible (variable) budget is a budget based upon the actual level of activity.

generally accepted accounting principles (GAAP) GAAP encompasses the accounting conventions, rules and procedures necessary to define accepted accounting practice at a particular time.

graphical (scatter diagram) method Involves plotting observations, visually fitting a line to the plot of the observations and estimating variable costs per unit and fixed costs.

gross margin Gross margin (gross profit) represents the difference between revenues and the cost of goods sold using absorption costing.

high-low method The high-low method uses two observations (usually the high and the low observation) to compute the variable cost per unit and the fixed cost.

internal rate of return The internal rate of return (time adjusted rate of return) is the interest rate which equates the present value of cash inflows with the present value of cash outflows.

job-ordering costing Job-order costing systems are used by organizations whose products and services can be identified by individual jobs (or batches) where each job generally receives different amounts of inputs of direct material, direct labor, and factory overhead.

joint costs The costs of producing joint products that are incurred before the split-off point.

joint products Products that are produced together and are not readily identifiable as individual products until a certain point in the production process known as the split-off point.

least-squares regression method A statistical method that can be used to estimate the variable cost per unit and the fixed cost.

management accounting The process of identification, measurement, accumulation, analysis, preparation, interpretation, and communication of financial information used by management to plan, evaluate, and control within an organization and to assure appropriate use of and accountability for its resources.

management control The process of assuring that resources are used effectively and efficiently to implement organizational strategies and attain the organizational goals.

master budget The master budget encompasses the planned operating and financial activities of a firm and includes two components: (1) the operating budget and (2) the financial budget.

minimum acceptable rate of return The minimum acceptable rate of return is sometimes referred to as the hurdle rate or minimum required rate of return. The minimum acceptable rate of return represents the minimum rate of return which management has determined.

mixed costs Costs which have both a fixed component and a variable component.

net present value method The net present value is equal to the present value of cash inflows minus the present value of cash outflows, discounted at the minimum acceptable rate of return.

net realizable value allocation method A method which allocates joint costs based on the relative net realizable value at the split-off point of the joint products. The net realizable value at the split-off point is computed by taking the sales value at completion minus the separable costs.

operational control The process of assuring specific operations or tasks are completed effectively and efficiently.

payback The payback of a project measures the amount of time necessary to recover the initial investment of a project.

period costs Costs that are expensed immediately in the period in which they are incurred and are not inventoried in inventory accounts.

physical units allocation method A method that uses some physical measure such as pounds, gallons, or units of production to allocate joint costs to joint products.

prime costs Prime costs consist of direct material costs plus direct labor costs.

process costing Process costing is used by organizations whose products or services are mass-produced through a continuous series of production steps.

product costs Costs of producing a product that are inventoried until those units of output are sold.

production departments Departments that are directly involved in the production process.

relevant costs Relevant costs are expected future costs that differ between the alternatives being considered.

relevant range The range of activity in which the firm expects to operate. The relevant range is the range of activity in which the classification of costs as variable and fixed is valid.

sales value allocation method A method which allocates joint costs based on the relative sales value at the split-off point of each joint product.

separable costs The cost of producing joint products after the split-off point.

service departments Departments that provide services to other departments within a factory but are not directly involved in the production process.

split-off point The point in the production process where joint products become separately identifiable.

spoilage Spoilage represents units of production that do not meet production quality standards and cannot be reworked to meet the quality standards. Normal spoilage occurs under efficient production operations. Abnormal spoilage is not expected to arise under efficient production operations.

standard costs Predetermined unit costs which are used for planning and control. Standard costs are used to develop budgets and are compared with actual costs to compute cost variances.

static budget A static (fixed) budget is based on a predetermined level of activity.

step allocation method The step (step down, sequential) method of service department cost allocation involves the allocation of service department costs in a particular sequence (order) of service departments and may involve the allocation of costs from one service department to another.

strategic planning The process of identifying organizational goals and the strategies for achieving those goals.

sunk costs A cost that has already been incurred (a past cost).

treasurer The treasurer is in an accounting position which is primarily responsible for the financial activities of an organization.

variable costs Variable costs are costs, which in total, change in direct proportion to changes in production activity within the relevant range.

variable overhead costs Variable overhead costs are assumed to change in direct proportion to changes in production activity.

INDEX